Ryan Ferrier ♪ *Daniel Bayliss* ♪ *Adam Metcalfe*

KENNEL BLOCK
Blues™

BOOM!™
STUDIOS

KENNEL BLOCK BLUES, January 2017. Published by
BOOM! Studios, a division of Boom Entertainment, Inc.
Kennel Block Blues is ™ & © 2017 Ryan Ferrier & Daniel
Bayliss. Originally published in single magazine form as
KENNEL BLOCK BLUES No. 1-4. ™ & © 2016 Ryan Ferrier
& Daniel Bayliss. All rights reserved. BOOM! Studios™
and the BOOM! Studios logo are trademarks of Boom
Entertainment, Inc., registered in various countries and
categories. All characters, events, and institutions depicted
herein are fictional. Any similarity between any of the
names, characters, persons, events, and/or institutions in
this publication to actual names, characters, and persons,
whether living or dead, events, and/or institutions is
unintended and purely coincidental. BOOM! Studios does
not read or accept unsolicited submissions of ideas, stories,
or artwork.

A catalog record of this book is available from OCLC and
from the BOOM! Studios website, www.boom-studios.com,
on the Librarians Page.

BOOM! Studios, 5670 Wilshire Boulevard, Suite 450, Los
Angeles, CA 90036-5679. Printed in China. First Printing.

ISBN: 978-1-60886-933-6, eISBN: 978-1-61398-604-2

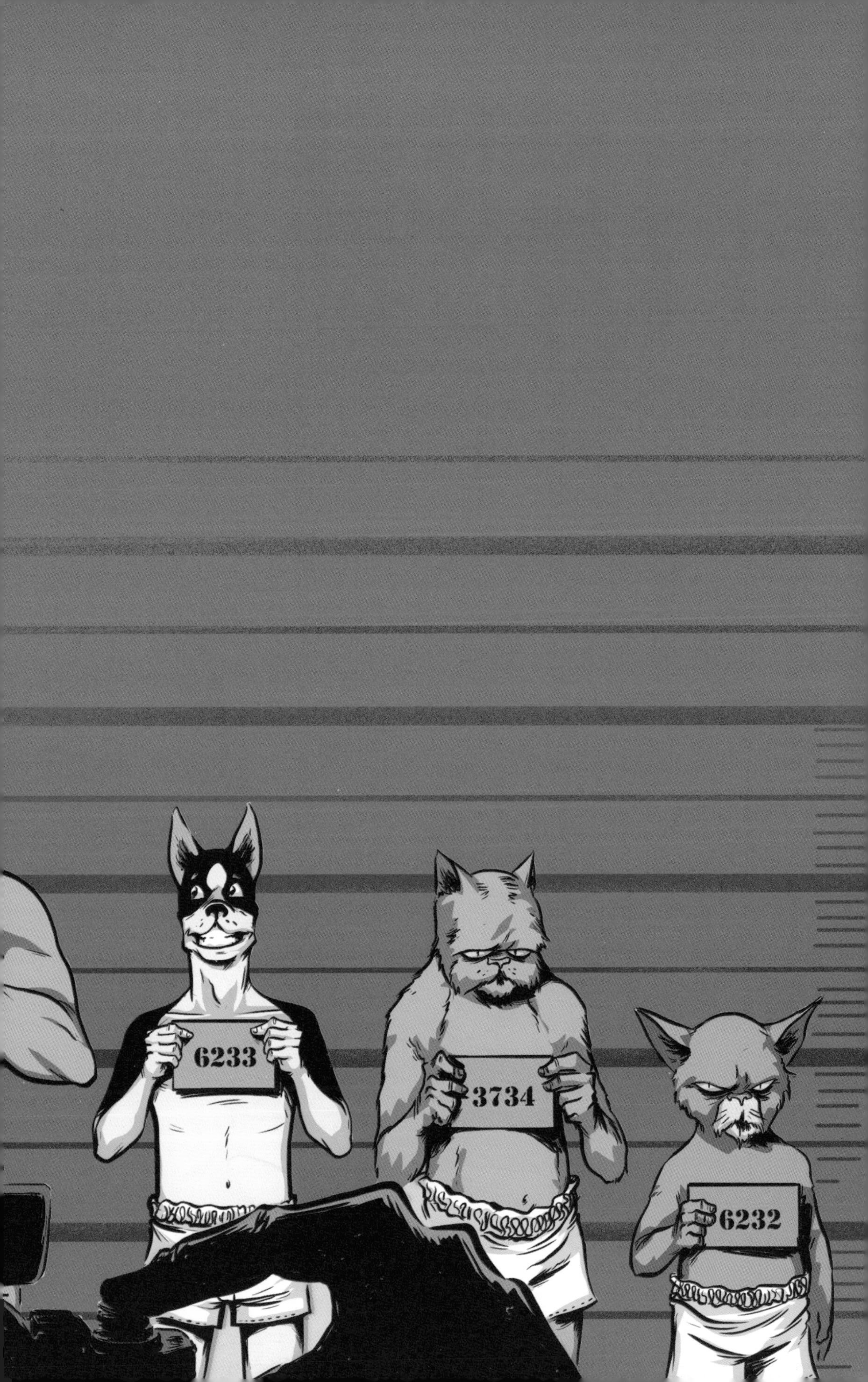
6233
3734
6232

KENNEL BLOCK *Blues*™

Created by
FERRIER & BAYLISS

Dedicated to those we love the most, who know but cannot say it.

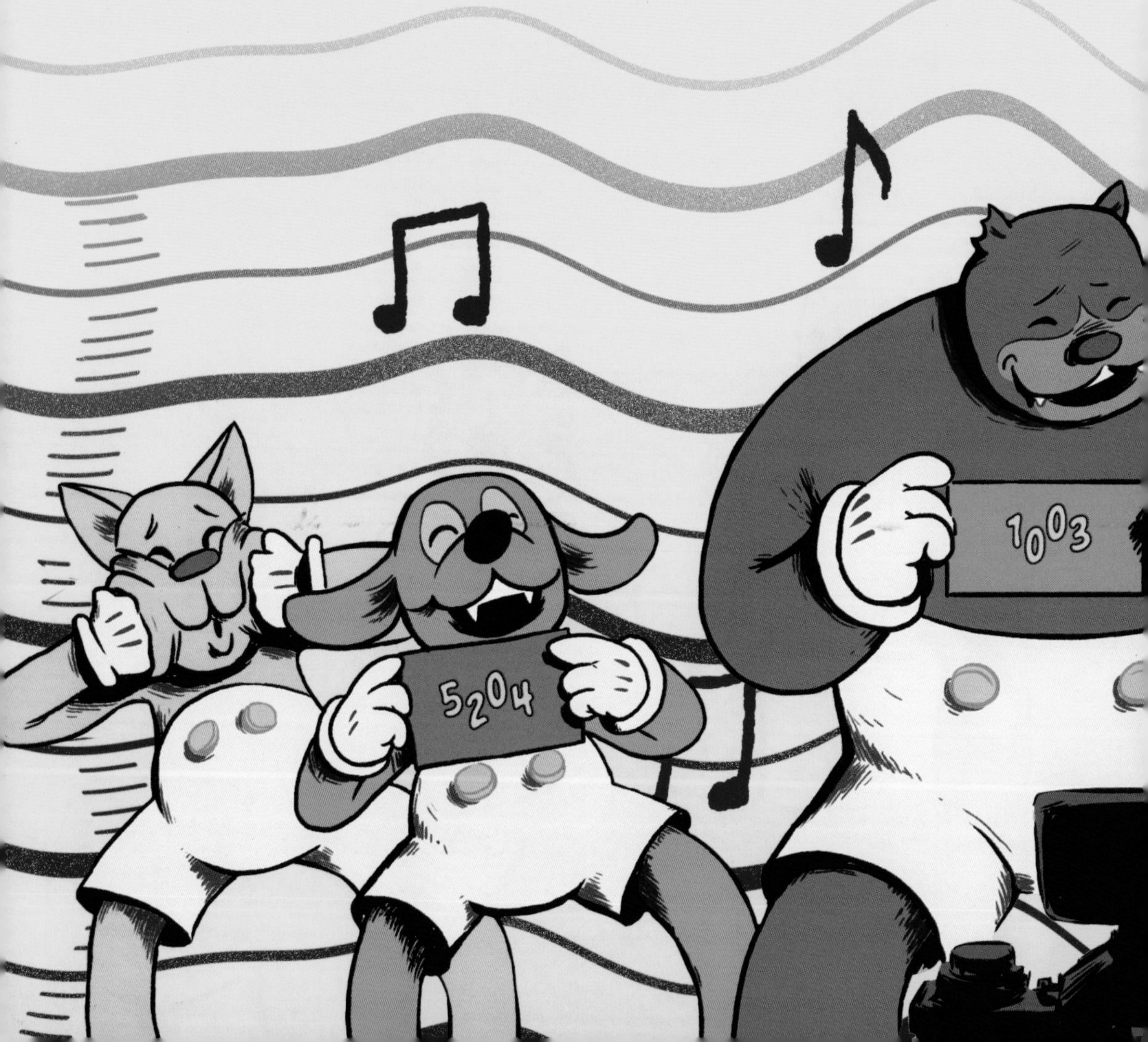
1003
5204

Written by
RYAN FERRIER

Illustrated by
DANIEL BAYLISS

Colored by
ADAM METCALFE

Lettered by
COLIN BELL

Cover by
DANIEL BAYLISS

Designer
MICHELLE ANKLEY

Assistant Editor
MARY GUMPORT

Editor
ERIC HARBURN

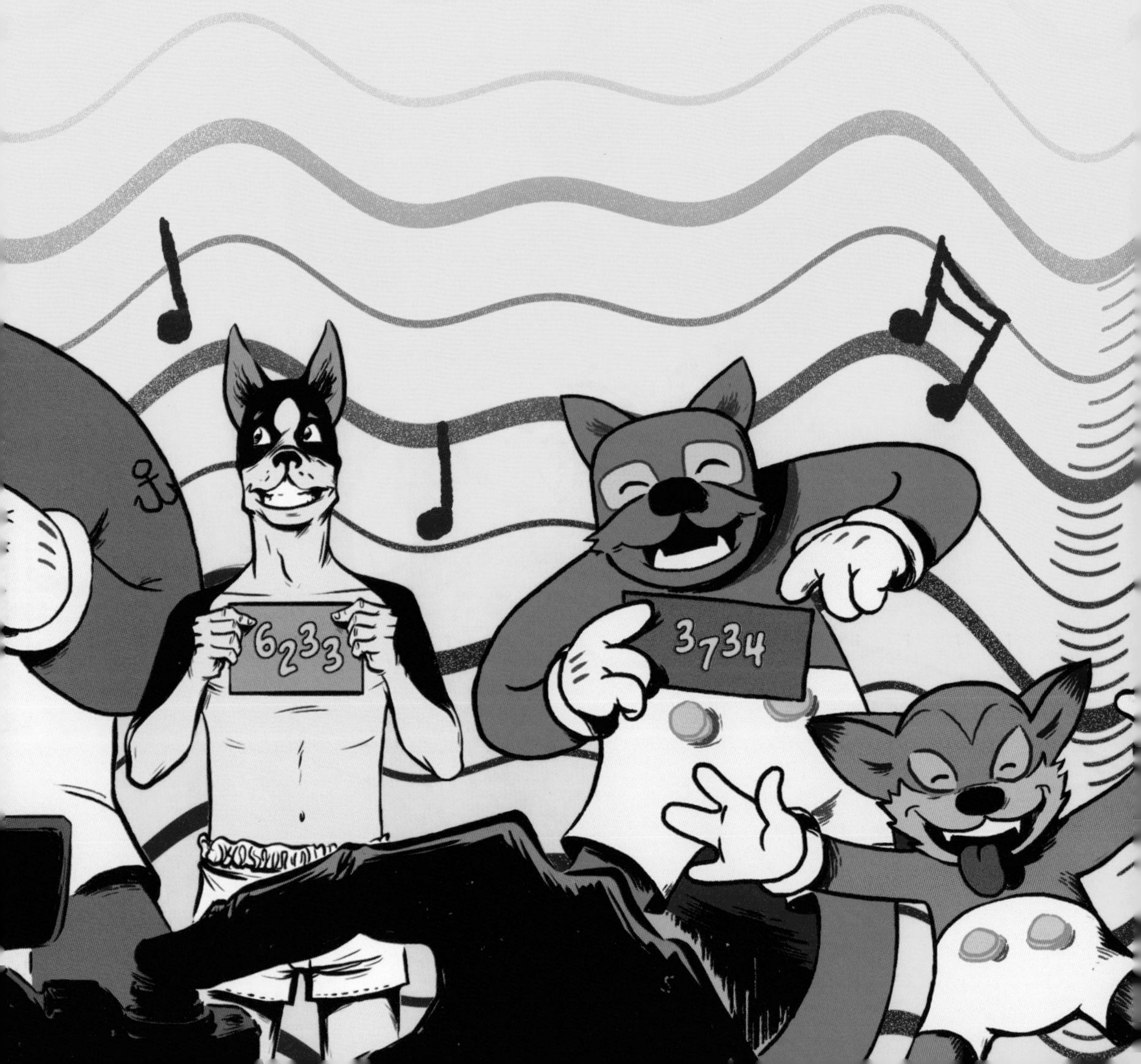
6233
3734

Chapter One

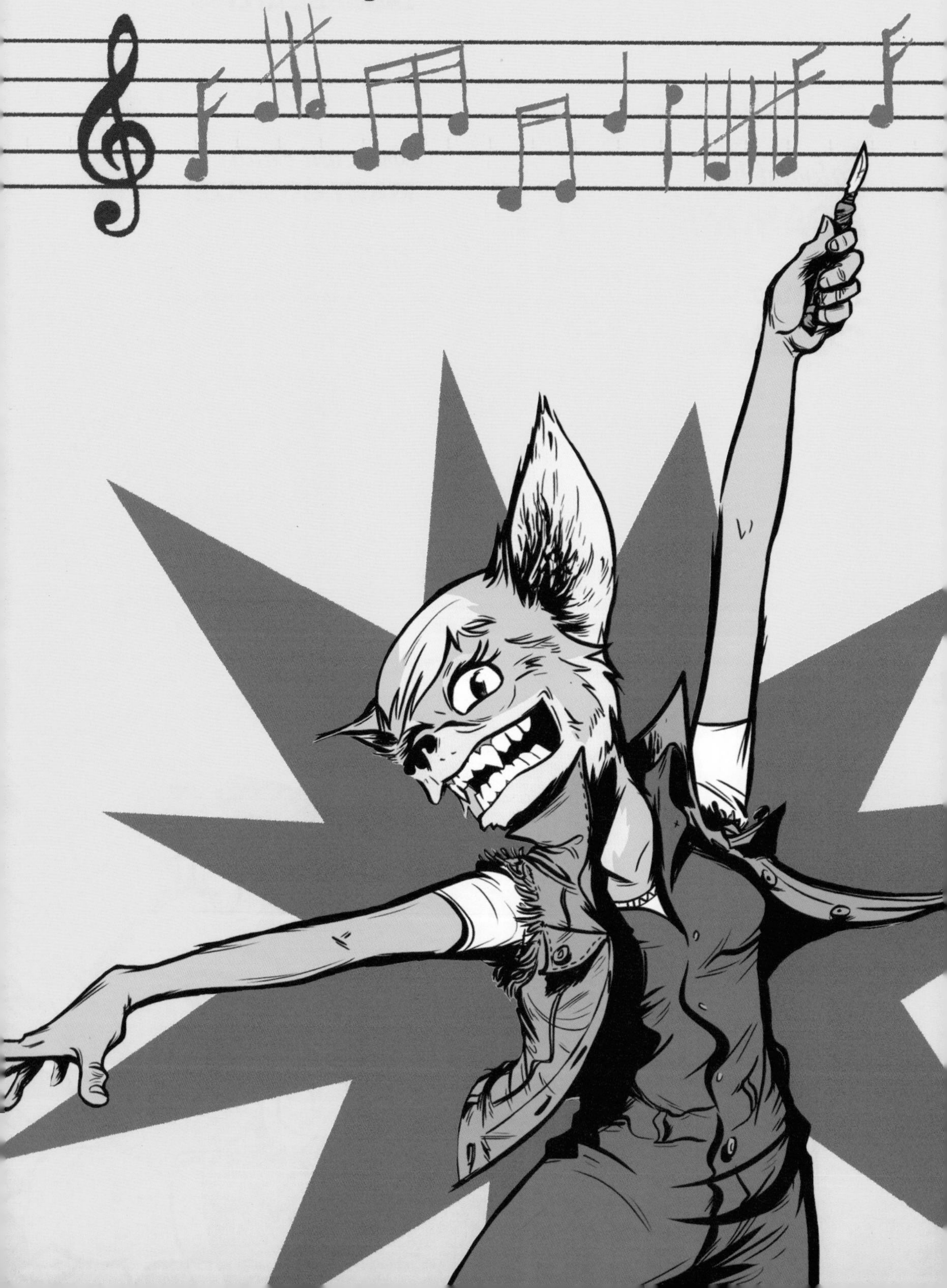

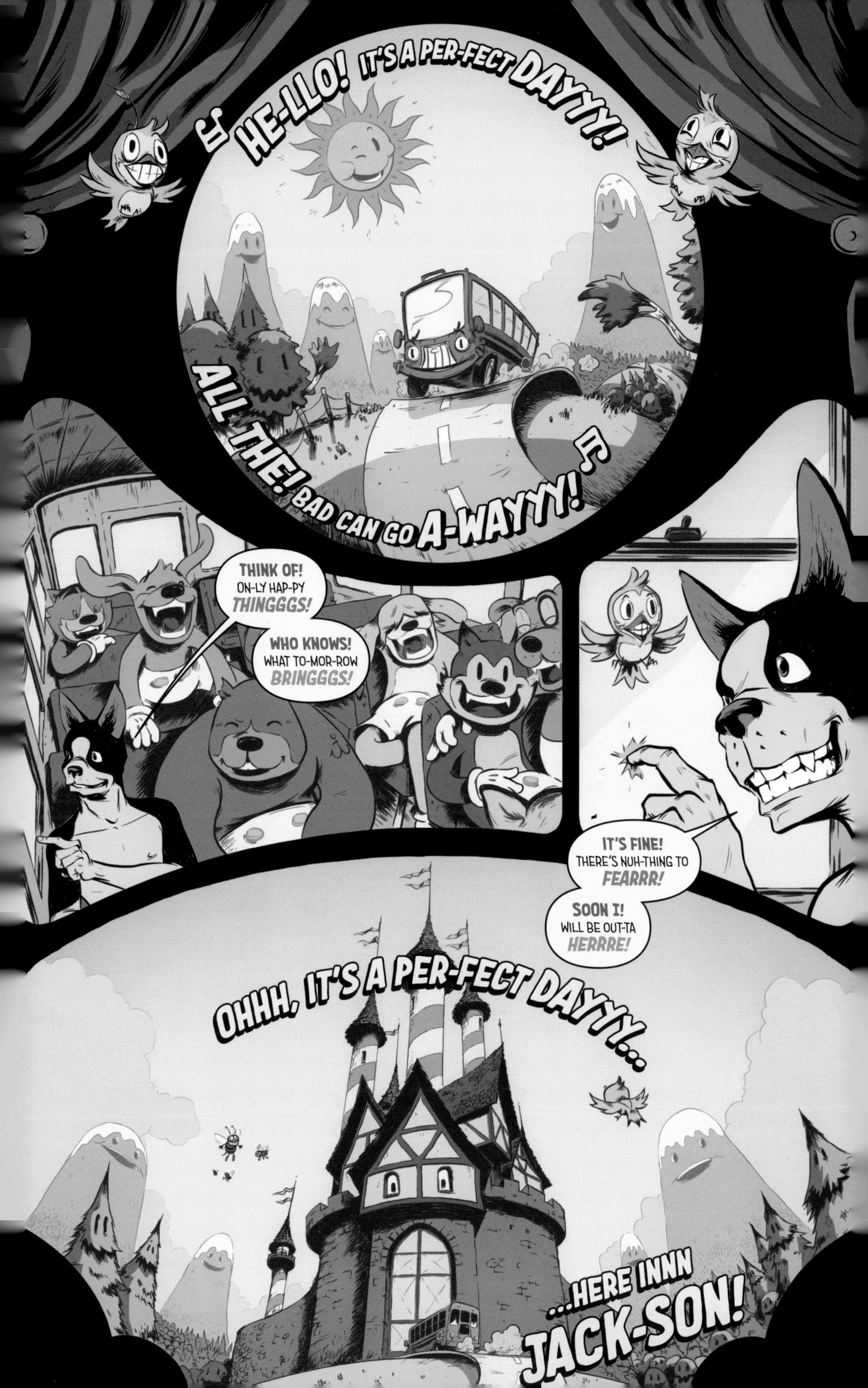
HE-LLO! IT'S A PER-FECT DAYYY!
ALL THE! BAD CAN GO A-WAYYY!
THINK OF! ON-LY HAP-PY THINGGGS!
WHO KNOWS! WHAT TO-MOR-ROW BRINGGGS!
IT'S FINE! THERE'S NUH-THING TO FEARRR!
SOON I! WILL BE OUT-TA HERRRE!
OHHH, IT'S A PER-FECT DAYYY...
...HERE INNN JACK-SON!

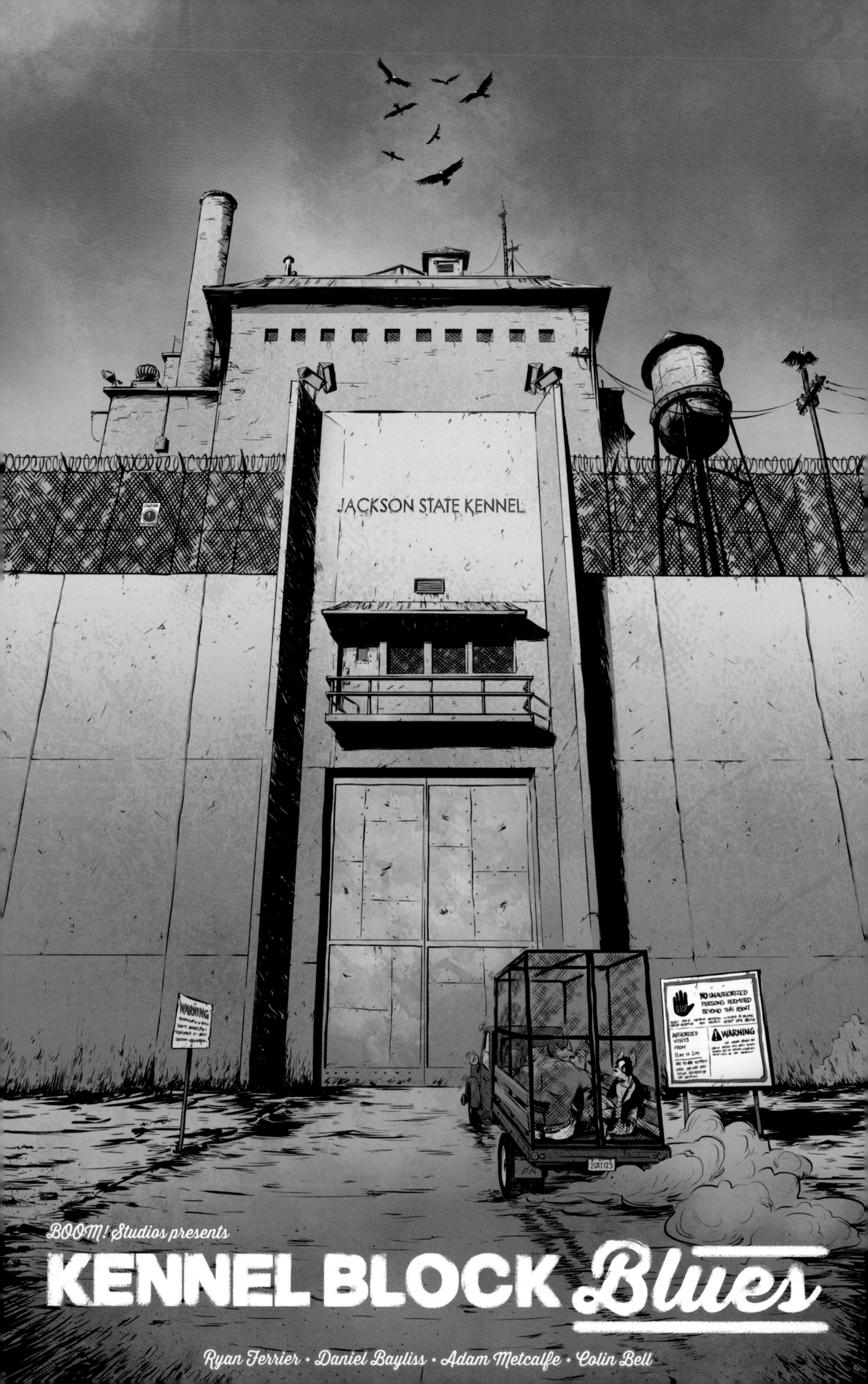
JACKSON STATE KENNEL
NO UNAUTHORIZED PERSONS PERMITTED BEYOND THIS POINT
STOP
WARNING
AUTHORIZED VISITS FROM
WARNING
2GAT123
BOOM! Studios presents
KENNEL BLOCK Blues
Ryan Ferrier • Daniel Bayliss • Adam Metcalfe • Colin Bell

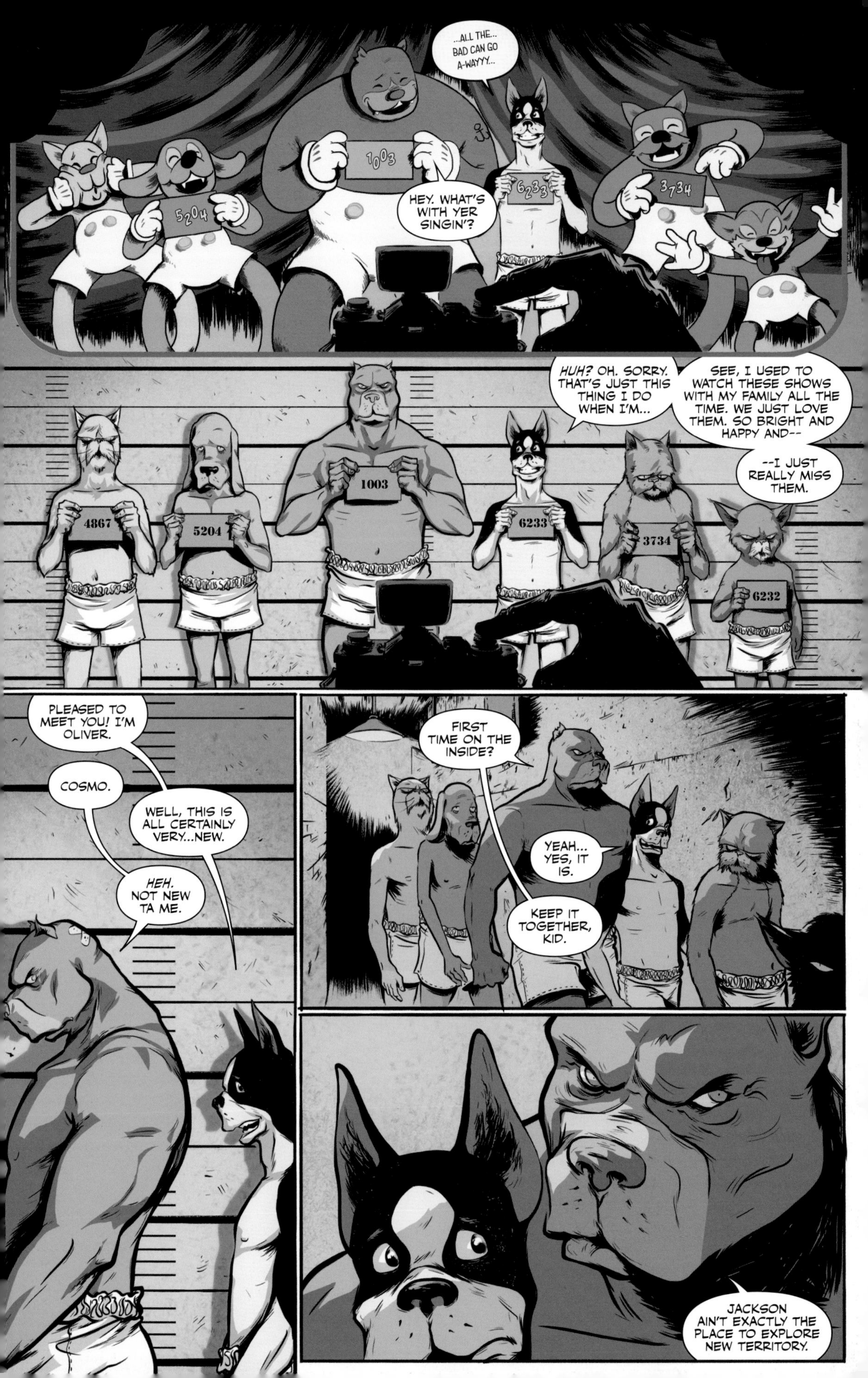
...ALL THE... BAD CAN GO A-WAYYY...
1003
5204
6233
3734
HEY. WHAT'S WITH YER SINGIN'?
4867
5204
1003
6233
3734
6232
HUH? OH. SORRY. THAT'S JUST THIS THING I DO WHEN I'M...
SEE, I USED TO WATCH THESE SHOWS WITH MY FAMILY ALL THE TIME. WE JUST LOVE THEM. SO BRIGHT AND HAPPY AND--
--I JUST REALLY MISS THEM.
PLEASED TO MEET YOU! I'M OLIVER.
COSMO.
WELL, THIS IS ALL CERTAINLY VERY...NEW.
HEH. NOT NEW TA ME.
FIRST TIME ON THE INSIDE?
YEAH... YES, IT IS.
KEEP IT TOGETHER, KID.
JACKSON AIN'T EXACTLY THE PLACE TO EXPLORE NEW TERRITORY.

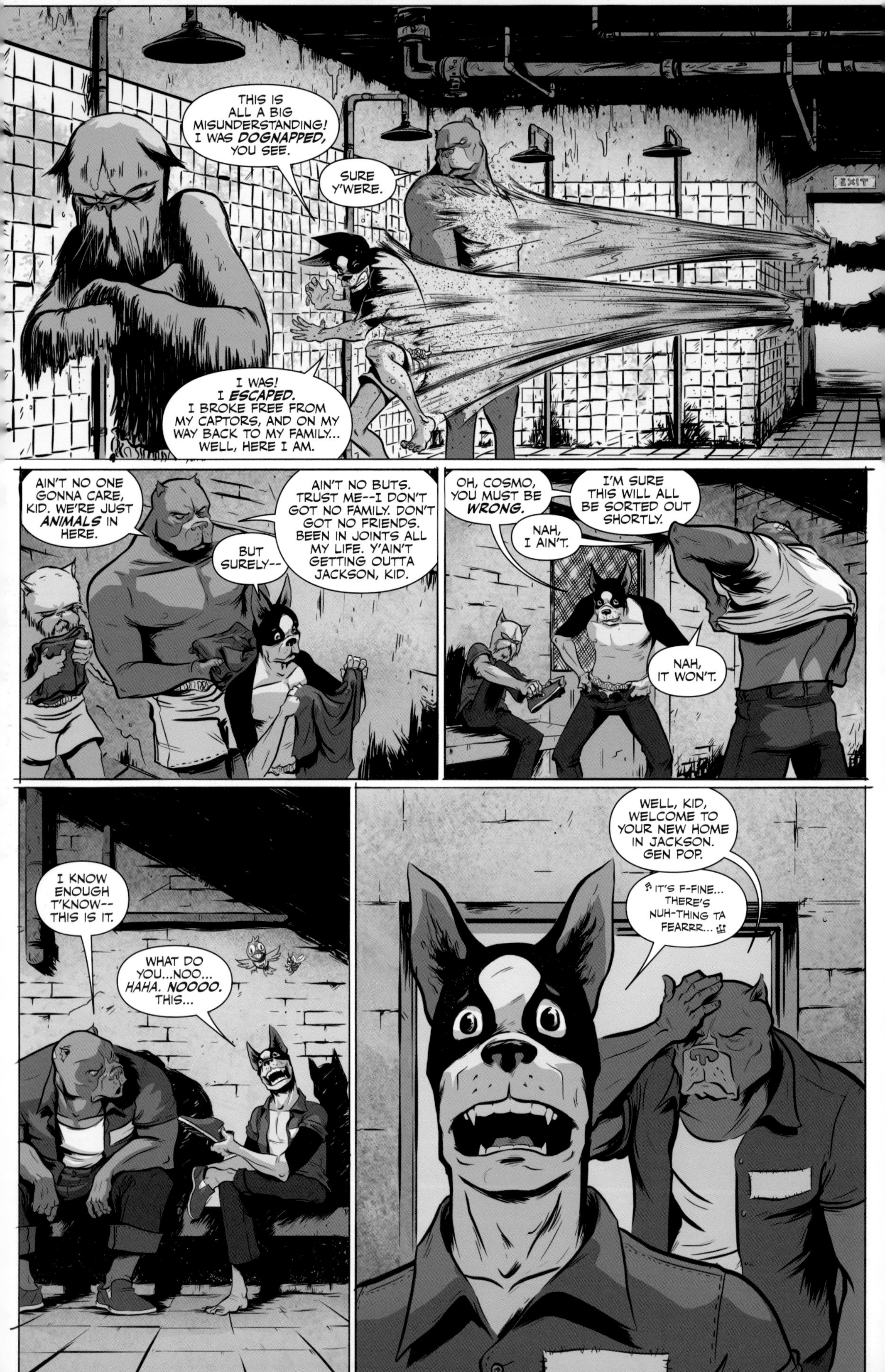

THIS IS ALL A BIG MISUNDERSTANDING! I WAS DOGNAPPED, YOU SEE.
SURE Y'WERE.
EXIT
I WAS! I ESCAPED. I BROKE FREE FROM MY CAPTORS, AND ON MY WAY BACK TO MY FAMILY... WELL, HERE I AM.
AIN'T NO ONE GONNA CARE, KID. WE'RE JUST ANIMALS IN HERE.
BUT SURELY--
AIN'T NO BUTS. TRUST ME--I DON'T GOT NO FAMILY. DON'T GOT NO FRIENDS. BEEN IN JOINTS ALL MY LIFE. Y'AIN'T GETTING OUTTA JACKSON, KID.
OH, COSMO, YOU MUST BE WRONG.
I'M SURE THIS WILL ALL BE SORTED OUT SHORTLY.
NAH, I AIN'T.
NAH, IT WON'T.
I KNOW ENOUGH T'KNOW-- THIS IS IT.
WHAT DO YOU...NOO... HAHA. NOOOO. THIS...
WELL, KID, WELCOME TO YOUR NEW HOME IN JACKSON. GEN POP.
IT'S F-FINE... THERE'S NUH-THING TA FEARRR...

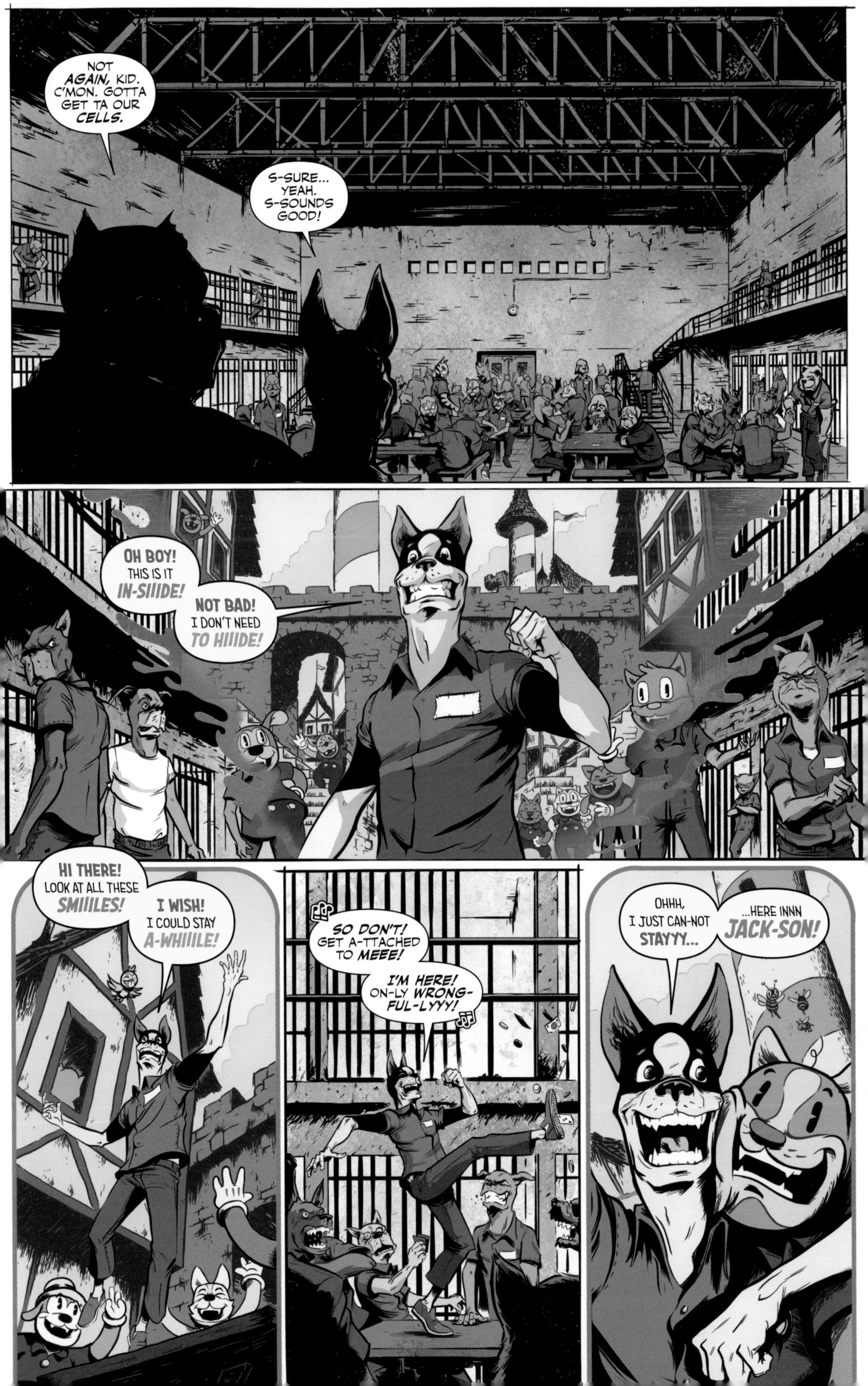
NOT AGAIN, KID. C'MON. GOTTA GET TA OUR CELLS.
S-SURE... YEAH. S-SOUNDS GOOD!
OH BOY! THIS IS IT IN-SIIIDE!
NOT BAD! I DON'T NEED TO HIIIDE!
HI THERE! LOOK AT ALL THESE SMIIILES!
I WISH! I COULD STAY A-WHIIILE!
SO DON'T! GET A-TTACHED TO MEEE!
I'M HERE! ON-LY WRONG-FUL-LYYY!
OHHH, I JUST CAN-NOT STAYYY...
...HERE INNN JACK-SON!

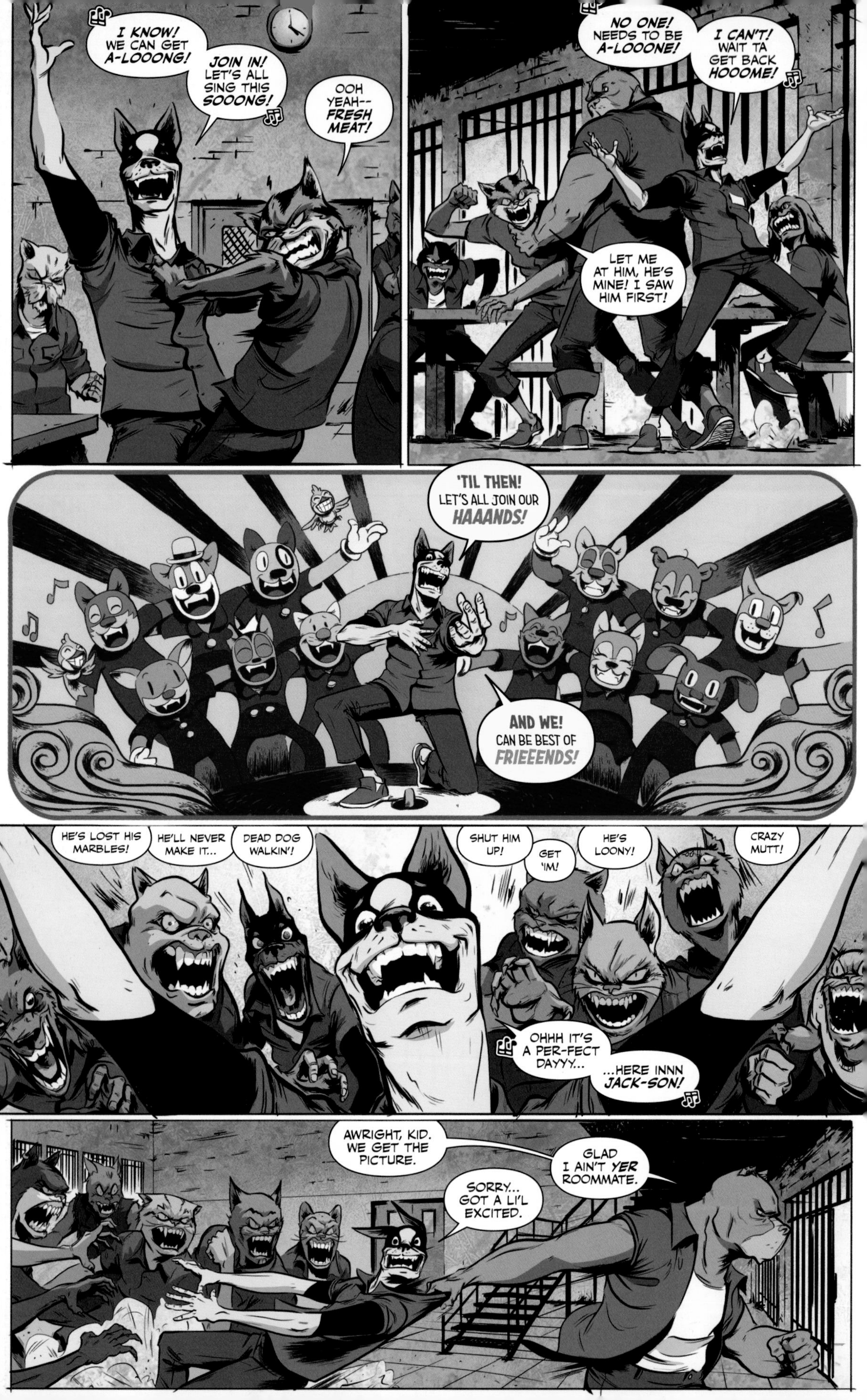
I KNOW! WE CAN GET A-LOOONG!
JOIN IN! LET'S ALL SING THIS SOOONG!
OOH YEAH-- FRESH MEAT!
NO ONE! NEEDS TO BE A-LOOONE!
I CAN'T! WAIT TA GET BACK HOOOME!
LET ME AT HIM, HE'S MINE! I SAW HIM FIRST!
'TIL THEN! LET'S ALL JOIN OUR HAAANDS!
AND WE! CAN BE BEST OF FRIEEENDS!
HE'S LOST HIS MARBLES!
HE'LL NEVER MAKE IT...
DEAD DOG WALKIN'!
SHUT HIM UP!
GET 'IM!
HE'S LOONY!
CRAZY MUTT!
OHHH IT'S A PER-FECT DAYYY...
...HERE INNN JACK-SON!
AWRIGHT, KID. WE GET THE PICTURE.
GLAD I AIN'T YER ROOMMATE.
SORRY... GOT A LI'L EXCITED.

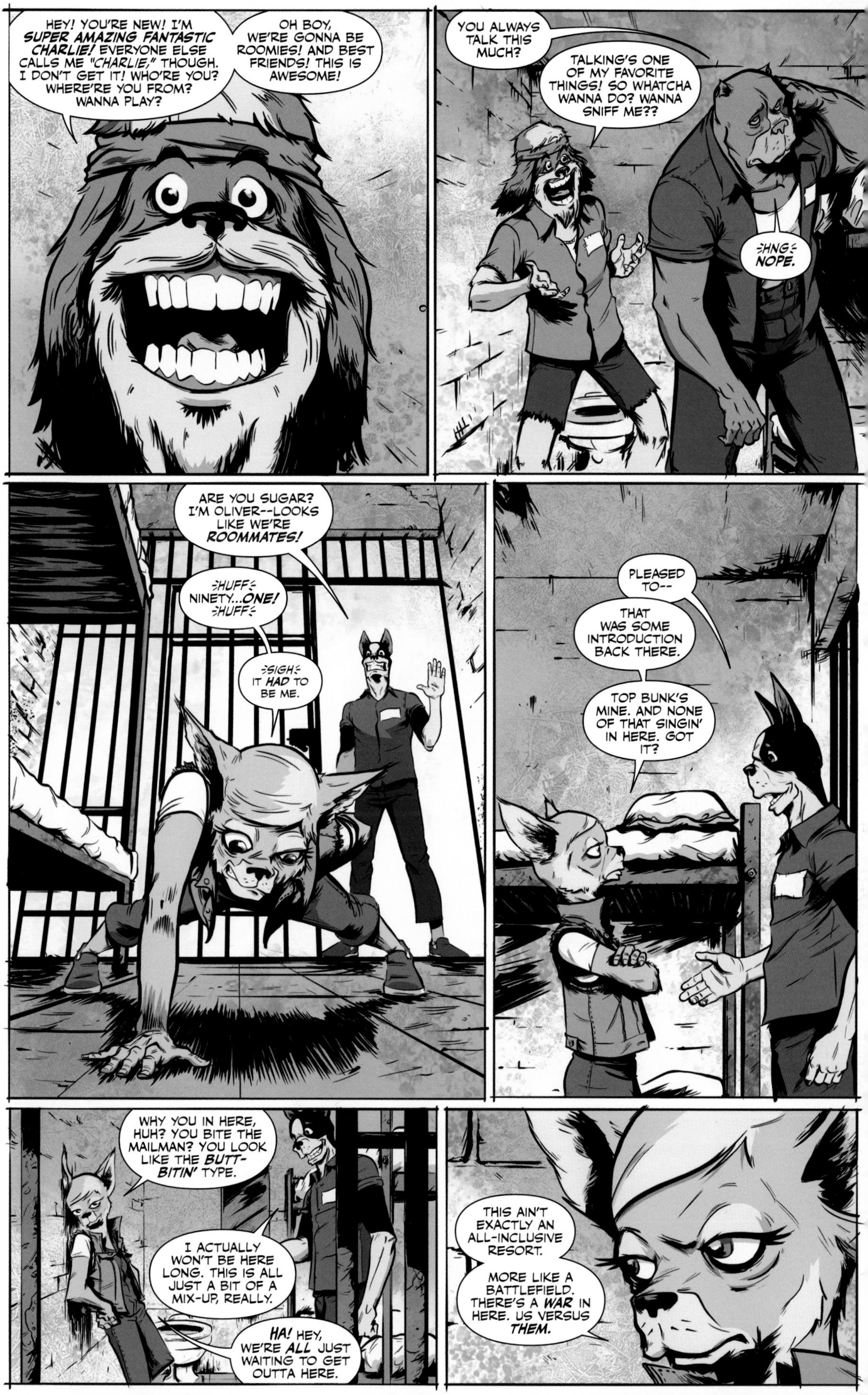
HEY! YOU'RE NEW! I'M SUPER AMAZING FANTASTIC CHARLIE! EVERYONE ELSE CALLS ME "CHARLIE," THOUGH. I DON'T GET IT! WHO'RE YOU? WHERE'RE YOU FROM? WANNA PLAY?
OH BOY, WE'RE GONNA BE ROOMIES! AND BEST FRIENDS! THIS IS AWESOME!
YOU ALWAYS TALK THIS MUCH?
TALKING'S ONE OF MY FAVORITE THINGS! SO WHATCHA WANNA DO? WANNA SNIFF ME??
HNG NOPE.
ARE YOU SUGAR? I'M OLIVER--LOOKS LIKE WE'RE ROOMMATES!
HUFF NINETY...ONE! HUFF
SIGH IT HAD TO BE ME.
PLEASED TO--
THAT WAS SOME INTRODUCTION BACK THERE.
TOP BUNK'S MINE. AND NONE OF THAT SINGIN' IN HERE. GOT IT?
WHY YOU IN HERE, HUH? YOU BITE THE MAILMAN? YOU LOOK LIKE THE BUTT-BITIN' TYPE.
I ACTUALLY WON'T BE HERE LONG. THIS IS ALL JUST A BIT OF A MIX-UP, REALLY.
HA! HEY, WE'RE ALL JUST WAITING TO GET OUTTA HERE.
THIS AIN'T EXACTLY AN ALL-INCLUSIVE RESORT.
MORE LIKE A BATTLEFIELD. THERE'S A WAR IN HERE. US VERSUS THEM.

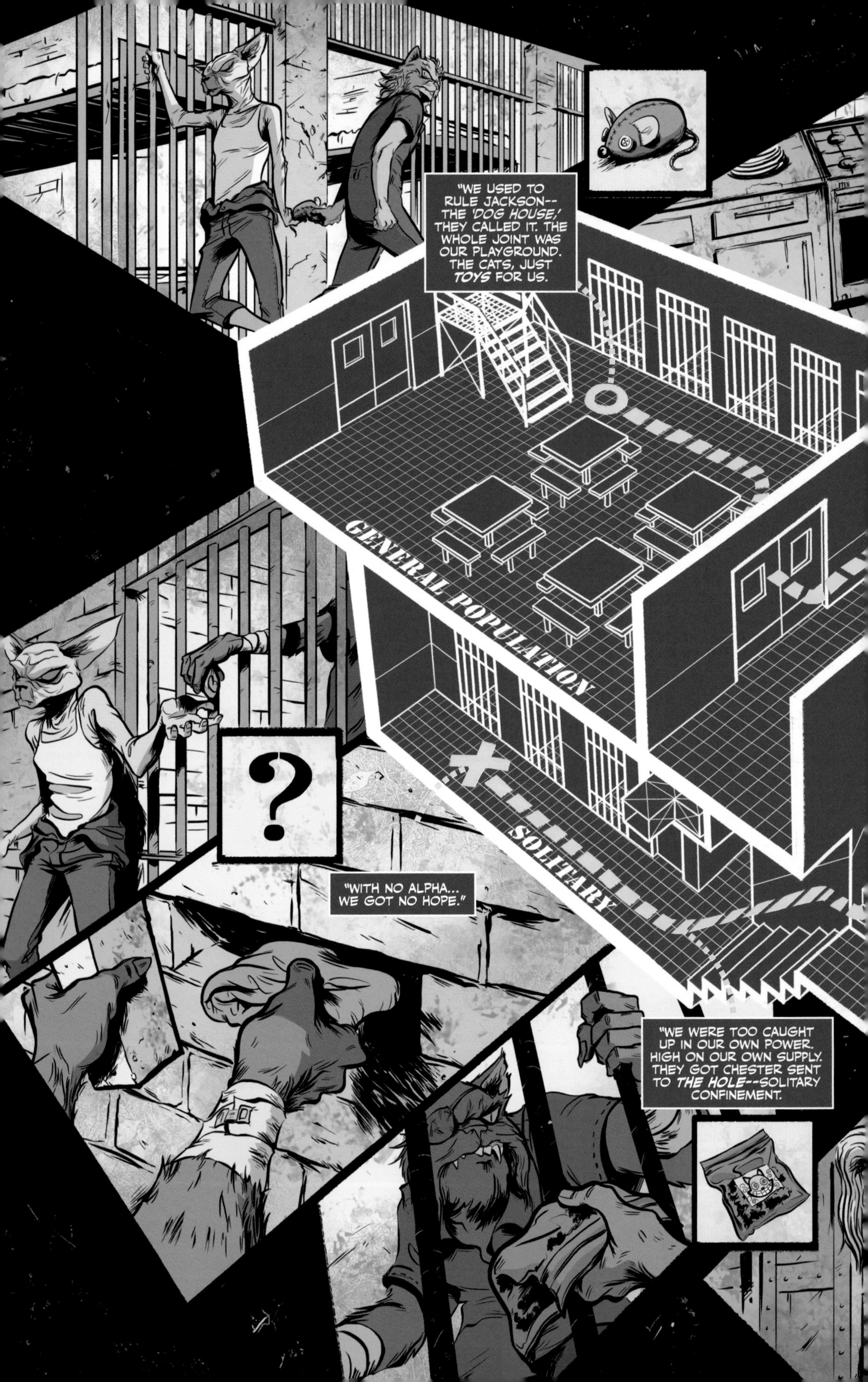
"WE USED TO RULE JACKSON-- THE 'DOG HOUSE,' THEY CALLED IT. THE WHOLE JOINT WAS OUR PLAYGROUND. THE CATS, JUST *TOYS* FOR US.
GENERAL POPULATION
SOLITARY
?
"WITH NO ALPHA... WE GOT NO HOPE."
"WE WERE TOO CAUGHT UP IN OUR OWN POWER. HIGH ON OUR OWN SUPPLY. THEY GOT CHESTER SENT TO *THE HOLE*--SOLITARY CONFINEMENT.

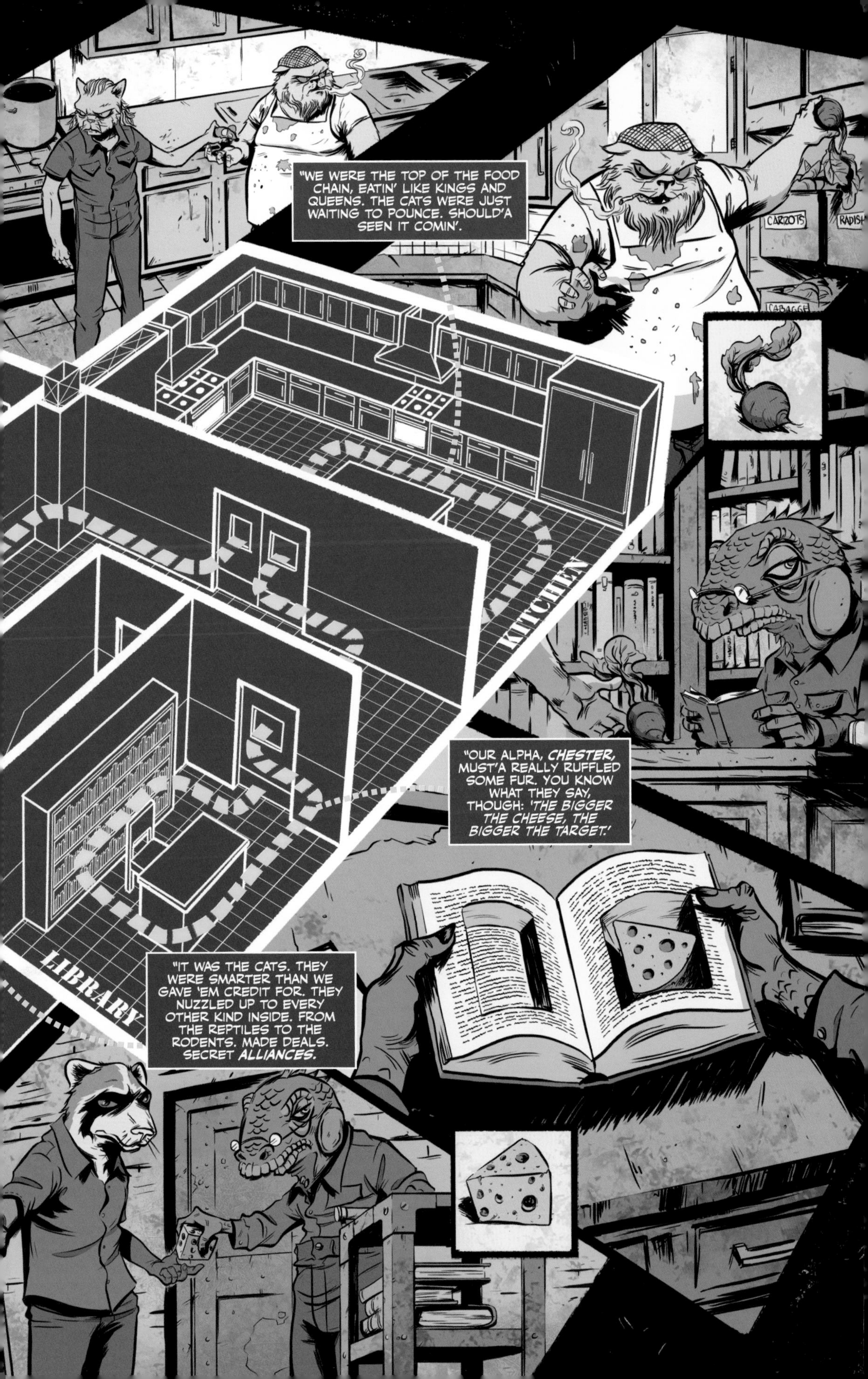
"WE WERE THE TOP OF THE FOOD CHAIN, EATIN' LIKE KINGS AND QUEENS. THE CATS WERE JUST WAITING TO POUNCE. SHOULD'A SEEN IT COMIN'.
CARROTS
RADISH
CABAGGE
KITCHEN
LIBRARY
"OUR ALPHA, *CHESTER,* MUST'A REALLY RUFFLED SOME FUR. YOU KNOW WHAT THEY SAY, THOUGH: *'THE BIGGER THE CHEESE, THE BIGGER THE TARGET.'*
"IT WAS THE CATS. THEY WERE SMARTER THAN WE GAVE 'EM CREDIT FOR. THEY NUZZLED UP TO EVERY OTHER KIND INSIDE. FROM THE REPTILES TO THE RODENTS. MADE DEALS. SECRET *ALLIANCES.*

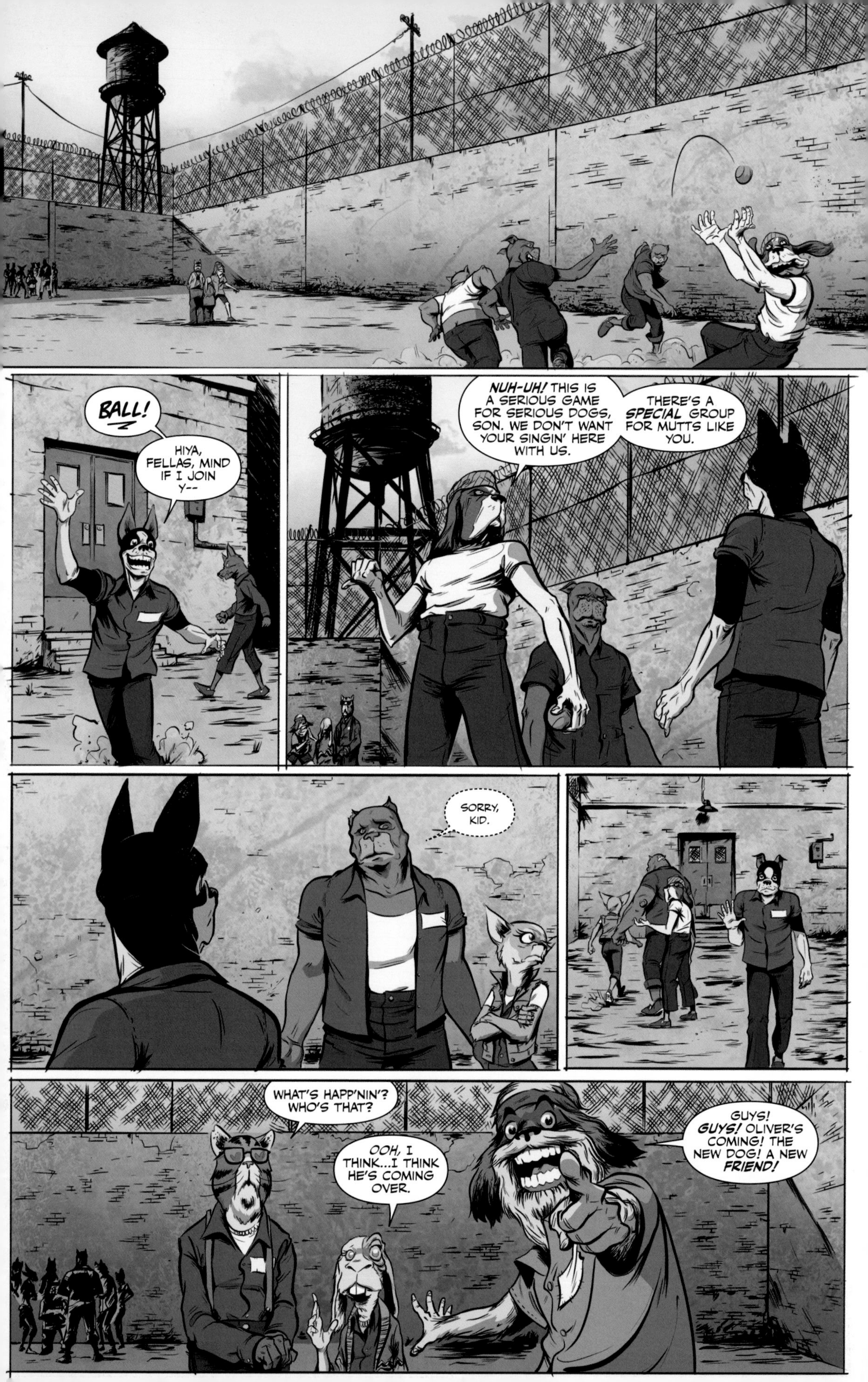
BALL!
HIYA, FELLAS, MIND IF I JOIN Y--
NUH-UH! THIS IS A SERIOUS GAME FOR SERIOUS DOGS, SON. WE DON'T WANT YOUR SINGIN' HERE WITH US.
THERE'S A SPECIAL GROUP FOR MUTTS LIKE YOU.
SORRY, KID.
WHAT'S HAPP'NIN'? WHO'S THAT?
OOH, I THINK...I THINK HE'S COMING OVER.
GUYS! GUYS! OLIVER'S COMING! THE NEW DOG! A NEW FRIEND!

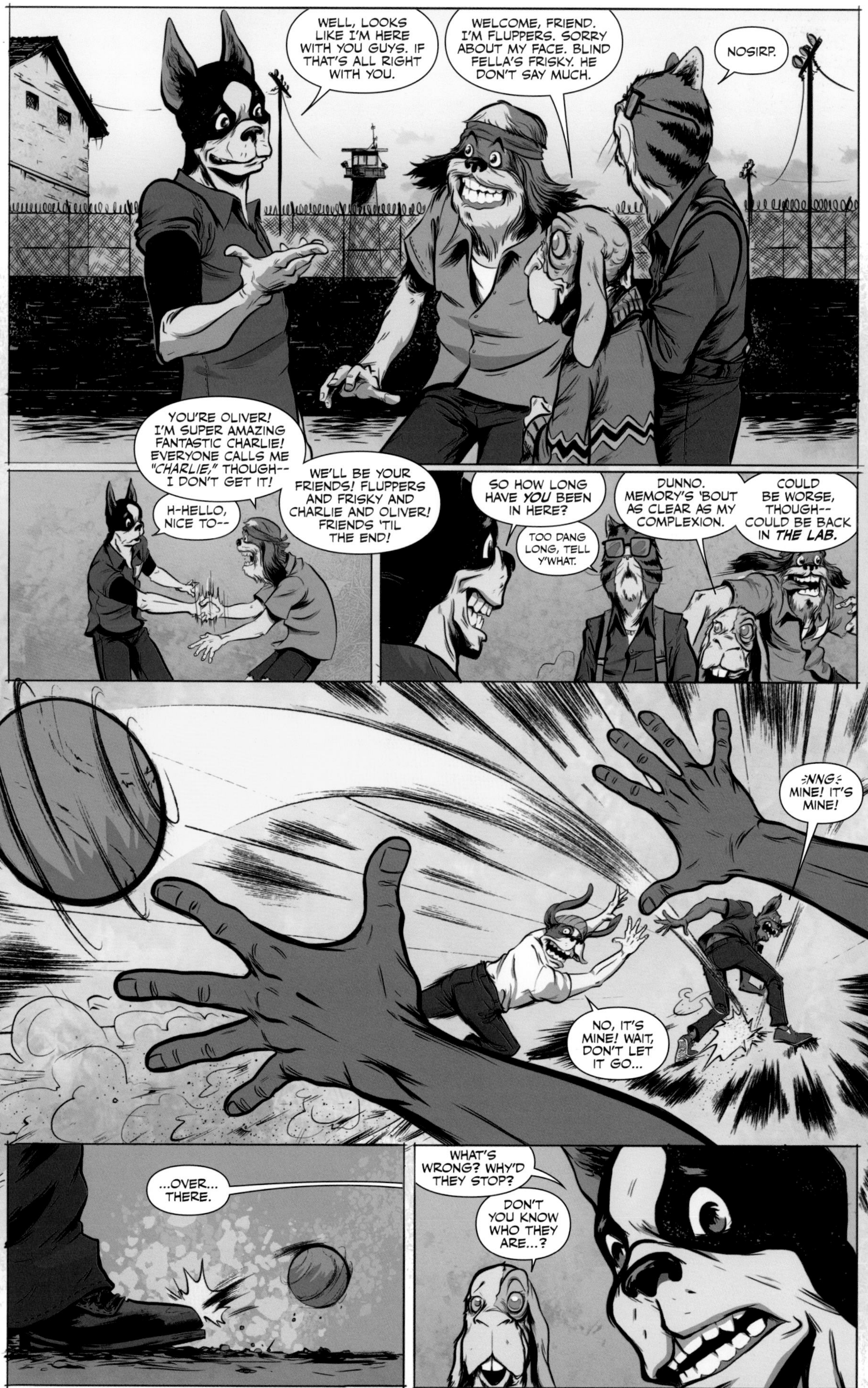
WELL, LOOKS LIKE I'M HERE WITH YOU GUYS. IF THAT'S ALL RIGHT WITH YOU.
WELCOME, FRIEND. I'M FLUPPERS. SORRY ABOUT MY FACE. BLIND FELLA'S FRISKY. HE DON'T SAY MUCH.
NOSIRP.
YOU'RE OLIVER! I'M SUPER AMAZING FANTASTIC CHARLIE! EVERYONE CALLS ME "CHARLIE," THOUGH-- I DON'T GET IT!
H-HELLO, NICE TO--
WE'LL BE YOUR FRIENDS! FLUPPERS AND FRISKY AND CHARLIE AND OLIVER! FRIENDS 'TIL THE END!
SO HOW LONG HAVE YOU BEEN IN HERE?
TOO DANG LONG, TELL Y'WHAT.
DUNNO. MEMORY'S 'BOUT AS CLEAR AS MY COMPLEXION.
COULD BE WORSE, THOUGH-- COULD BE BACK IN THE LAB.
NNG MINE! IT'S MINE!
NO, IT'S MINE! WAIT, DON'T LET IT GO...
...OVER... THERE.
WHAT'S WRONG? WHY'D THEY STOP?
DON'T YOU KNOW WHO THEY ARE...?

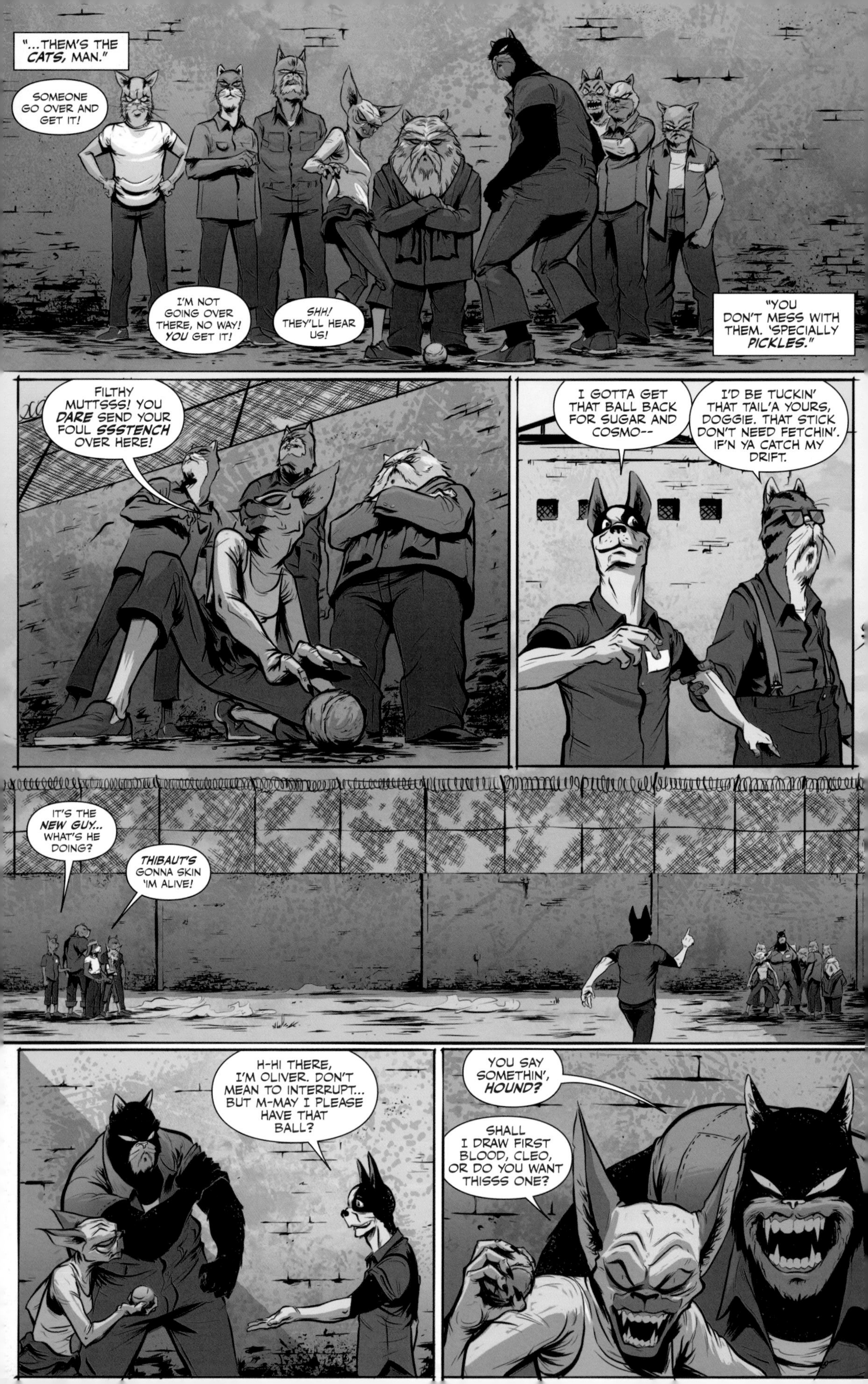
"...THEM'S THE CATS, MAN."
SOMEONE GO OVER AND GET IT!
I'M NOT GOING OVER THERE, NO WAY! YOU GET IT!
SHH! THEY'LL HEAR US!
"YOU DON'T MESS WITH THEM. 'SPECIALLY PICKLES."
FILTHY MUTTSSS! YOU DARE SEND YOUR FOUL SSSTENCH OVER HERE!
I GOTTA GET THAT BALL BACK FOR SUGAR AND COSMO--
I'D BE TUCKIN' THAT TAIL'A YOURS, DOGGIE. THAT STICK DON'T NEED FETCHIN'. IF'N YA CATCH MY DRIFT.
IT'S THE NEW GUY... WHAT'S HE DOING?
THIBAUT'S GONNA SKIN 'IM ALIVE!
H-HI THERE, I'M OLIVER. DON'T MEAN TO INTERRUPT... BUT M-MAY I PLEASE HAVE THAT BALL?
YOU SAY SOMETHIN', HOUND?
SHALL I DRAW FIRST BLOOD, CLEO, OR DO YOU WANT THISSS ONE?

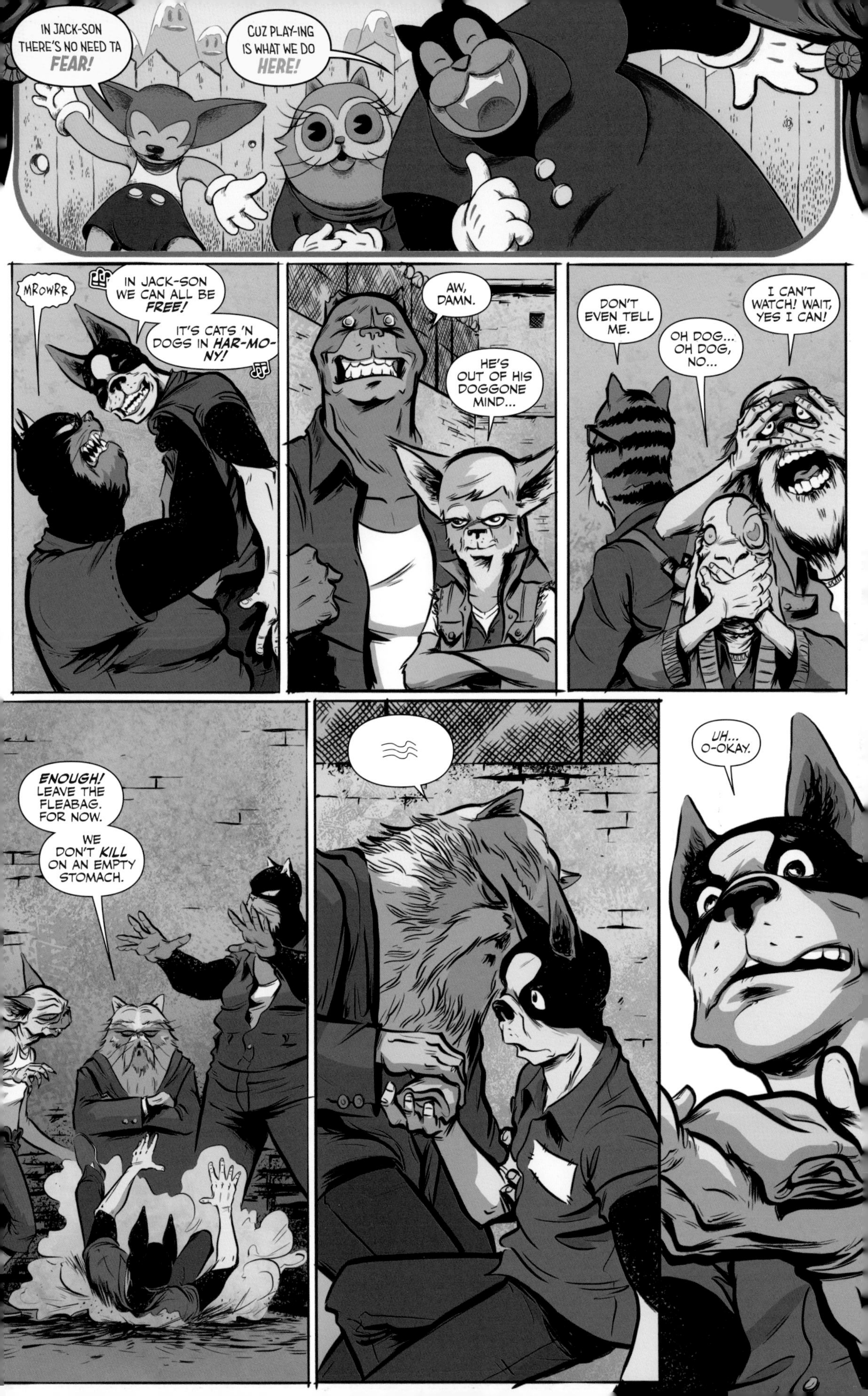
IN JACK-SON THERE'S NO NEED TA FEAR!
CUZ PLAY-ING IS WHAT WE DO HERE!
MROWRR
IN JACK-SON WE CAN ALL BE FREE!
IT'S CATS 'N DOGS IN HAR-MO-NY!
AW, DAMN.
HE'S OUT OF HIS DOGGONE MIND...
DON'T EVEN TELL ME.
OH DOG... OH DOG, NO...
I CAN'T WATCH! WAIT, YES I CAN!
ENOUGH! LEAVE THE FLEABAG. FOR NOW.
WE DON'T KILL ON AN EMPTY STOMACH.
UH... O-OKAY.

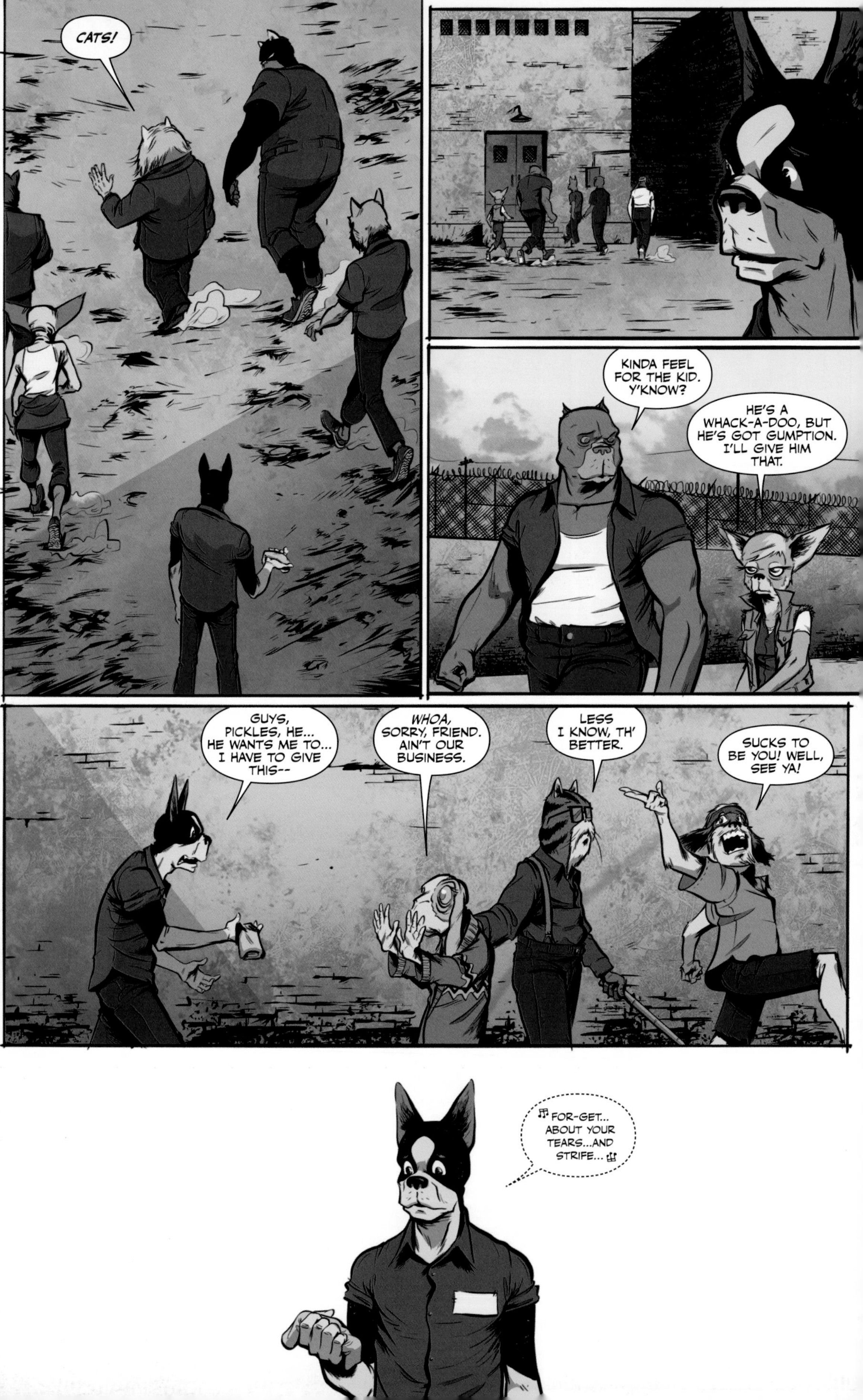
CATS!
KINDA FEEL FOR THE KID. Y'KNOW?
HE'S A WHACK-A-DOO, BUT HE'S GOT GUMPTION. I'LL GIVE HIM THAT.
GUYS, PICKLES, HE... HE WANTS ME TO... I HAVE TO GIVE THIS--
WHOA, SORRY, FRIEND. AIN'T OUR BUSINESS.
LESS I KNOW, TH' BETTER.
SUCKS TO BE YOU! WELL, SEE YA!
FOR-GET... ABOUT YOUR TEARS...AND STRIFE...

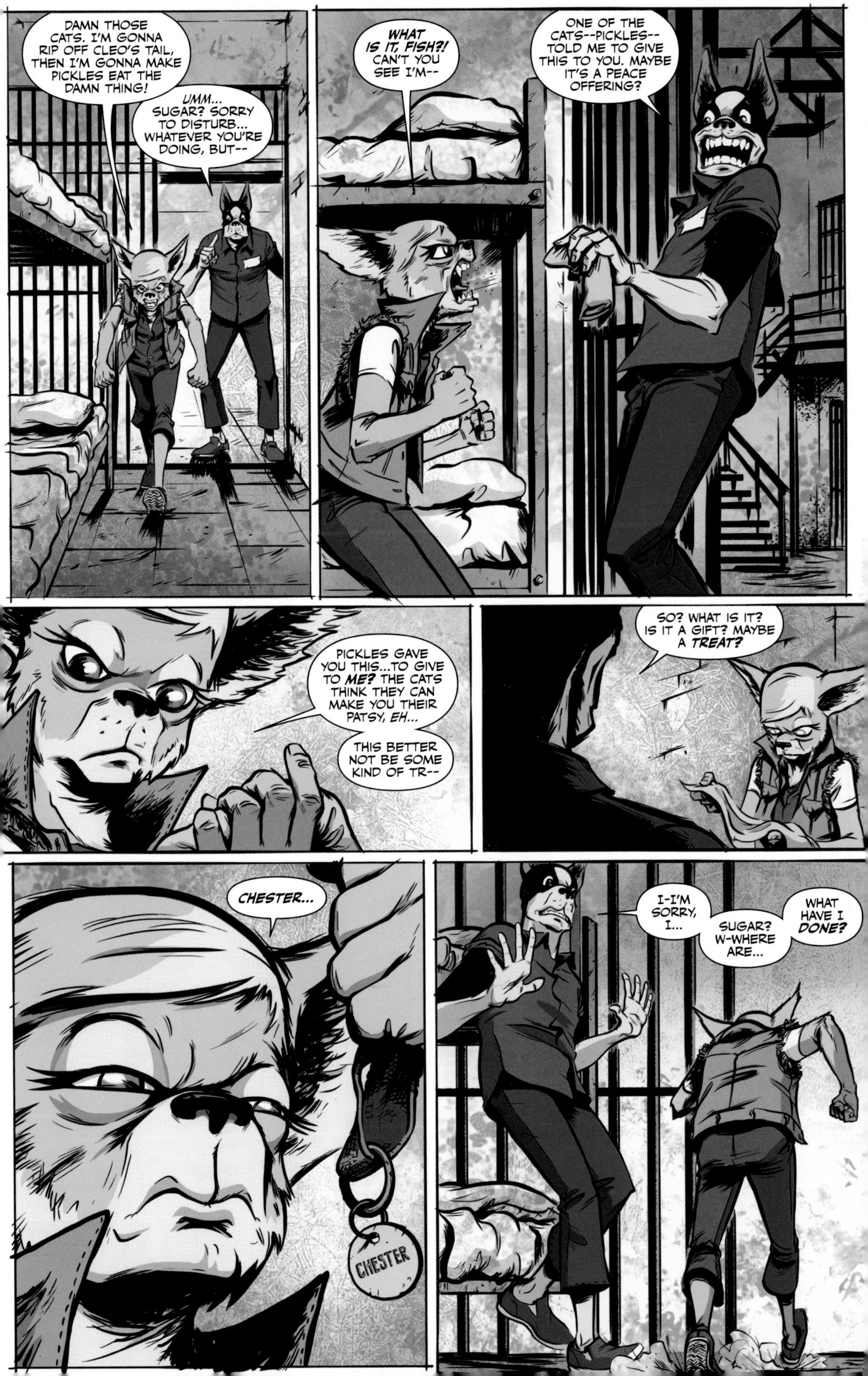

DAMN THOSE CATS. I'M GONNA RIP OFF CLEO'S TAIL, THEN I'M GONNA MAKE PICKLES EAT THE DAMN THING!
UMM... SUGAR? SORRY TO DISTURB... WHATEVER YOU'RE DOING, BUT--
WHAT IS IT, FISH?! CAN'T YOU SEE I'M--
ONE OF THE CATS--PICKLES--TOLD ME TO GIVE THIS TO YOU. MAYBE IT'S A PEACE OFFERING?
PICKLES GAVE YOU THIS...TO GIVE TO ME? THE CATS THINK THEY CAN MAKE YOU THEIR PATSY, EH...
THIS BETTER NOT BE SOME KIND OF TR--
SO? WHAT IS IT? IS IT A GIFT? MAYBE A TREAT?
CHESTER...
CHESTER
I-I'M SORRY, I...
SUGAR? W-WHERE ARE...
WHAT HAVE I DONE?

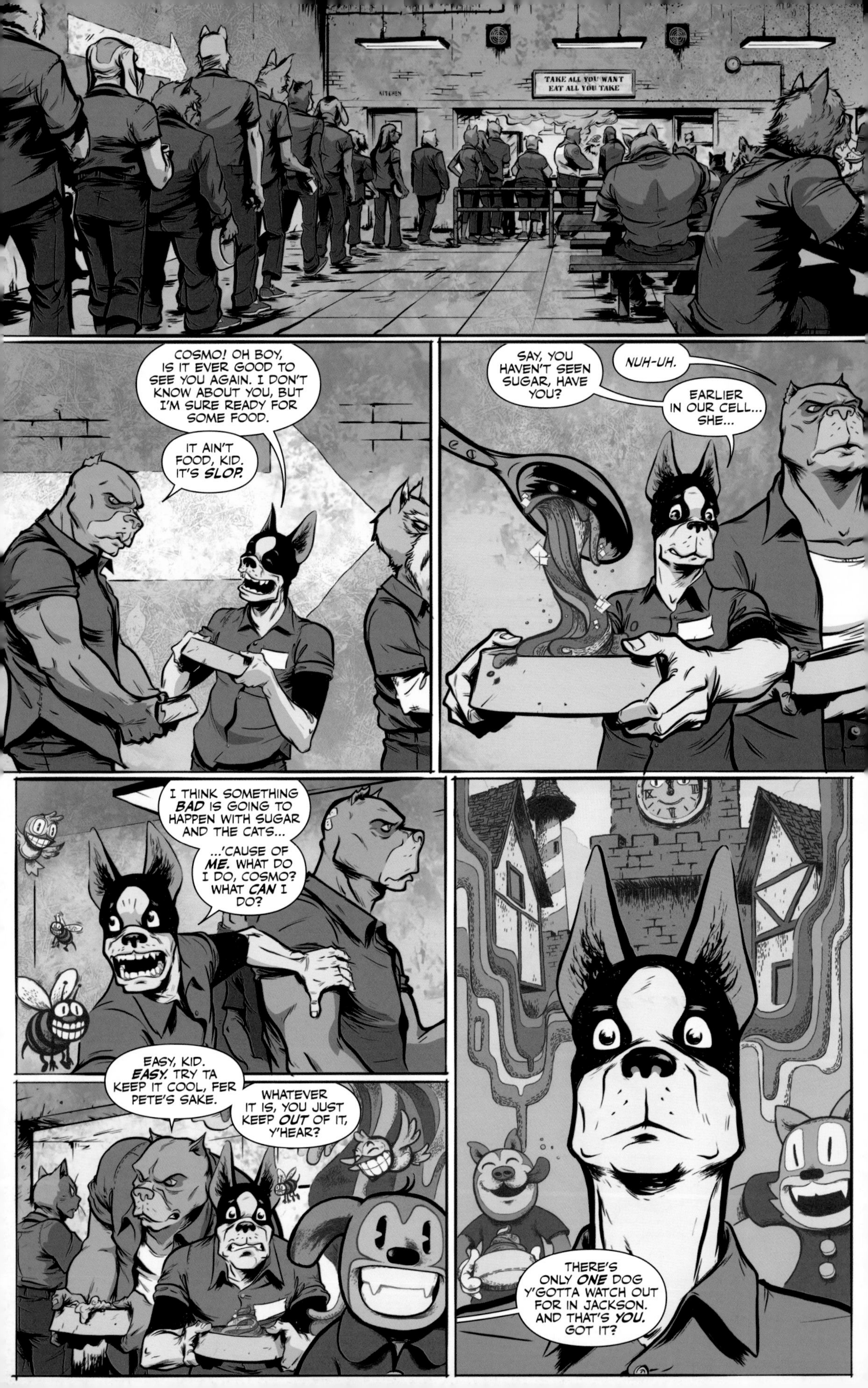
TAKE ALL YOU WANT
EAT ALL YOU TAKE
KITCHEN
COSMO! OH BOY, IS IT EVER GOOD TO SEE YOU AGAIN. I DON'T KNOW ABOUT YOU, BUT I'M SURE READY FOR SOME FOOD.
IT AIN'T FOOD, KID. IT'S *SLOP.*
SAY, YOU HAVEN'T SEEN SUGAR, HAVE YOU?
NUH-UH.
EARLIER IN OUR CELL... SHE...
I THINK SOMETHING *BAD* IS GOING TO HAPPEN WITH SUGAR AND THE CATS...
...'CAUSE OF *ME.* WHAT DO I DO, COSMO? WHAT *CAN* I DO?
EASY, KID. *EASY.* TRY TA KEEP IT COOL, FER PETE'S SAKE.
WHATEVER IT IS, YOU JUST KEEP *OUT* OF IT, Y'HEAR?
THERE'S ONLY *ONE* DOG Y'GOTTA WATCH OUT FOR IN JACKSON. AND THAT'S *YOU.* GOT IT?

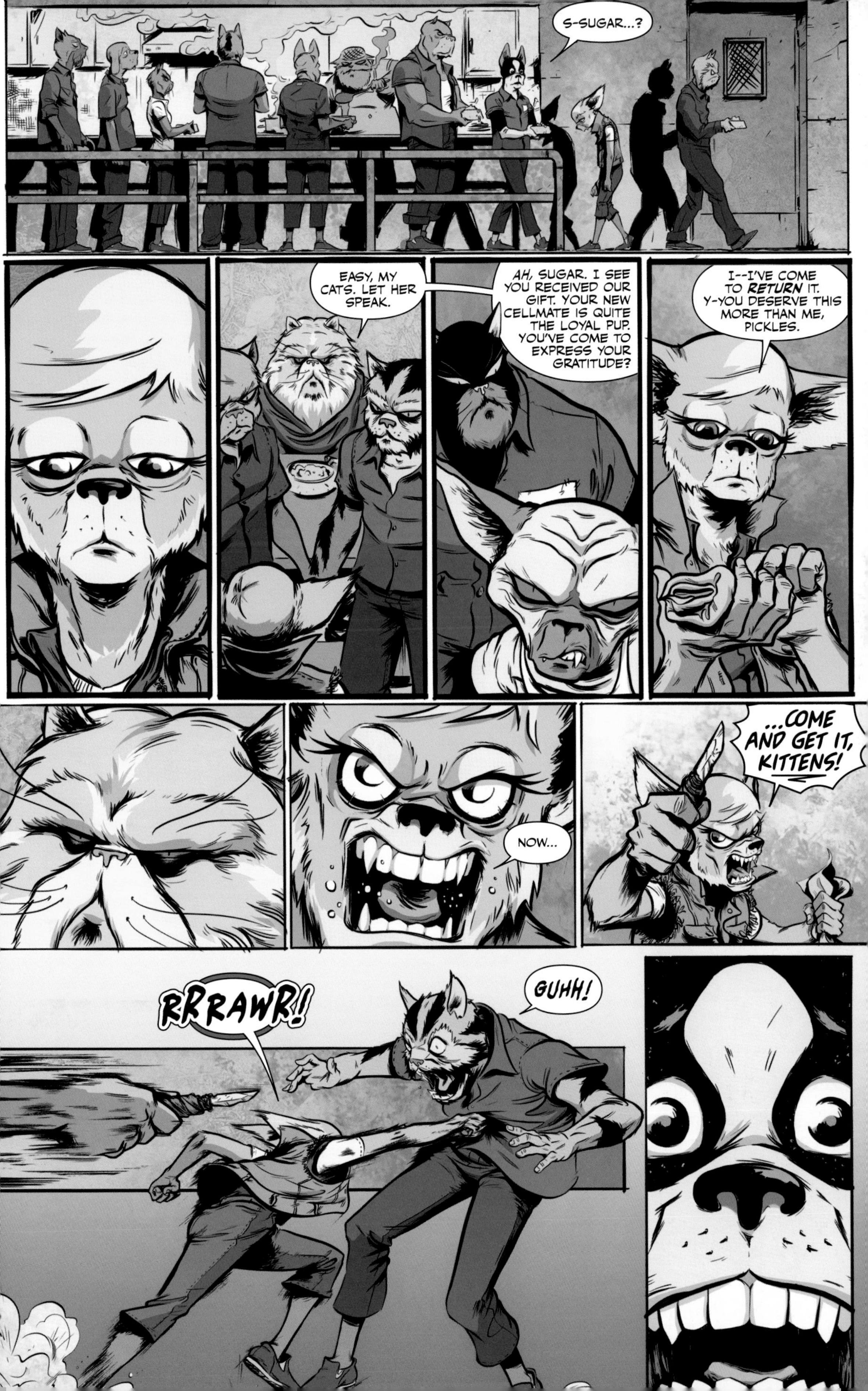
S-SUGAR...?
EASY, MY CATS. LET HER SPEAK.
AH, SUGAR. I SEE YOU RECEIVED OUR GIFT. YOUR NEW CELLMATE IS QUITE THE LOYAL PUP. YOU'VE COME TO EXPRESS YOUR GRATITUDE?
I--I'VE COME TO RETURN IT. Y-YOU DESERVE THIS MORE THAN ME, PICKLES.
NOW...
...COME AND GET IT, KITTENS!
RRRAWR!
GUHH!

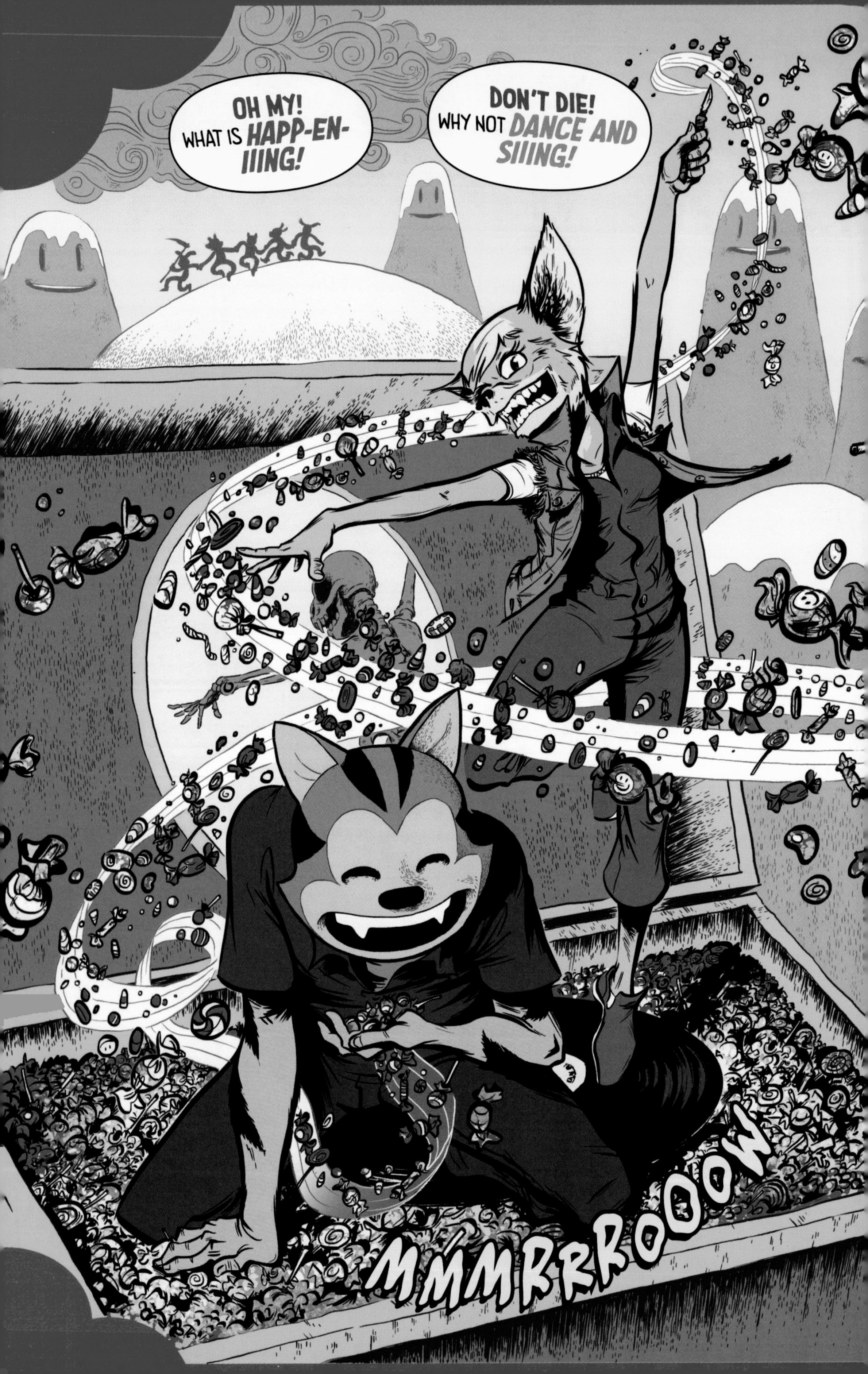
OH MY! WHAT IS HAPP-EN-IIING!
DON'T DIE! WHY NOT DANCE AND SIING!
MMMRRROOOW

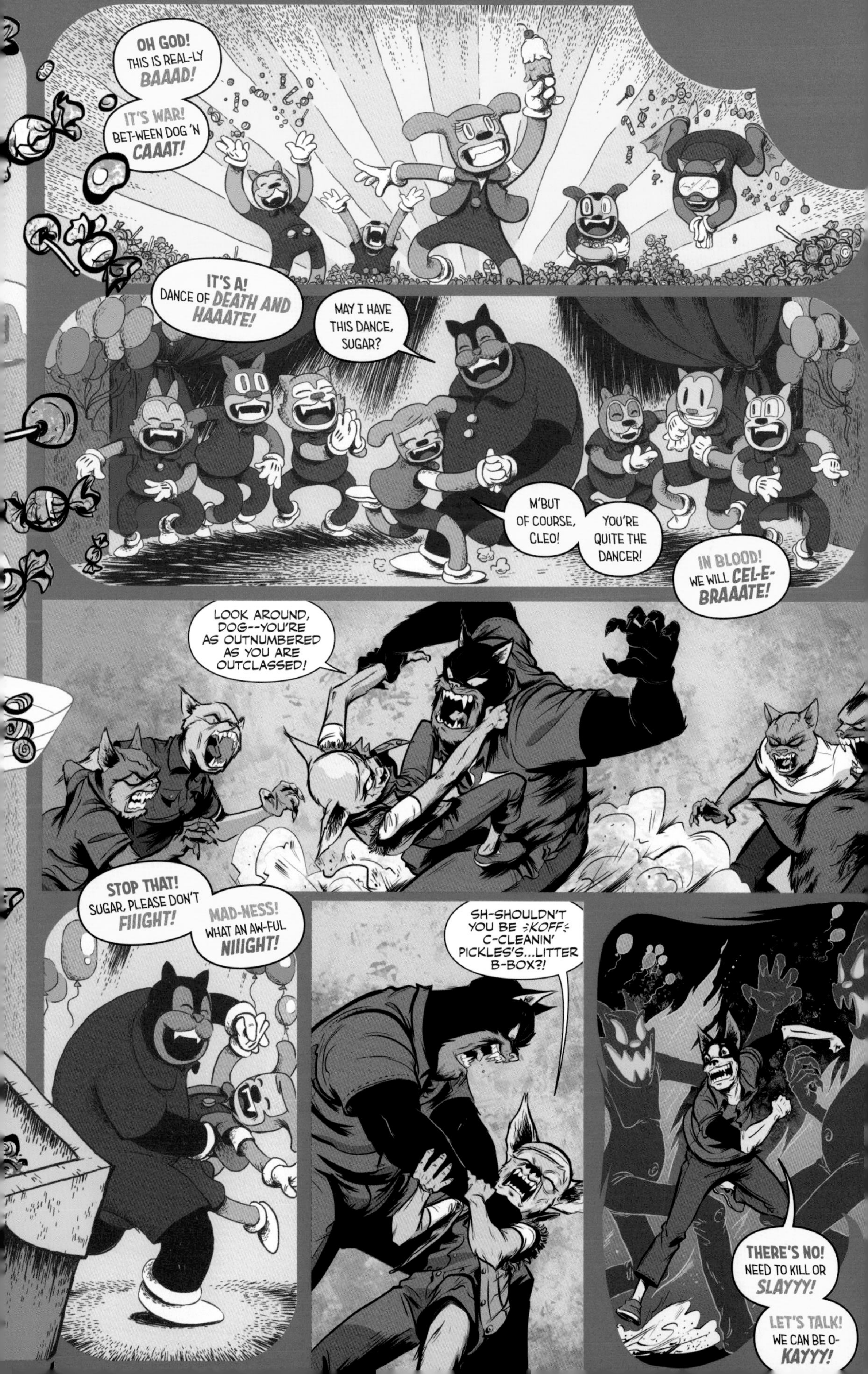
OH GOD! THIS IS REAL-LY BAAAD!
IT'S WAR! BET-WEEN DOG 'N CAAAT!
IT'S A! DANCE OF DEATH AND HAAATE!
MAY I HAVE THIS DANCE, SUGAR?
M'BUT OF COURSE, CLEO!
YOU'RE QUITE THE DANCER!
IN BLOOD! WE WILL CEL-E-BRAAATE!
LOOK AROUND, DOG--YOU'RE AS OUTNUMBERED AS YOU ARE OUTCLASSED!
STOP THAT! SUGAR, PLEASE DON'T FIIIGHT!
MAD-NESS! WHAT AN AW-FUL NIIIGHT!
SH-SHOULDN'T YOU BE KOFF C-CLEANIN' PICKLES'S...LITTER B-BOX?!
THERE'S NO! NEED TO KILL OR SLAYYY!
LET'S TALK! WE CAN BE O-KAYYY!

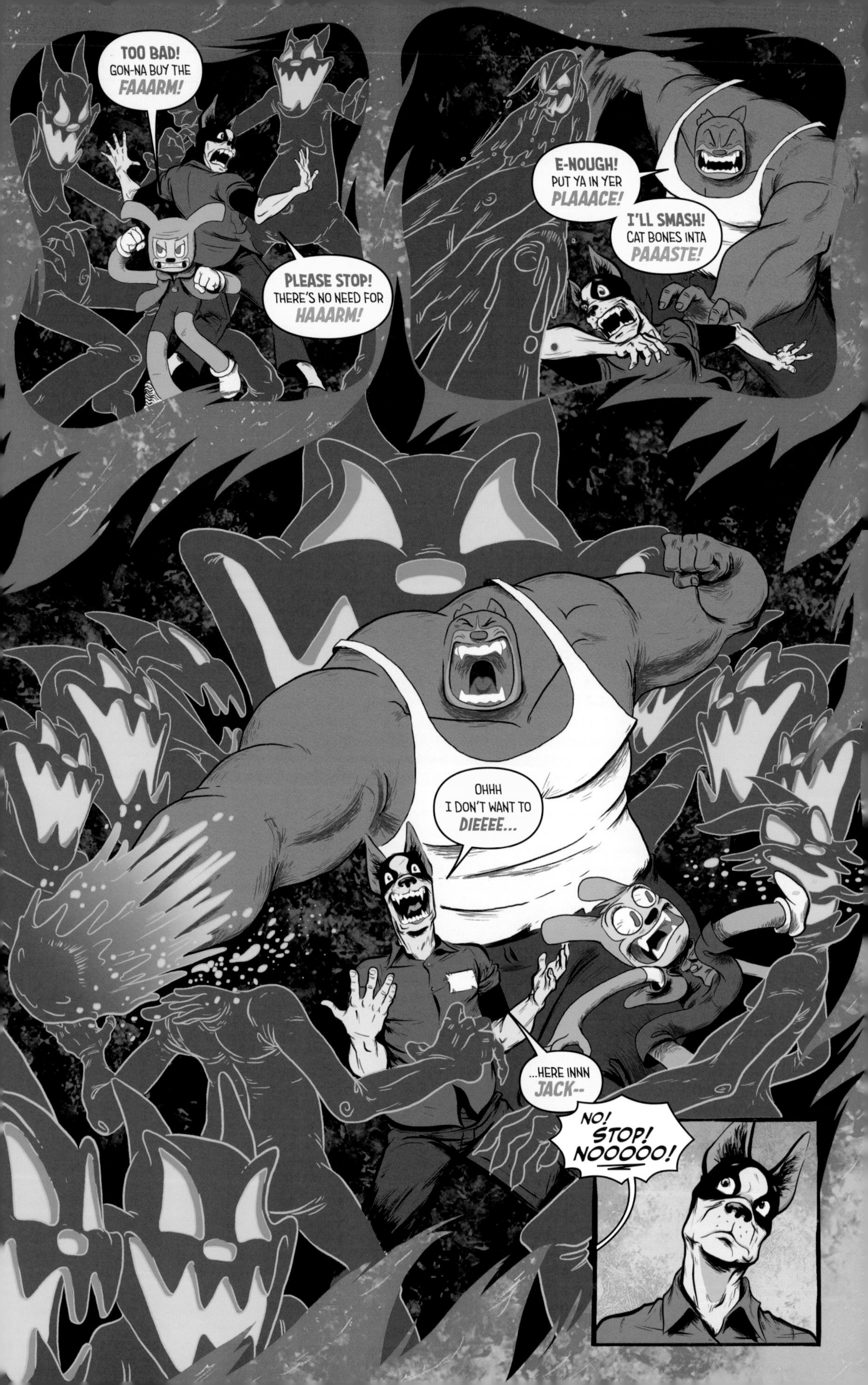
TOO BAD! GON-NA BUY THE FAAARM!
PLEASE STOP! THERE'S NO NEED FOR HAAARM!
E-NOUGH! PUT YA IN YER PLAAACE!
I'LL SMASH! CAT BONES INTA PAAASTE!
OHHH I DON'T WANT TO DIEEEE...
...HERE INNN JACK--
NO! STOP! NOOOOO!

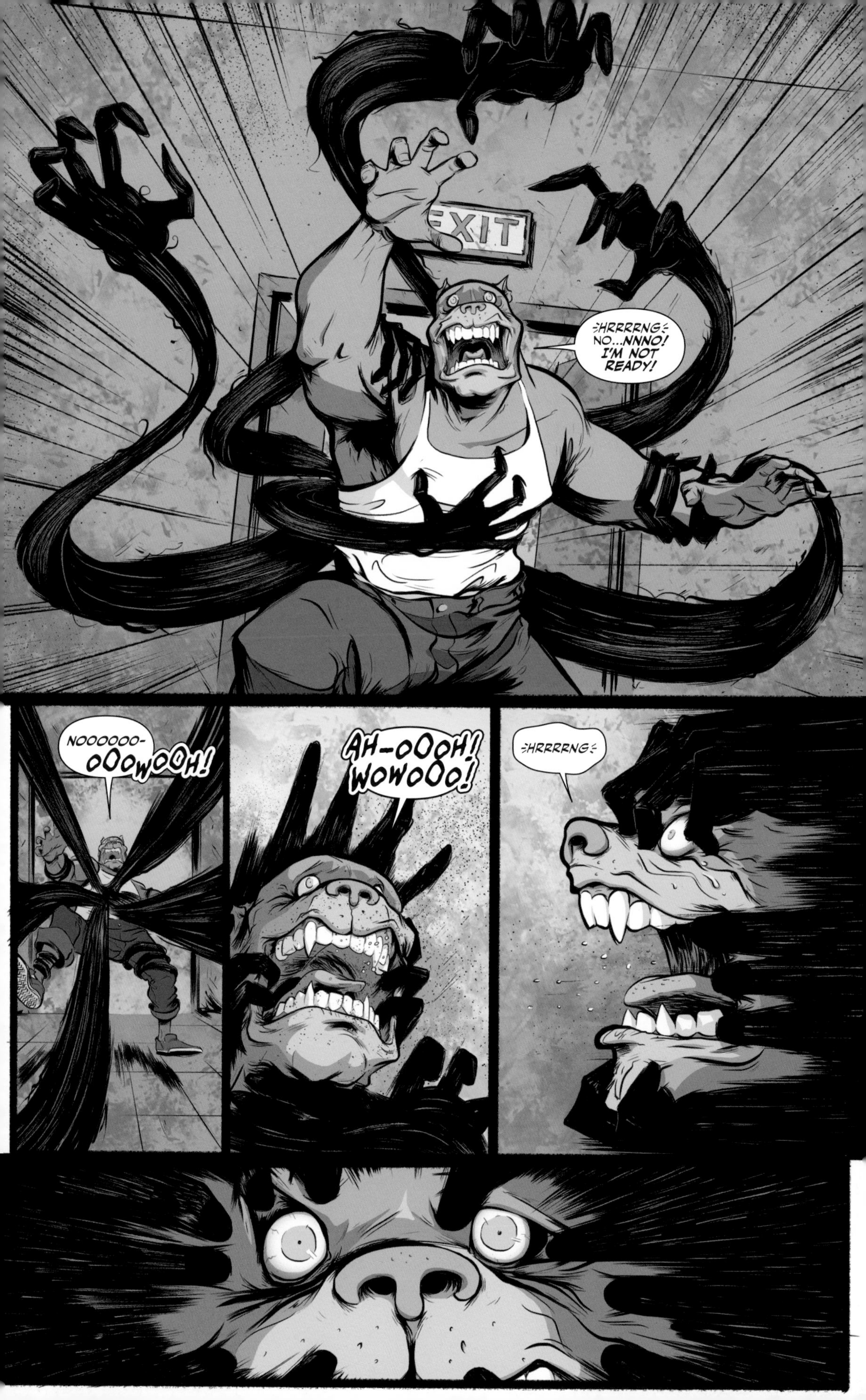

=HRRRRNG= NO...NNNO! I'M NOT READY!
NOOOOOO-OOOWOOOH!
AH-OOOH! WOWOOO!
=HRRRRNG=

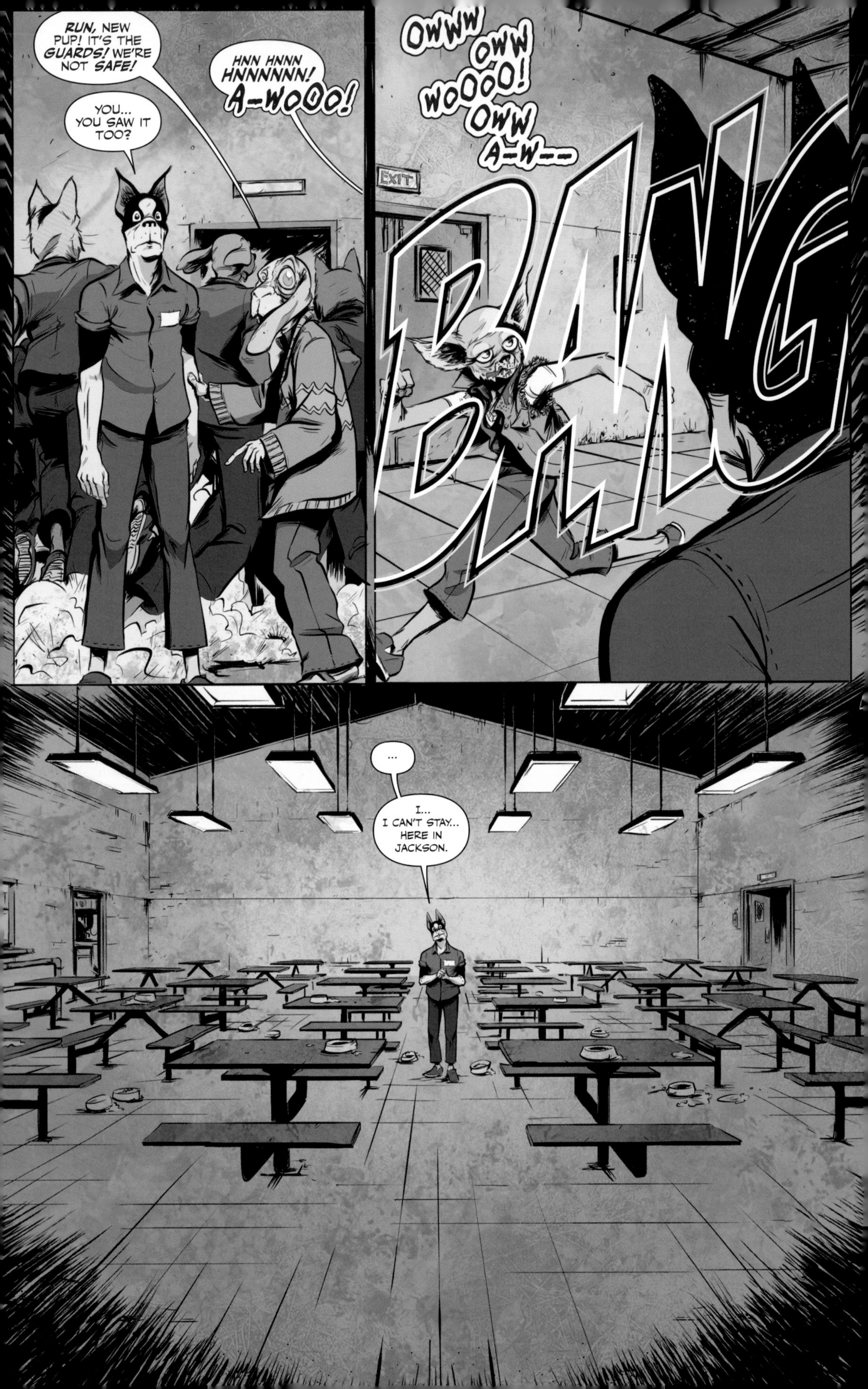
RUN, NEW PUP! IT'S THE GUARDS! WE'RE NOT SAFE!
YOU... YOU SAW IT TOO?
HNN HNNN HNNNNNN! A-WOOO!
OWWW OWW WOOOO! OWW A-W--
BANG
...
I... I CAN'T STAY... HERE IN JACKSON.
EXIT

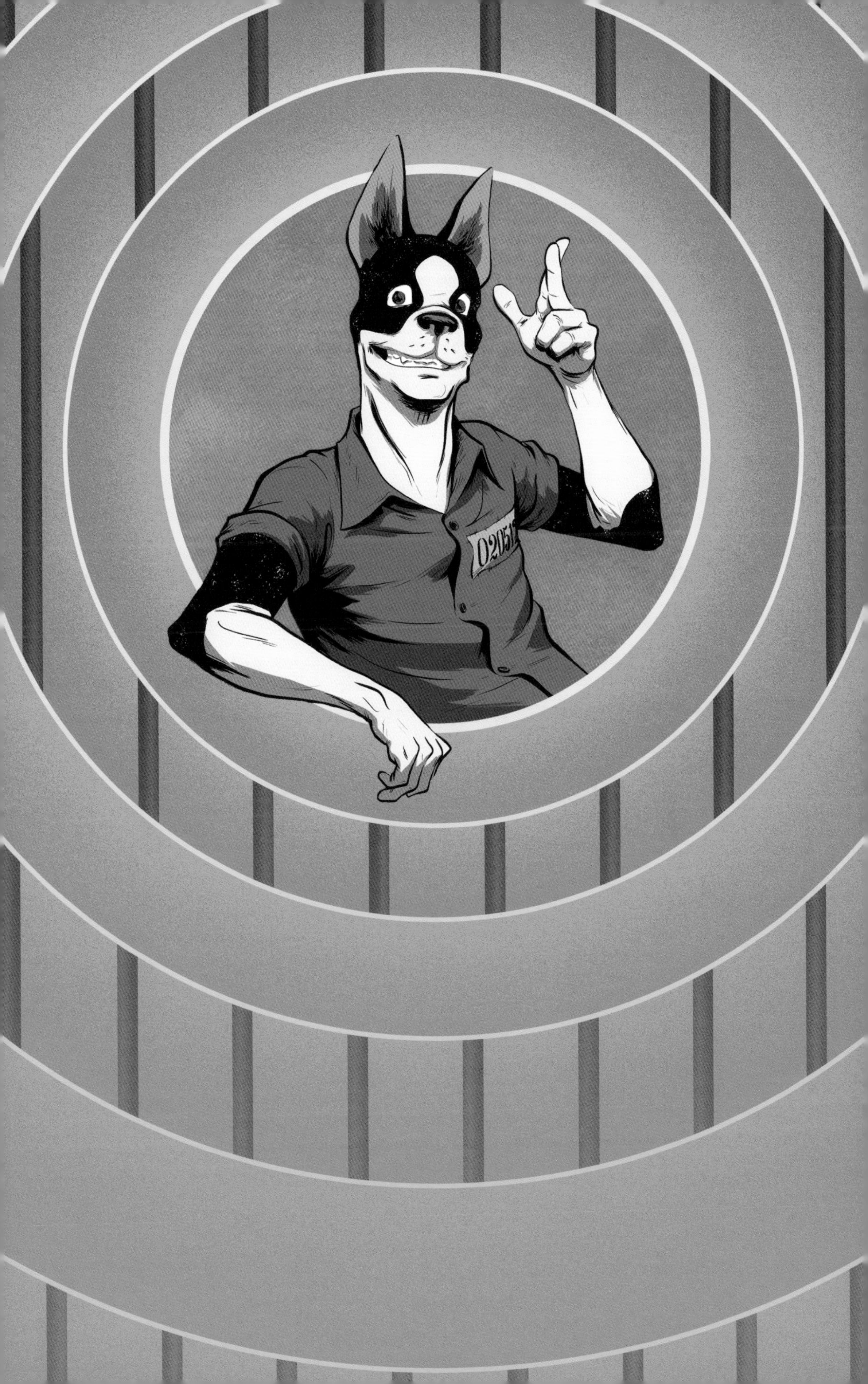
02051

Chapter Two

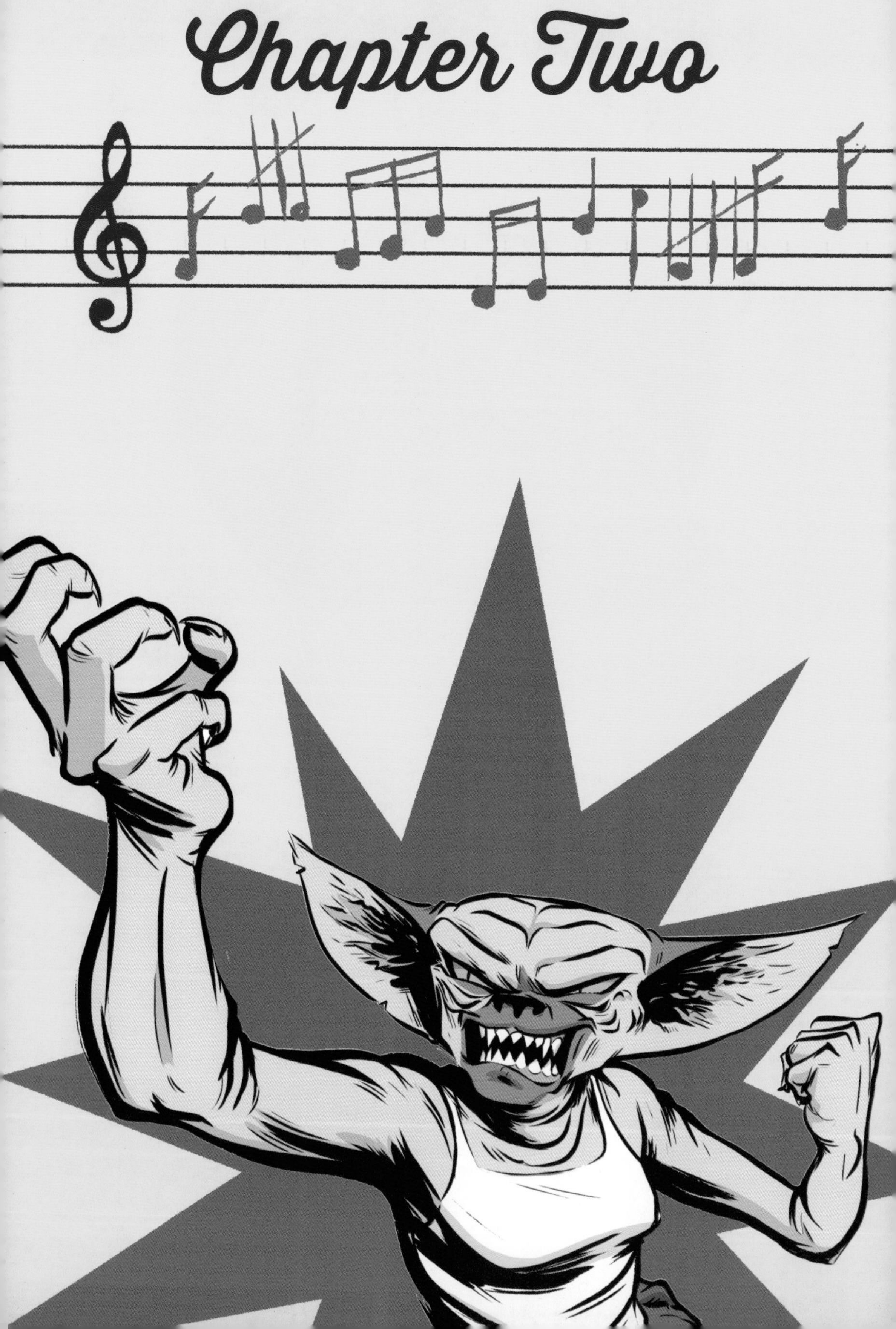

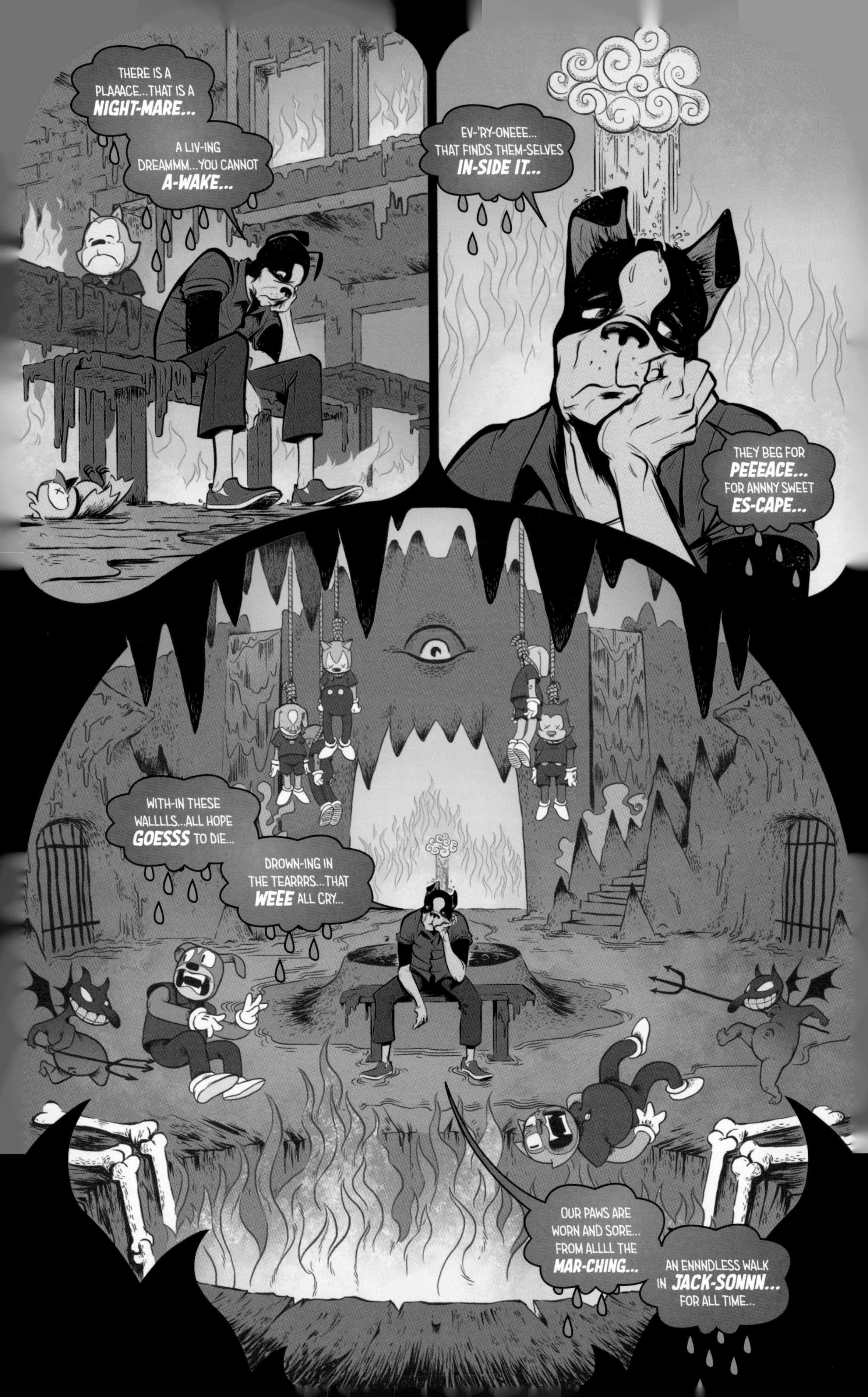
THERE IS A PLAAACE...THAT IS A NIGHT-MARE...
A LIV-ING DREAMMM...YOU CANNOT A-WAKE...
EV-'RY-ONEEE... THAT FINDS THEM-SELVES IN-SIDE IT...
THEY BEG FOR PEEEACE... FOR ANNNY SWEET ES-CAPE...
WITH-IN THESE WALLLLS...ALL HOPE GOESSS TO DIE...
DROWN-ING IN THE TEARRRS...THAT WEEE ALL CRY...
OUR PAWS ARE WORN AND SORE... FROM ALLLL THE MAR-CHING...
AN ENNNDLESS WALK IN JACK-SONNN... FOR ALL TIME...

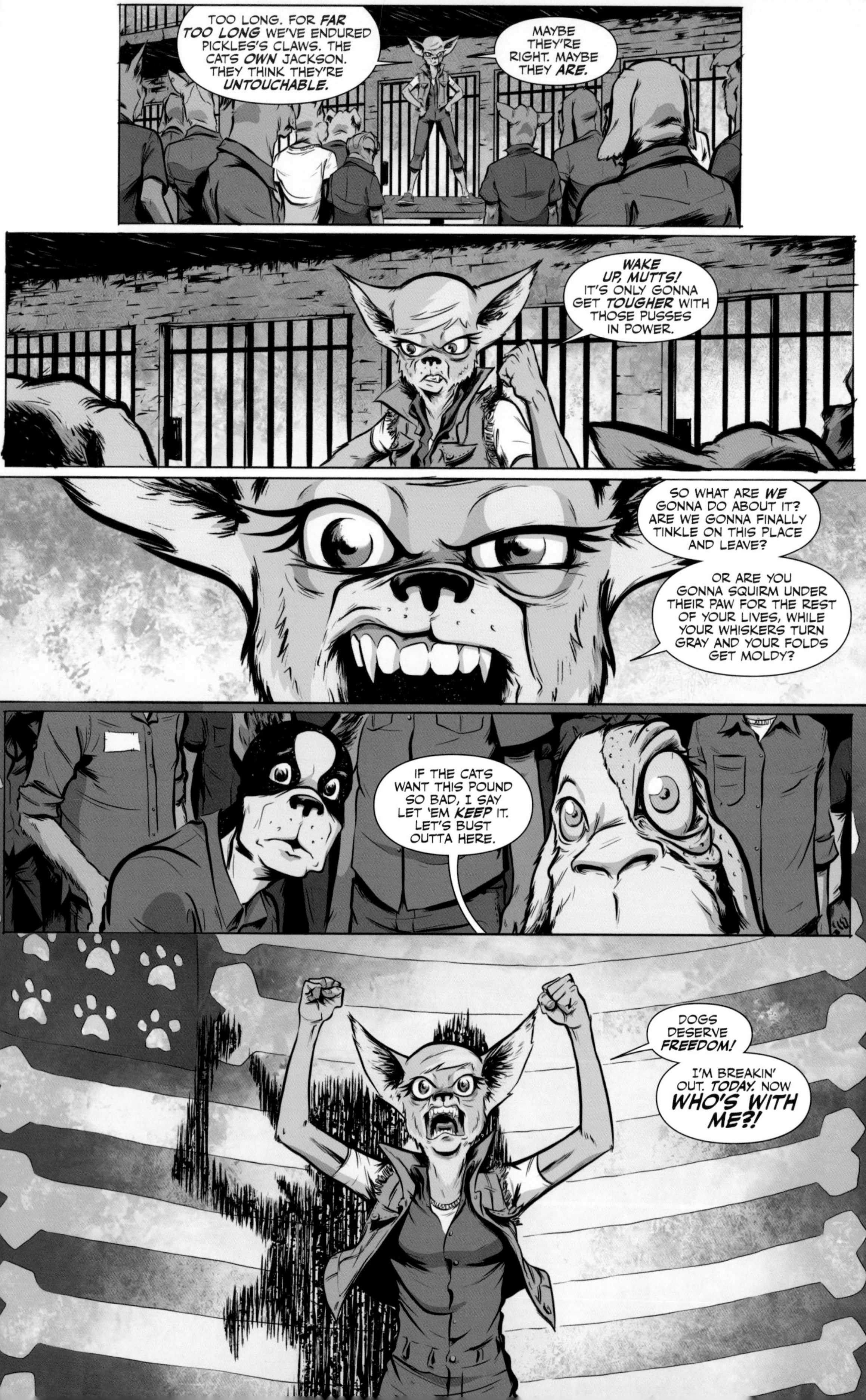
TOO LONG. FOR FAR TOO LONG WE'VE ENDURED PICKLES'S CLAWS. THE CATS OWN JACKSON. THEY THINK THEY'RE UNTOUCHABLE.
MAYBE THEY'RE RIGHT. MAYBE THEY ARE.
WAKE UP, MUTTS! IT'S ONLY GONNA GET TOUGHER WITH THOSE PUSSES IN POWER.
SO WHAT ARE WE GONNA DO ABOUT IT? ARE WE GONNA FINALLY TINKLE ON THIS PLACE AND LEAVE?
OR ARE YOU GONNA SQUIRM UNDER THEIR PAW FOR THE REST OF YOUR LIVES, WHILE YOUR WHISKERS TURN GRAY AND YOUR FOLDS GET MOLDY?
IF THE CATS WANT THIS POUND SO BAD, I SAY LET 'EM KEEP IT. LET'S BUST OUTTA HERE.
DOGS DESERVE FREEDOM!
I'M BREAKIN' OUT. TODAY. NOW WHO'S WITH ME?!

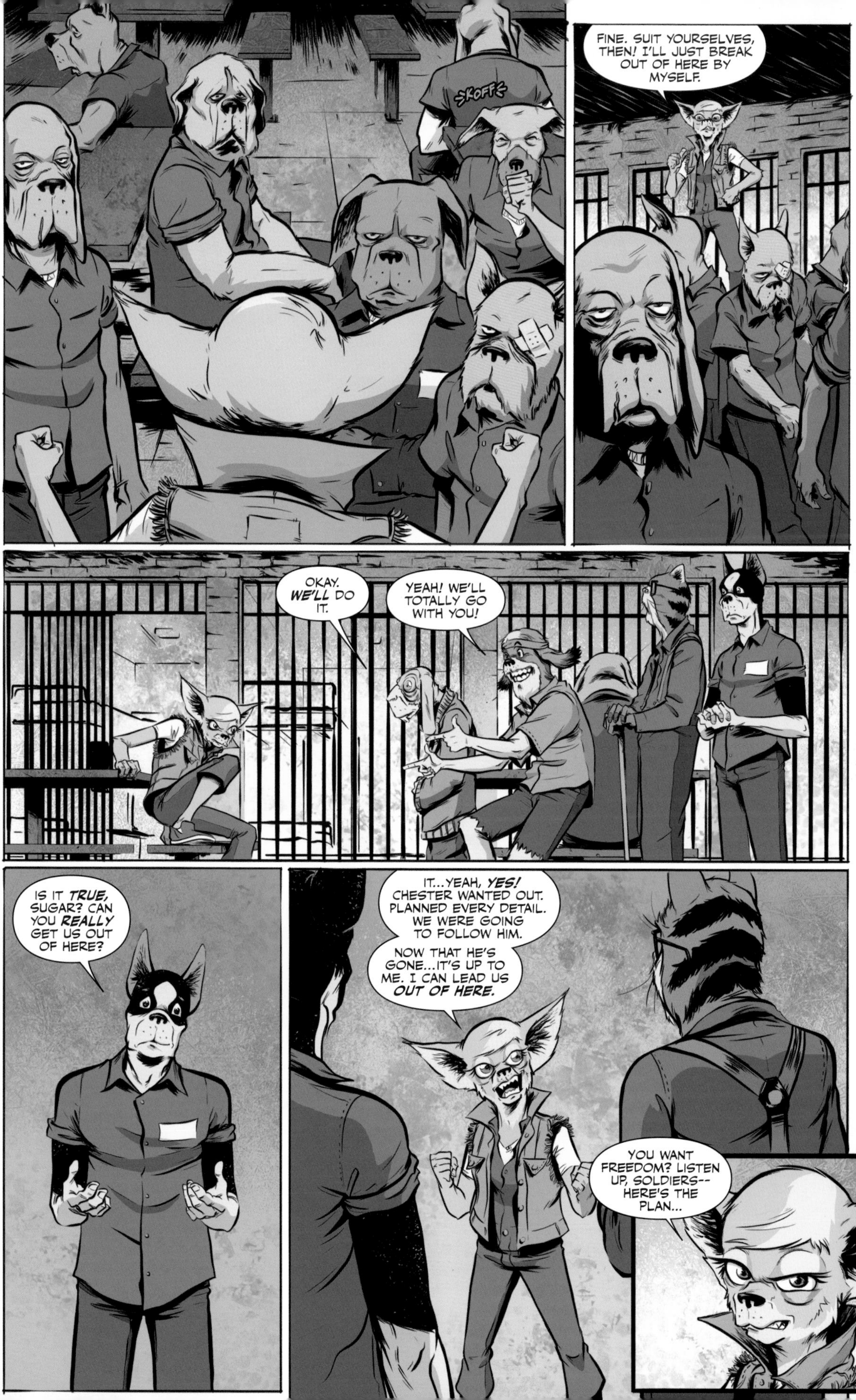

KOFF
FINE. SUIT YOURSELVES, THEN! I'LL JUST BREAK OUT OF HERE BY MYSELF.
OKAY. WE'LL DO IT.
YEAH! WE'LL TOTALLY GO WITH YOU!
IS IT TRUE, SUGAR? CAN YOU REALLY GET US OUT OF HERE?
IT...YEAH, YES! CHESTER WANTED OUT. PLANNED EVERY DETAIL. WE WERE GOING TO FOLLOW HIM.
NOW THAT HE'S GONE...IT'S UP TO ME. I CAN LEAD US OUT OF HERE.
YOU WANT FREEDOM? LISTEN UP, SOLDIERS--HERE'S THE PLAN...

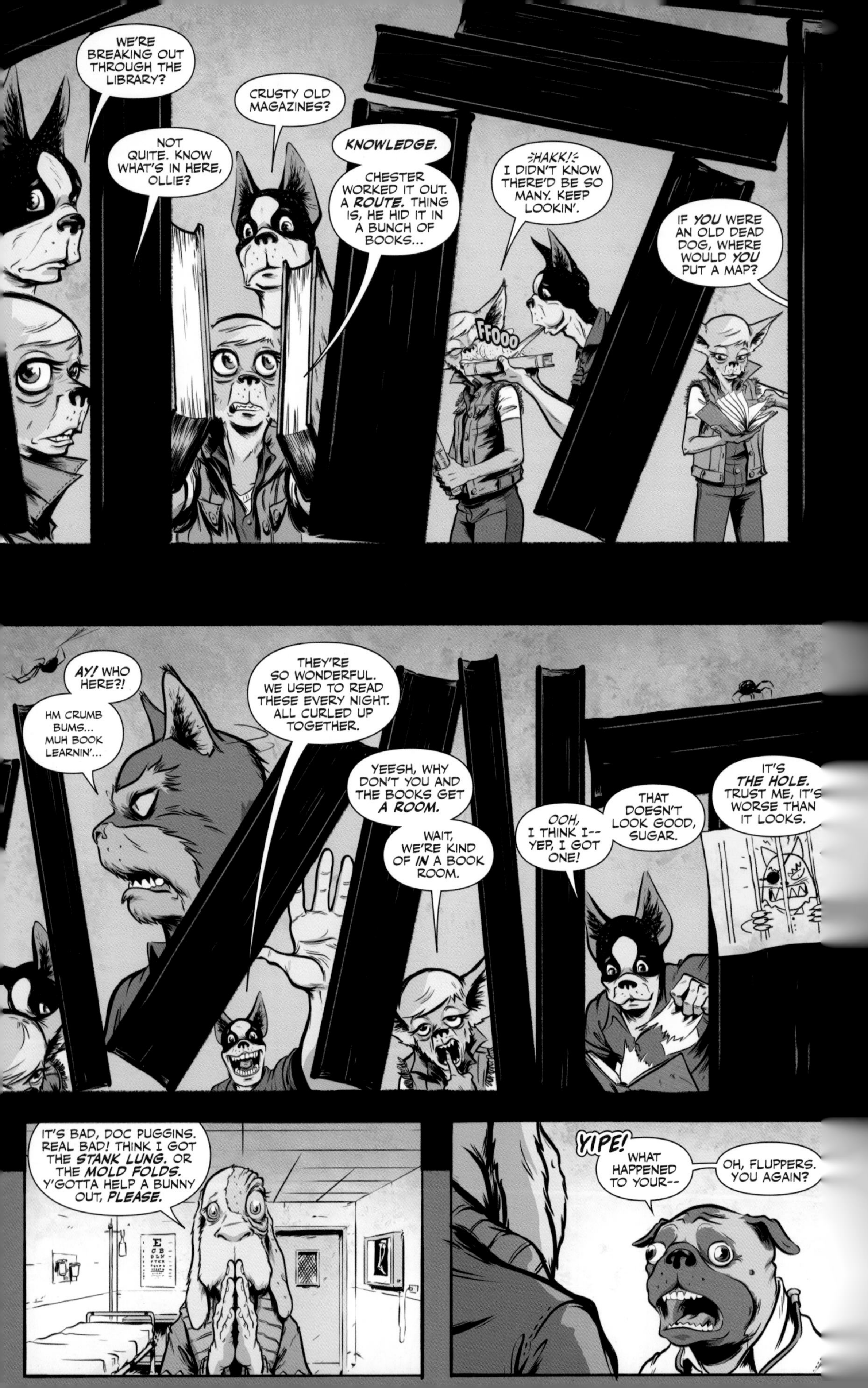

WE'RE BREAKING OUT THROUGH THE LIBRARY?
NOT QUITE. KNOW WHAT'S IN HERE, OLLIE?
CRUSTY OLD MAGAZINES?
KNOWLEDGE.
CHESTER WORKED IT OUT. A ROUTE. THING IS, HE HID IT IN A BUNCH OF BOOKS...
HAKK!
I DIDN'T KNOW THERE'D BE SO MANY. KEEP LOOKIN'.
FFOOO
IF YOU WERE AN OLD DEAD DOG, WHERE WOULD YOU PUT A MAP?
AY! WHO HERE?!
HM CRUMB BUMS... MUH BOOK LEARNIN'...
THEY'RE SO WONDERFUL. WE USED TO READ THESE EVERY NIGHT. ALL CURLED UP TOGETHER.
YEESH, WHY DON'T YOU AND THE BOOKS GET A ROOM.
WAIT, WE'RE KIND OF IN A BOOK ROOM.
OOH, I THINK I-- YEP, I GOT ONE!
THAT DOESN'T LOOK GOOD, SUGAR.
IT'S THE HOLE. TRUST ME, IT'S WORSE THAN IT LOOKS.
IT'S BAD, DOC PUGGINS. REAL BAD! THINK I GOT THE STANK LUNG. OR THE MOLD FOLDS. Y'GOTTA HELP A BUNNY OUT, PLEASE.
YIPE!
WHAT HAPPENED TO YOUR--
OH, FLUPPERS. YOU AGAIN?

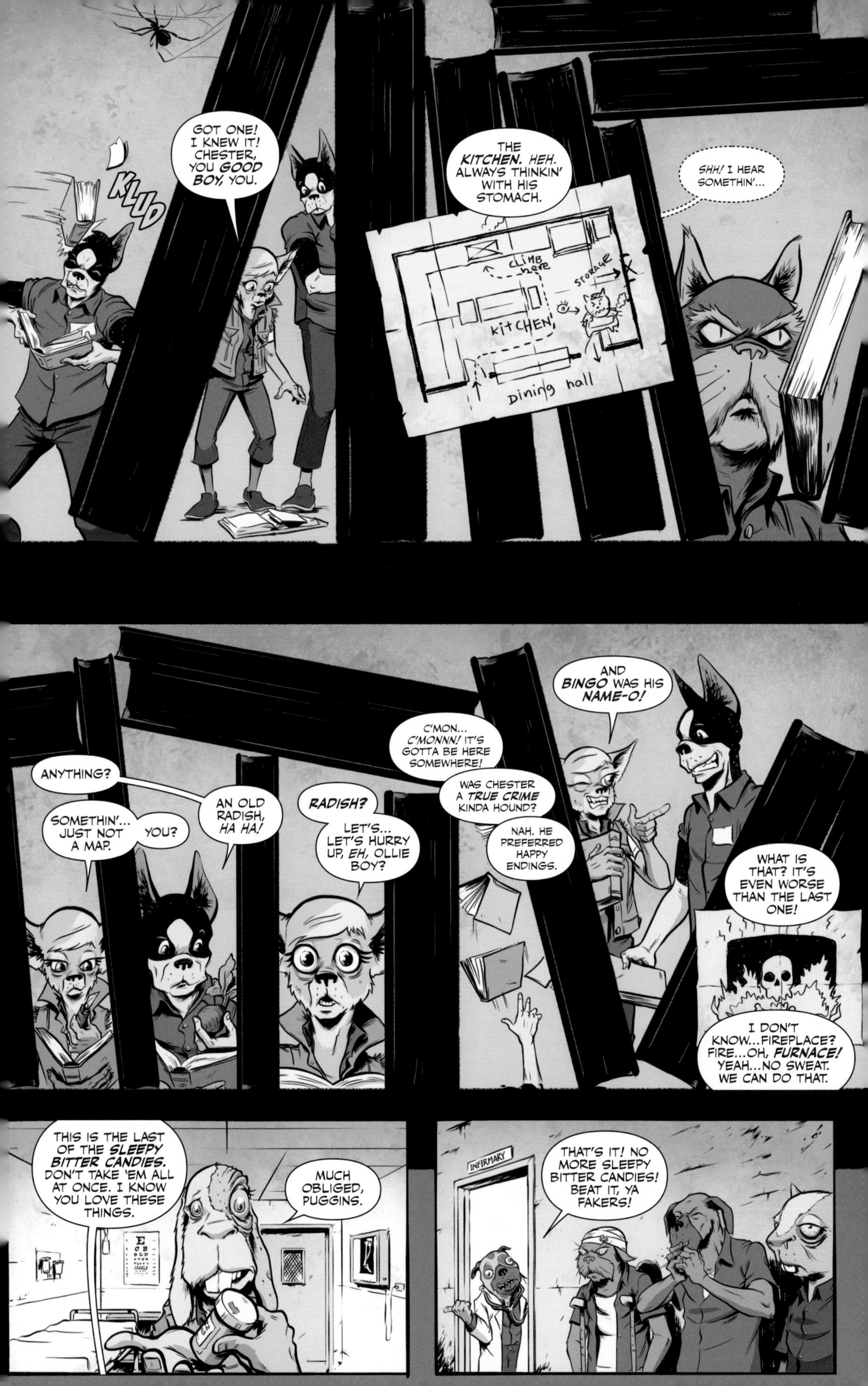
KLUD
GOT ONE! I KNEW IT! CHESTER, YOU GOOD BOY, YOU.
THE KITCHEN. HEH. ALWAYS THINKIN' WITH HIS STOMACH.
CLIMB here
STORAGE
KITCHEN
Dining hall
SHH! I HEAR SOMETHIN'...
ANYTHING?
SOMETHIN'... JUST NOT A MAP.
YOU?
AN OLD RADISH, HA HA!
RADISH?
LET'S... LET'S HURRY UP, EH, OLLIE BOY?
C'MON... C'MONNN! IT'S GOTTA BE HERE SOMEWHERE!
AND BINGO WAS HIS NAME-O!
WAS CHESTER A TRUE CRIME KINDA HOUND?
NAH. HE PREFERRED HAPPY ENDINGS.
WHAT IS THAT? IT'S EVEN WORSE THAN THE LAST ONE!
I DON'T KNOW...FIREPLACE? FIRE...OH, FURNACE! YEAH...NO SWEAT. WE CAN DO THAT.
THIS IS THE LAST OF THE SLEEPY BITTER CANDIES. DON'T TAKE 'EM ALL AT ONCE. I KNOW YOU LOVE THESE THINGS.
MUCH OBLIGED, PUGGINS.
INFIRMARY
THAT'S IT! NO MORE SLEEPY BITTER CANDIES! BEAT IT, YA FAKERS!

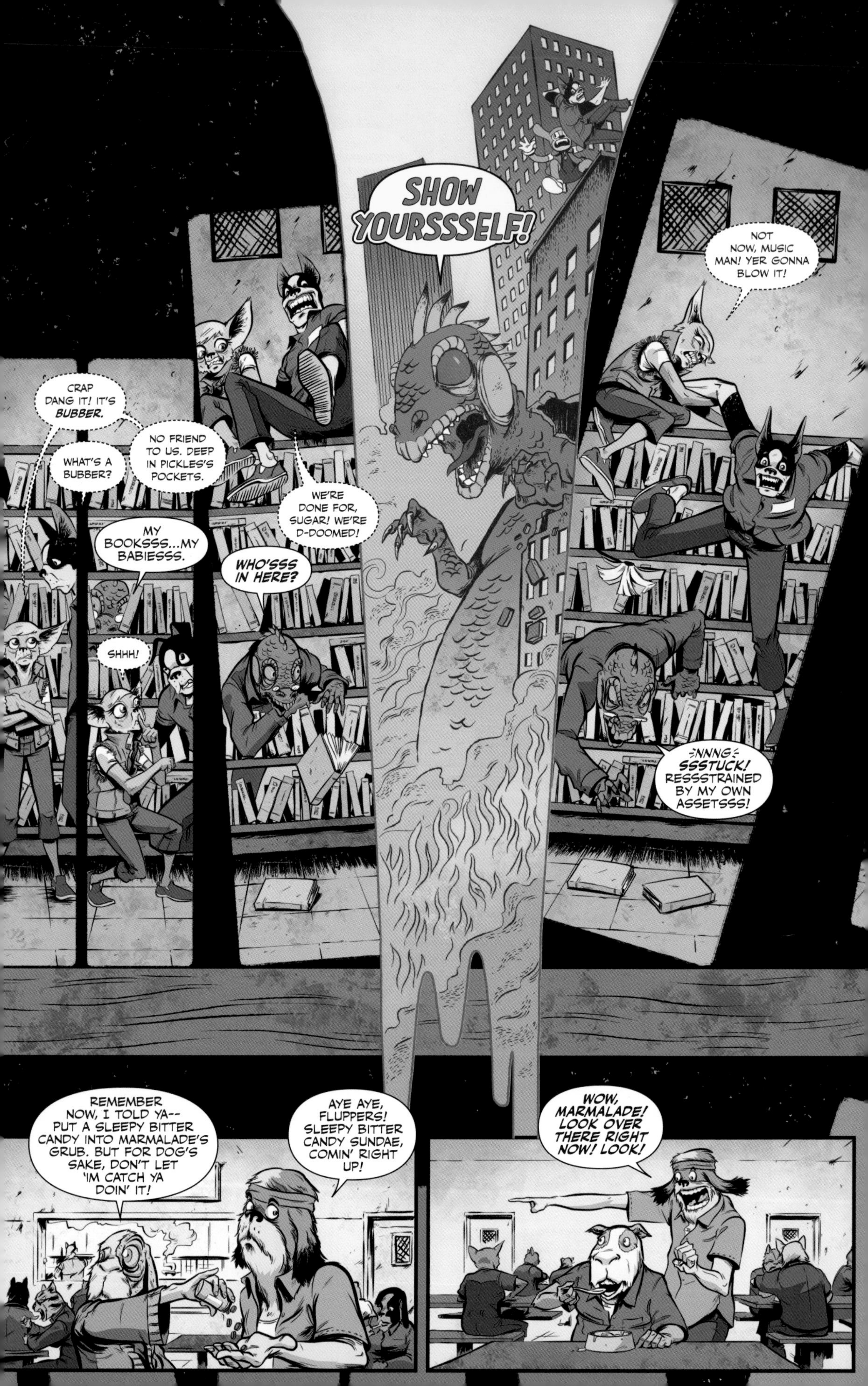
SHOW YOURSSSELF!
CRAP DANG IT! IT'S BUBBER.
WHAT'S A BUBBER?
NO FRIEND TO US. DEEP IN PICKLES'S POCKETS.
MY BOOKSSS...MY BABIESSS.
SHHH!
WE'RE DONE FOR, SUGAR! WE'RE D-DOOMED!
WHO'SSS IN HERE?
NOT NOW, MUSIC MAN! YER GONNA BLOW IT!
NNNG SSSTUCK! RESSSTRAINED BY MY OWN ASSETSSS!
REMEMBER NOW, I TOLD YA-- PUT A SLEEPY BITTER CANDY INTO MARMALADE'S GRUB. BUT FOR DOG'S SAKE, DON'T LET 'IM CATCH YA DOIN' IT!
AYE AYE, FLUPPERS! SLEEPY BITTER CANDY SUNDAE, COMIN' RIGHT UP!
WOW, MARMALADE! LOOK OVER THERE RIGHT NOW! LOOK!

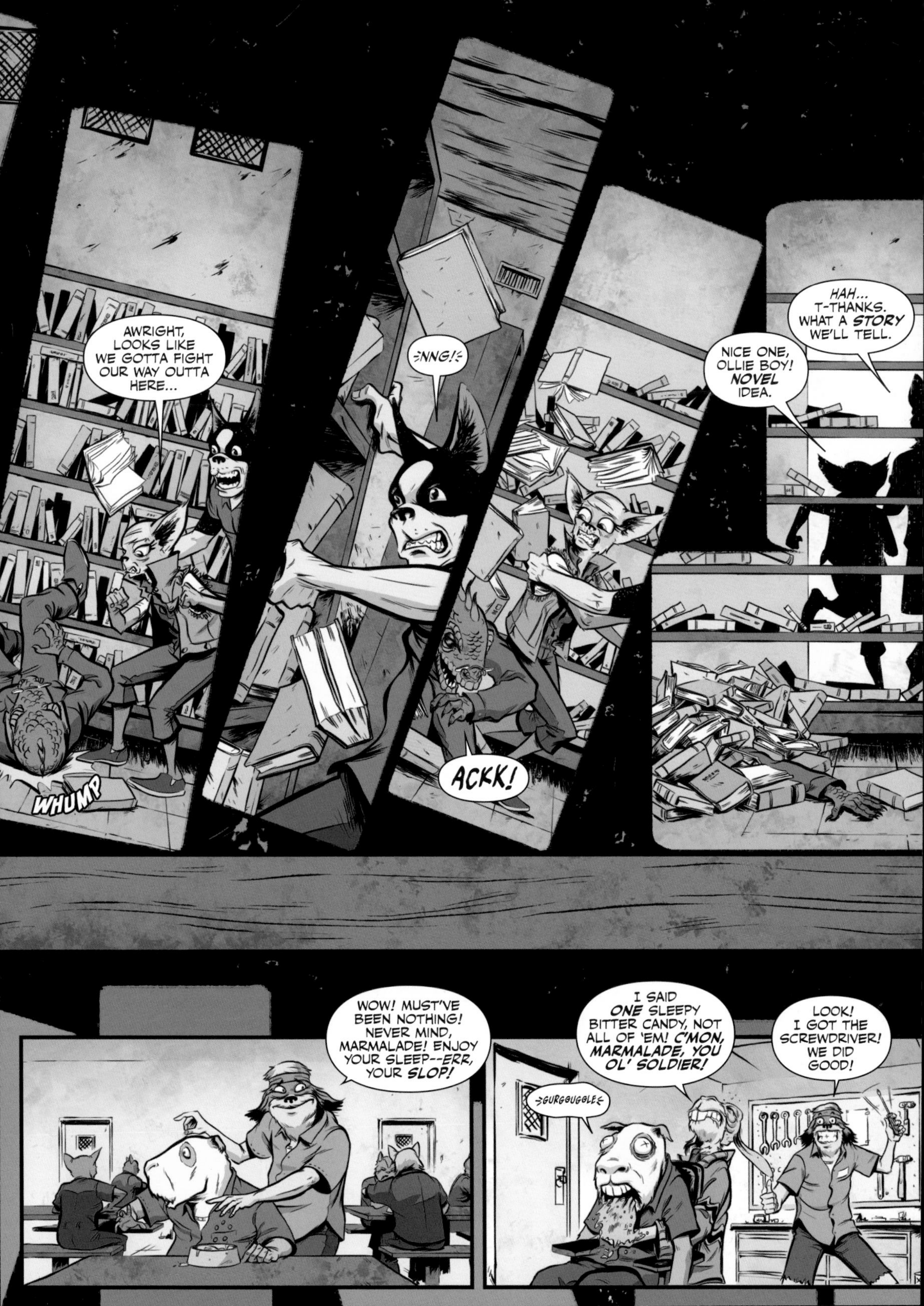
AWRIGHT, LOOKS LIKE WE GOTTA FIGHT OUR WAY OUTTA HERE...
WHUMP
NNG!
ACKK!
NICE ONE, OLLIE BOY! NOVEL IDEA.
HAH... T-THANKS. WHAT A STORY WE'LL TELL.
WOW! MUST'VE BEEN NOTHING! NEVER MIND, MARMALADE! ENJOY YOUR SLEEP--ERR, YOUR SLOP!
GURGGUGGLE
I SAID ONE SLEEPY BITTER CANDY, NOT ALL OF 'EM! C'MON, MARMALADE, YOU OL' SOLDIER!
LOOK! I GOT THE SCREWDRIVER! WE DID GOOD!

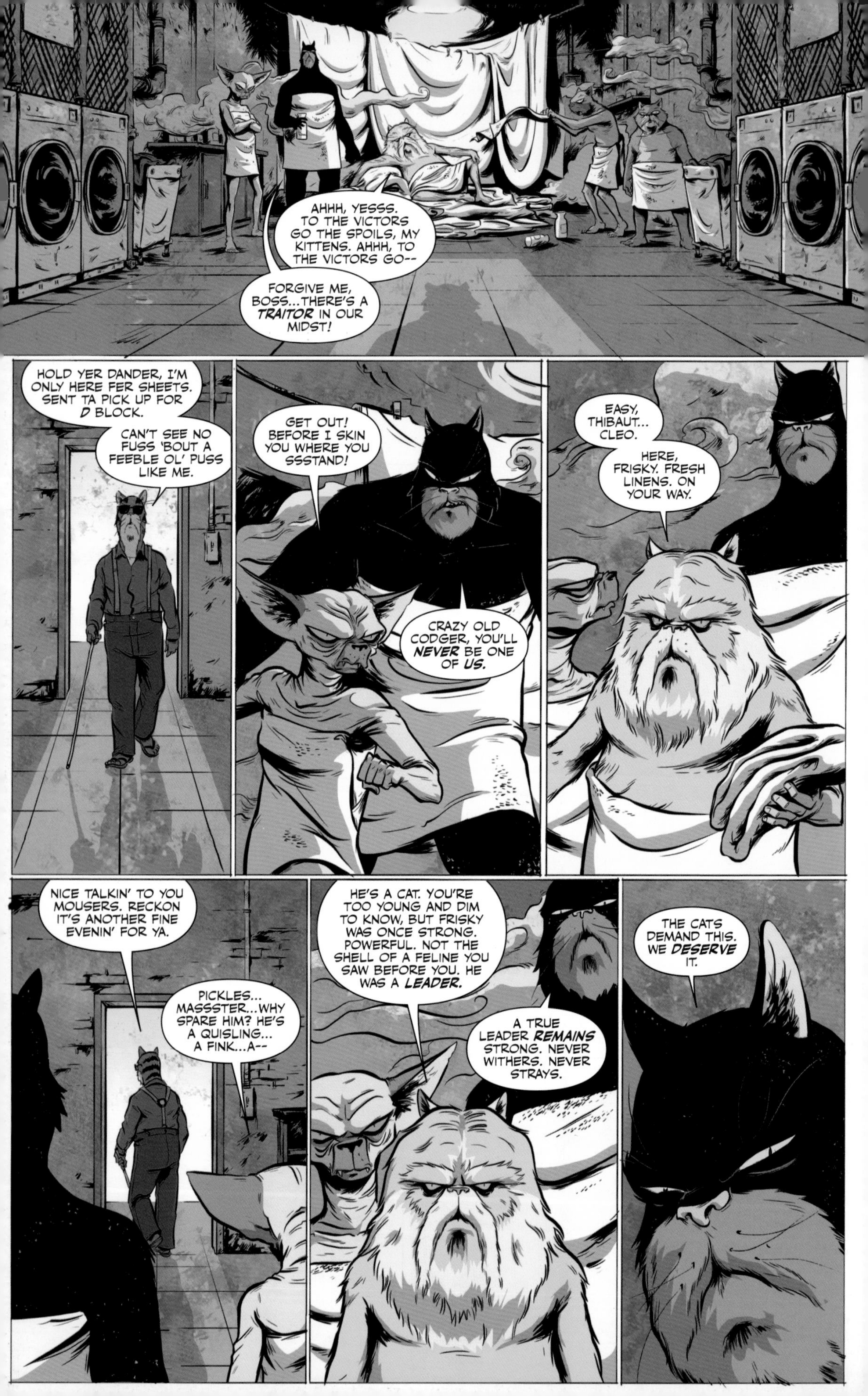
AHHH, YESSS. TO THE VICTORS GO THE SPOILS, MY KITTENS. AHHH, TO THE VICTORS GO--
FORGIVE ME, BOSS...THERE'S A TRAITOR IN OUR MIDST!
HOLD YER DANDER, I'M ONLY HERE FER SHEETS. SENT TA PICK UP FOR D BLOCK.
CAN'T SEE NO FUSS 'BOUT A FEEBLE OL' PUSS LIKE ME.
GET OUT! BEFORE I SKIN YOU WHERE YOU SSSTAND!
CRAZY OLD CODGER, YOU'LL NEVER BE ONE OF US.
EASY, THIBAUT... CLEO.
HERE, FRISKY. FRESH LINENS. ON YOUR WAY.
NICE TALKIN' TO YOU MOUSERS. RECKON IT'S ANOTHER FINE EVENIN' FOR YA.
PICKLES... MASSSTER...WHY SPARE HIM? HE'S A QUISLING... A FINK...A--
HE'S A CAT. YOU'RE TOO YOUNG AND DIM TO KNOW, BUT FRISKY WAS ONCE STRONG. POWERFUL. NOT THE SHELL OF A FELINE YOU SAW BEFORE YOU. HE WAS A LEADER.
A TRUE LEADER REMAINS STRONG. NEVER WITHERS. NEVER STRAYS.
THE CATS DEMAND THIS. WE DESERVE IT.

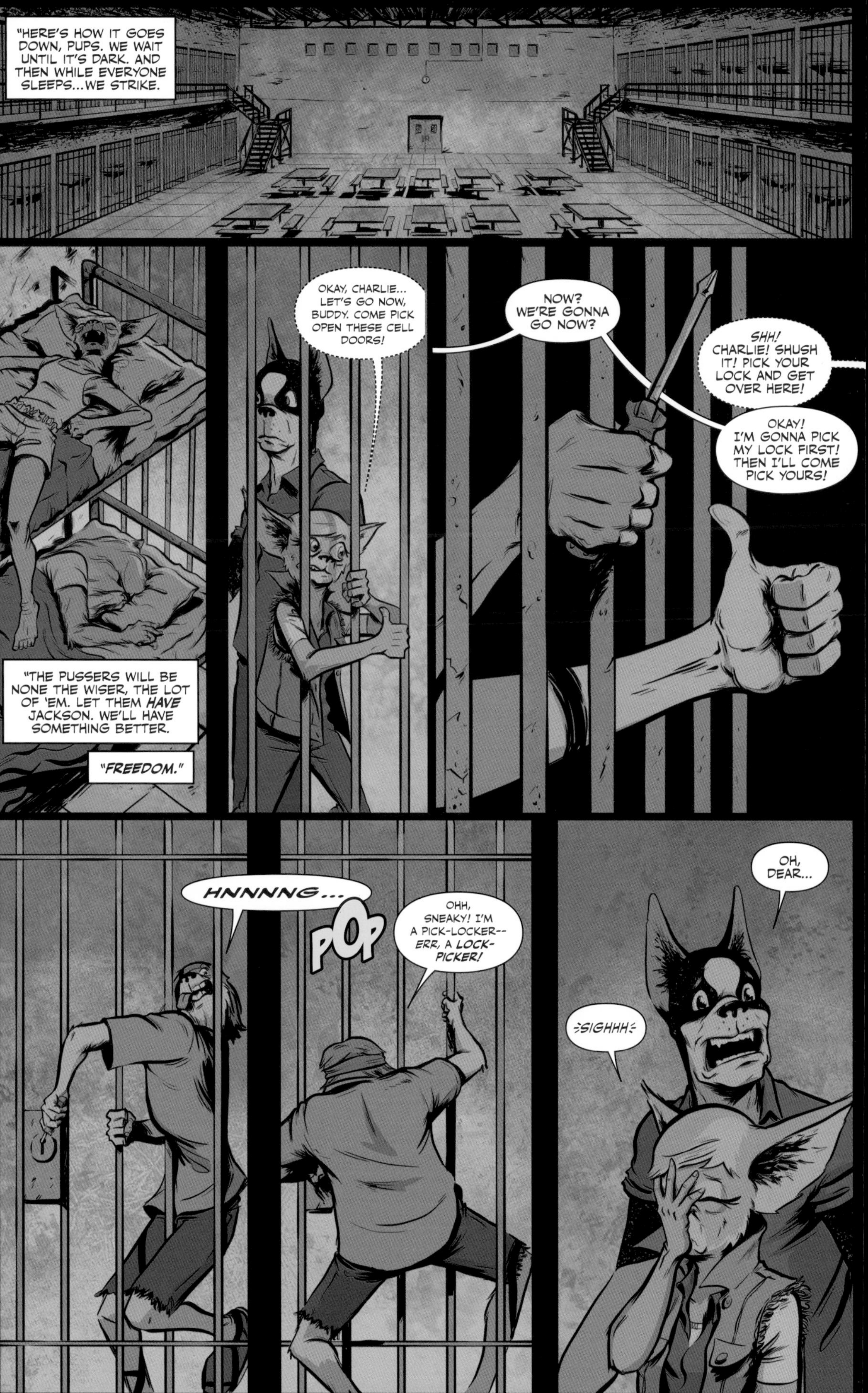
"HERE'S HOW IT GOES DOWN, PUPS. WE WAIT UNTIL IT'S DARK. AND THEN WHILE EVERYONE SLEEPS...WE STRIKE.
OKAY, CHARLIE... LET'S GO NOW, BUDDY. COME PICK OPEN THESE CELL DOORS!
NOW? WE'RE GONNA GO NOW?
SHH! CHARLIE! SHUSH IT! PICK YOUR LOCK AND GET OVER HERE!
OKAY! I'M GONNA PICK MY LOCK FIRST! THEN I'LL COME PICK YOURS!
"THE PUSSERS WILL BE NONE THE WISER, THE LOT OF 'EM. LET THEM *HAVE* JACKSON. WE'LL HAVE SOMETHING BETTER.
"FREEDOM."
HNNNNG...
POP
OHH, SNEAKY! I'M A PICK-LOCKER-- ERR, A *LOCK-PICKER!*
OH, DEAR...
SIGHHH

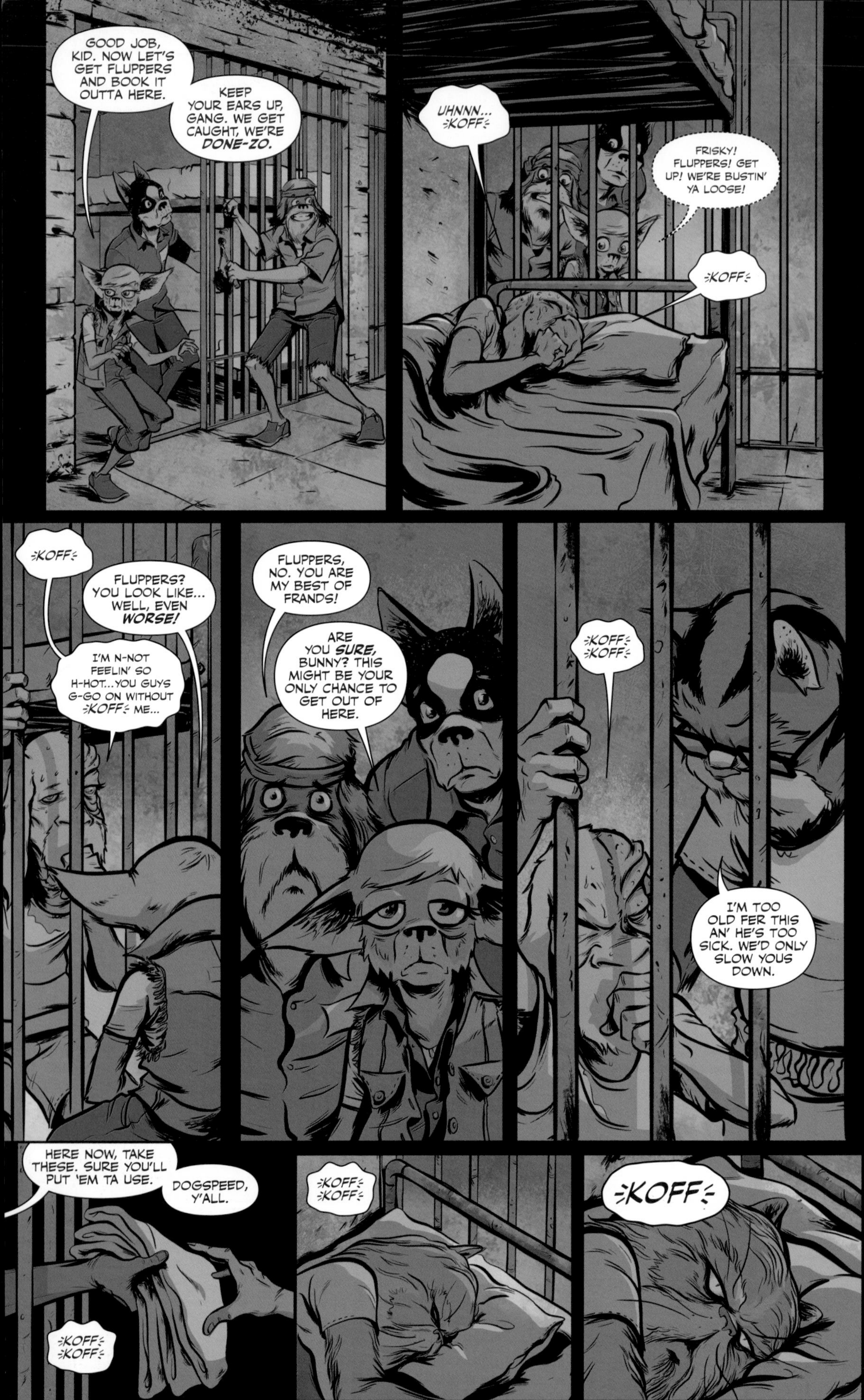
GOOD JOB, KID. NOW LET'S GET FLUPPERS AND BOOK IT OUTTA HERE.
KEEP YOUR EARS UP, GANG. WE GET CAUGHT, WE'RE DONE-ZO.
UHNNN... KOFF
FRISKY! FLUPPERS! GET UP! WE'RE BUSTIN' YA LOOSE!
KOFF
KOFF
FLUPPERS? YOU LOOK LIKE... WELL, EVEN WORSE!
I'M N-NOT FEELIN' SO H-HOT...YOU GUYS G-GO ON WITHOUT KOFF ME...
FLUPPERS, NO. YOU ARE MY BEST OF FRANDS!
ARE YOU SURE, BUNNY? THIS MIGHT BE YOUR ONLY CHANCE TO GET OUT OF HERE.
KOFF KOFF
I'M TOO OLD FER THIS AN' HE'S TOO SICK. WE'D ONLY SLOW YOUS DOWN.
HERE NOW, TAKE THESE. SURE YOU'LL PUT 'EM TA USE.
DOGSPEED, Y'ALL.
KOFF KOFF
KOFF KOFF
KOFF

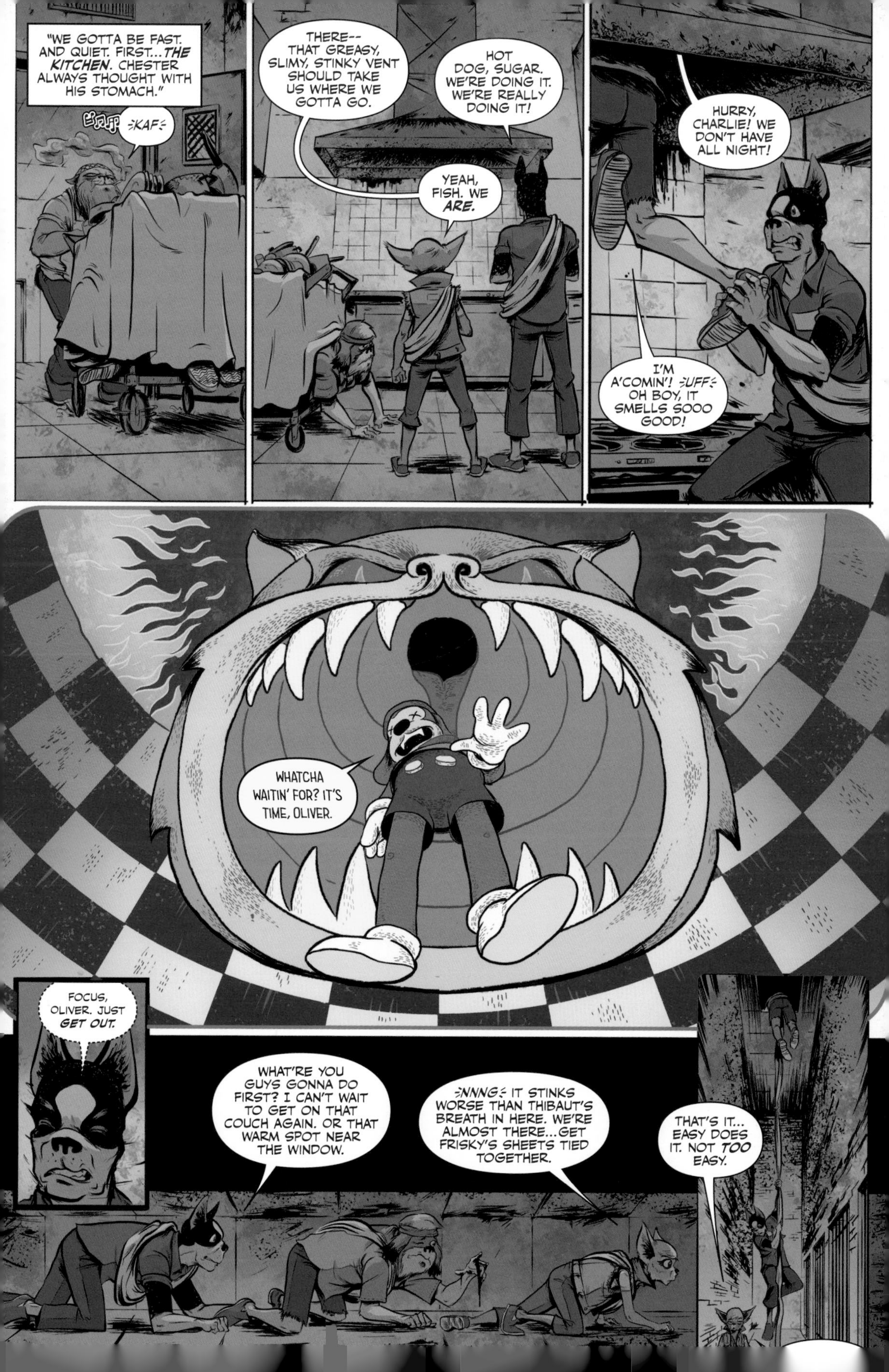
"WE GOTTA BE FAST. AND QUIET. FIRST... THE KITCHEN. CHESTER ALWAYS THOUGHT WITH HIS STOMACH."
KAF
THERE-- THAT GREASY, SLIMY, STINKY VENT SHOULD TAKE US WHERE WE GOTTA GO.
HOT DOG, SUGAR. WE'RE DOING IT. WE'RE REALLY DOING IT!
YEAH, FISH. WE ARE.
HURRY, CHARLIE! WE DON'T HAVE ALL NIGHT!
I'M A'COMIN'! UFF OH BOY, IT SMELLS SOOO GOOD!
WHATCHA WAITIN' FOR? IT'S TIME, OLIVER.
FOCUS, OLIVER. JUST GET OUT.
WHAT'RE YOU GUYS GONNA DO FIRST? I CAN'T WAIT TO GET ON THAT COUCH AGAIN. OR THAT WARM SPOT NEAR THE WINDOW.
NNNG IT STINKS WORSE THAN THIBAUT'S BREATH IN HERE. WE'RE ALMOST THERE... GET FRISKY'S SHEETS TIED TOGETHER.
THAT'S IT... EASY DOES IT. NOT TOO EASY.

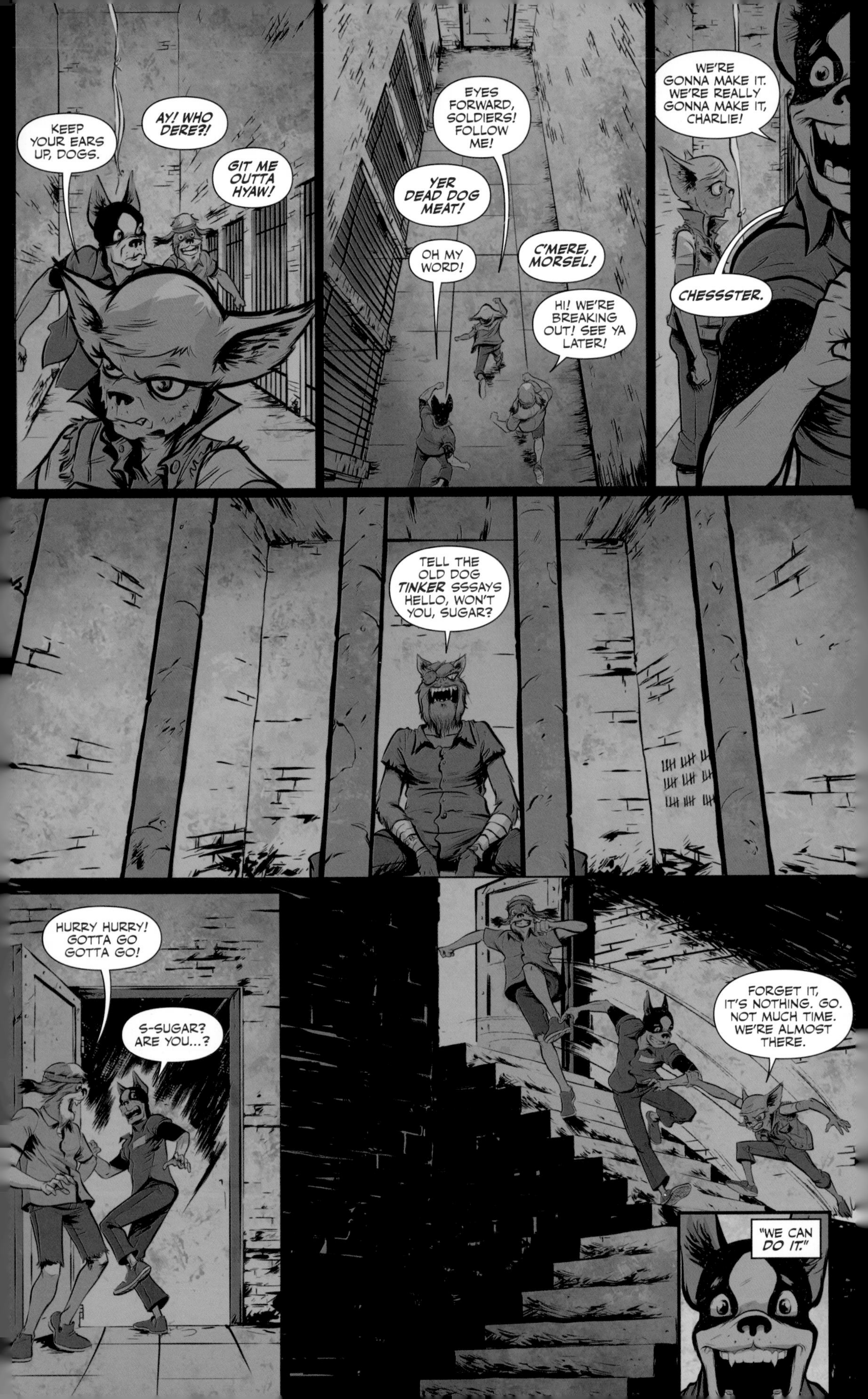
KEEP YOUR EARS UP, DOGS.
AY! WHO DERE?!
GIT ME OUTTA HYAW!
EYES FORWARD, SOLDIERS! FOLLOW ME!
YER DEAD DOG MEAT!
OH MY WORD!
C'MERE, MORSEL!
HI! WE'RE BREAKING OUT! SEE YA LATER!
WE'RE GONNA MAKE IT. WE'RE REALLY GONNA MAKE IT, CHARLIE!
CHESSSTER.
TELL THE OLD DOG TINKER SSSAYS HELLO, WON'T YOU, SUGAR?
HURRY HURRY! GOTTA GO GOTTA GO!
S-SUGAR? ARE YOU...?
FORGET IT, IT'S NOTHING. GO. NOT MUCH TIME. WE'RE ALMOST THERE.
"WE CAN DO IT."

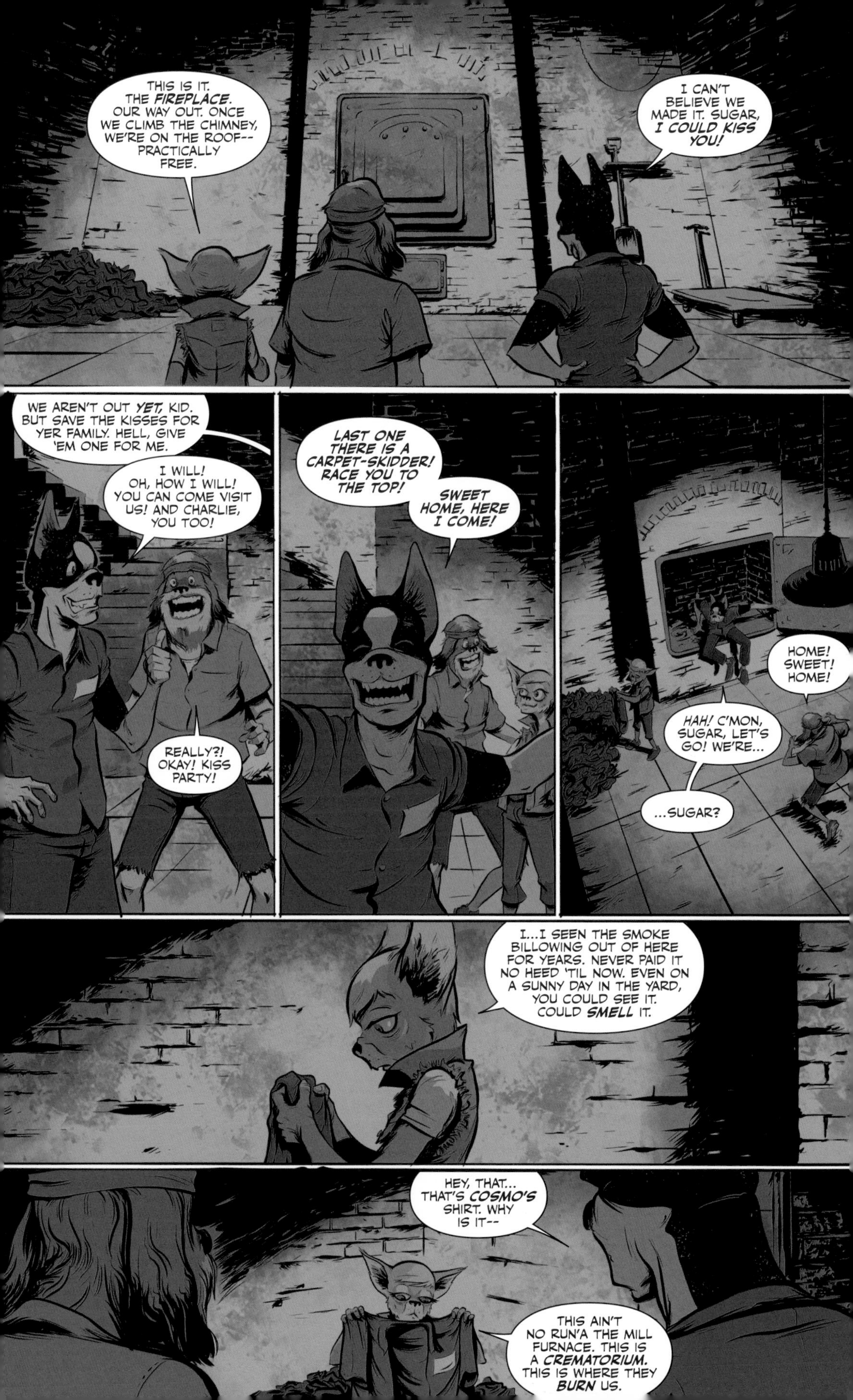
THIS IS IT. THE *FIREPLACE*. OUR WAY OUT. ONCE WE CLIMB THE CHIMNEY, WE'RE ON THE ROOF-- PRACTICALLY FREE.
I CAN'T BELIEVE WE MADE IT. SUGAR, *I COULD KISS YOU!*
WE AREN'T OUT *YET,* KID. BUT SAVE THE KISSES FOR YER FAMILY. HELL, GIVE 'EM ONE FOR ME.
I WILL! OH, HOW I WILL! YOU CAN COME VISIT US! AND CHARLIE, YOU TOO!
REALLY?! OKAY! KISS PARTY!
LAST ONE THERE IS A CARPET-SKIDDER! RACE YOU TO THE TOP!
SWEET HOME, HERE I COME!
HOME! SWEET! HOME!
HAH! C'MON, SUGAR, LET'S GO! WE'RE...
...SUGAR?
I...I SEEN THE SMOKE BILLOWING OUT OF HERE FOR YEARS. NEVER PAID IT NO HEED 'TIL NOW. EVEN ON A SUNNY DAY IN THE YARD, YOU COULD SEE IT. COULD *SMELL* IT.
HEY, THAT... THAT'S *COSMO'S* SHIRT. WHY IS IT--
THIS AIN'T NO RUN'A THE MILL FURNACE. THIS IS A *CREMATORIUM.* THIS IS WHERE THEY *BURN* US.

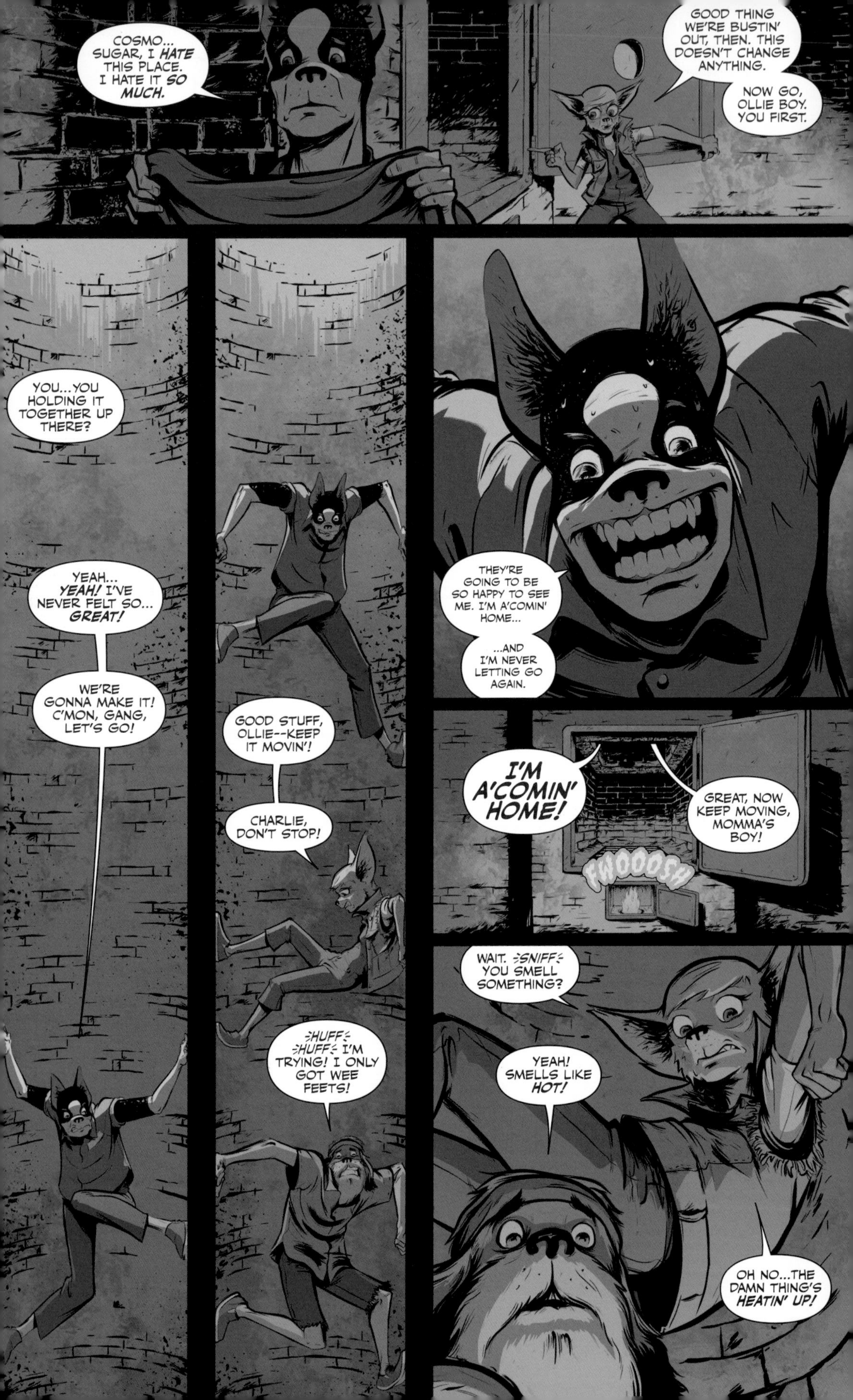
COSMO... SUGAR, I *HATE* THIS PLACE. I HATE IT *SO MUCH.*
GOOD THING WE'RE BUSTIN' OUT, THEN. THIS DOESN'T CHANGE ANYTHING.
NOW GO, OLLIE BOY. YOU FIRST.
YOU...YOU HOLDING IT TOGETHER UP THERE?
YEAH... *YEAH!* I'VE NEVER FELT SO... *GREAT!*
WE'RE GONNA MAKE IT! C'MON, GANG, LET'S GO!
GOOD STUFF, OLLIE--KEEP IT MOVIN'!
CHARLIE, DON'T STOP!
HUFF *HUFF* I'M TRYING! I ONLY GOT WEE FEETS!
THEY'RE GOING TO BE SO HAPPY TO SEE ME. I'M A'COMIN' HOME...
...AND I'M NEVER LETTING GO AGAIN.
I'M A'COMIN' HOME!
GREAT, NOW KEEP MOVING, MOMMA'S BOY!
FWOOOSH
WAIT. *SNIFF* YOU SMELL SOMETHING?
YEAH! SMELLS LIKE *HOT!*
OH NO...THE DAMN THING'S *HEATIN' UP!*

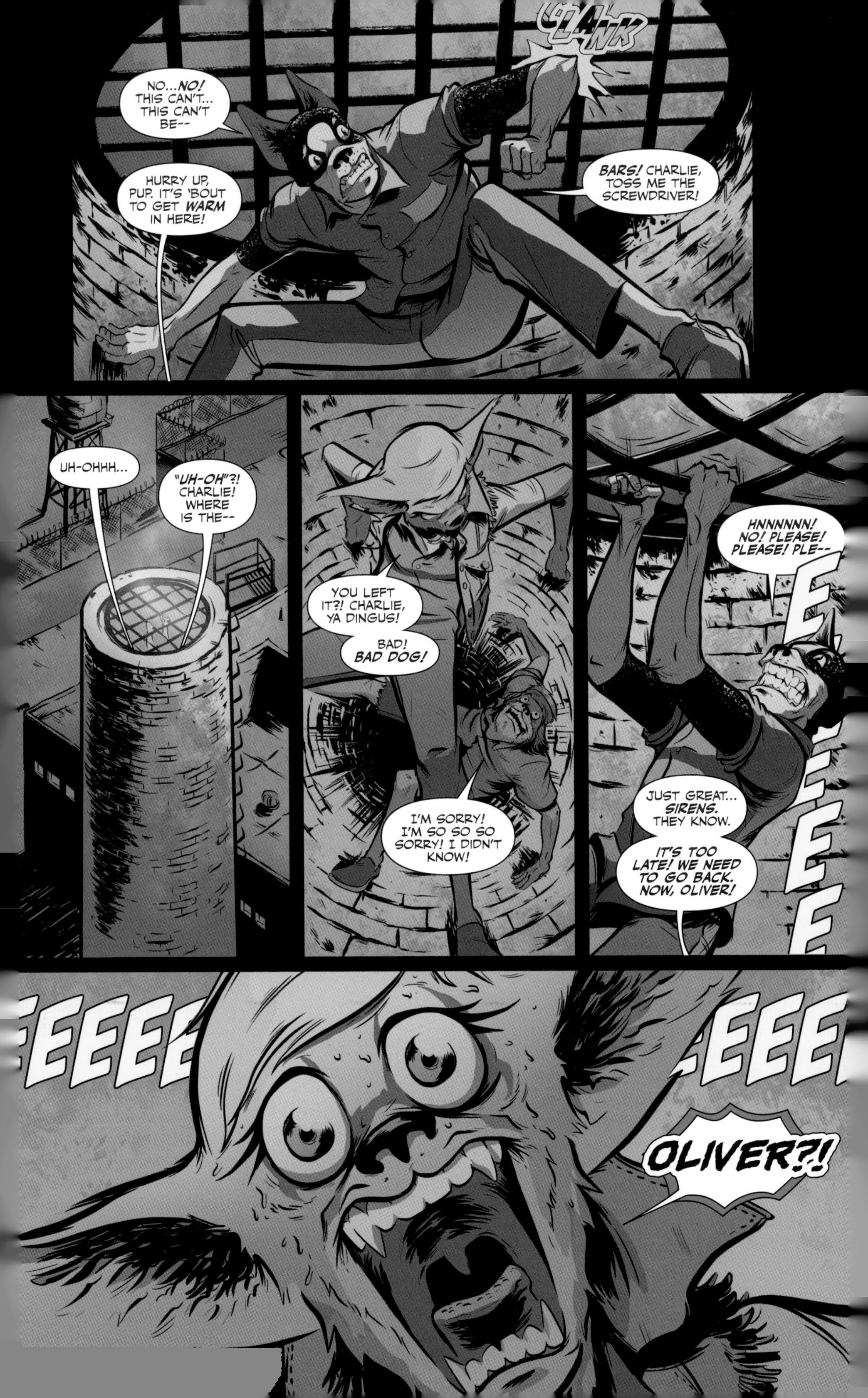
CLANK
NO...NO! THIS CAN'T... THIS CAN'T BE--
HURRY UP, PUP. IT'S 'BOUT TO GET WARM IN HERE!
BARS! CHARLIE, TOSS ME THE SCREWDRIVER!
UH-OHHH...
"UH-OH"?! CHARLIE! WHERE IS THE--
YOU LEFT IT?! CHARLIE, YA DINGUS!
BAD! BAD DOG!
I'M SORRY! I'M SO SO SO SORRY! I DIDN'T KNOW!
HNNNNNN! NO! PLEASE! PLEASE! PLE--
EEEEE
JUST GREAT... SIRENS. THEY KNOW.
IT'S TOO LATE! WE NEED TO GO BACK. NOW, OLIVER!
EEEEEEEEE
OLIVER?!

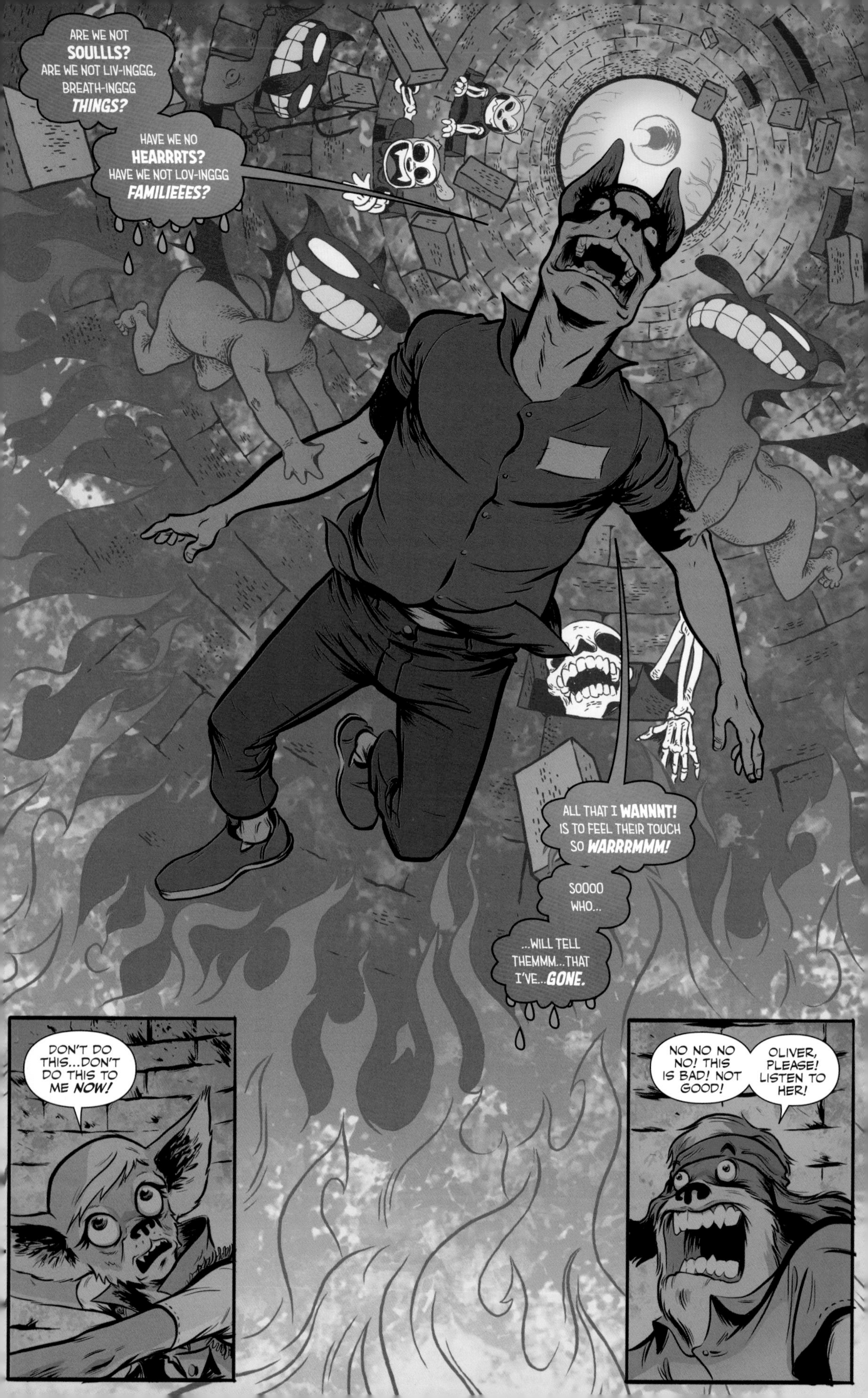
ARE WE NOT SOULLLS? ARE WE NOT LIV-INGGG, BREATH-INGGG THINGS?
HAVE WE NO HEARRRTS? HAVE WE NOT LOV-INGGG FAMILIEEES?
ALL THAT I WANNNT! IS TO FEEL THEIR TOUCH SO WARRRMMM!
SOOOO WHO...
...WILL TELL THEMMM...THAT I'VE...GONE.
DON'T DO THIS...DON'T DO THIS TO ME NOW!
NO NO NO NO! THIS IS BAD! NOT GOOD!
OLIVER, PLEASE! LISTEN TO HER!

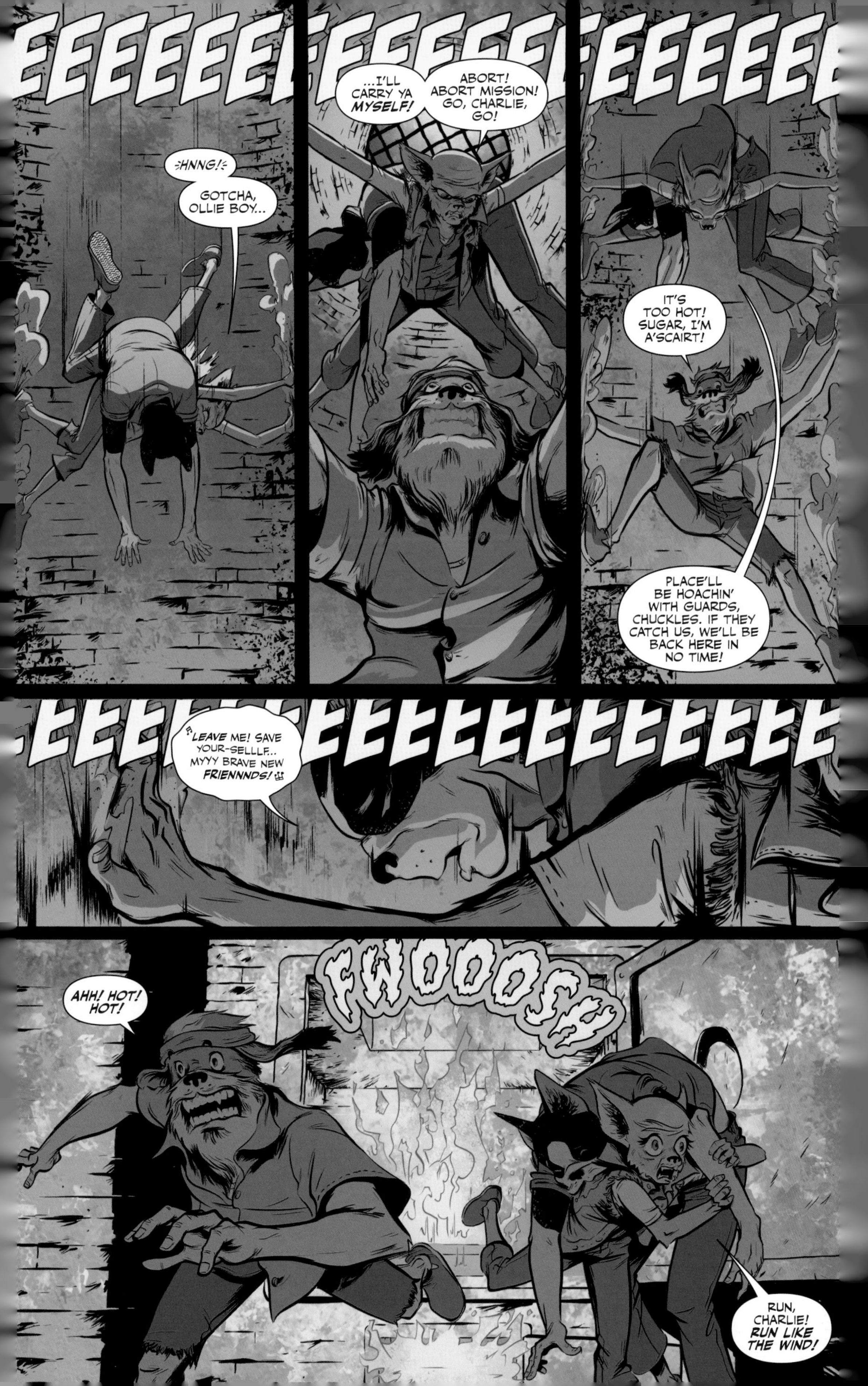
EEEEEEEEEEEEEEEEEEEEEEE
HNNG!
GOTCHA, OLLIE BOY...
...I'LL CARRY YA MYSELF!
ABORT! ABORT MISSION! GO, CHARLIE, GO!
IT'S TOO HOT! SUGAR, I'M A'SCAIRT!
PLACE'LL BE HOACHIN' WITH GUARDS, CHUCKLES. IF THEY CATCH US, WE'LL BE BACK HERE IN NO TIME!
EEEEEEEEEEEEEEEEEEEEEE
LEAVE ME! SAVE YOUR-SELLLF... MYYY BRAVE NEW FRIENNNDS!
FWOOOSH
AHH! HOT! HOT!
RUN, CHARLIE! RUN LIKE THE WIND!

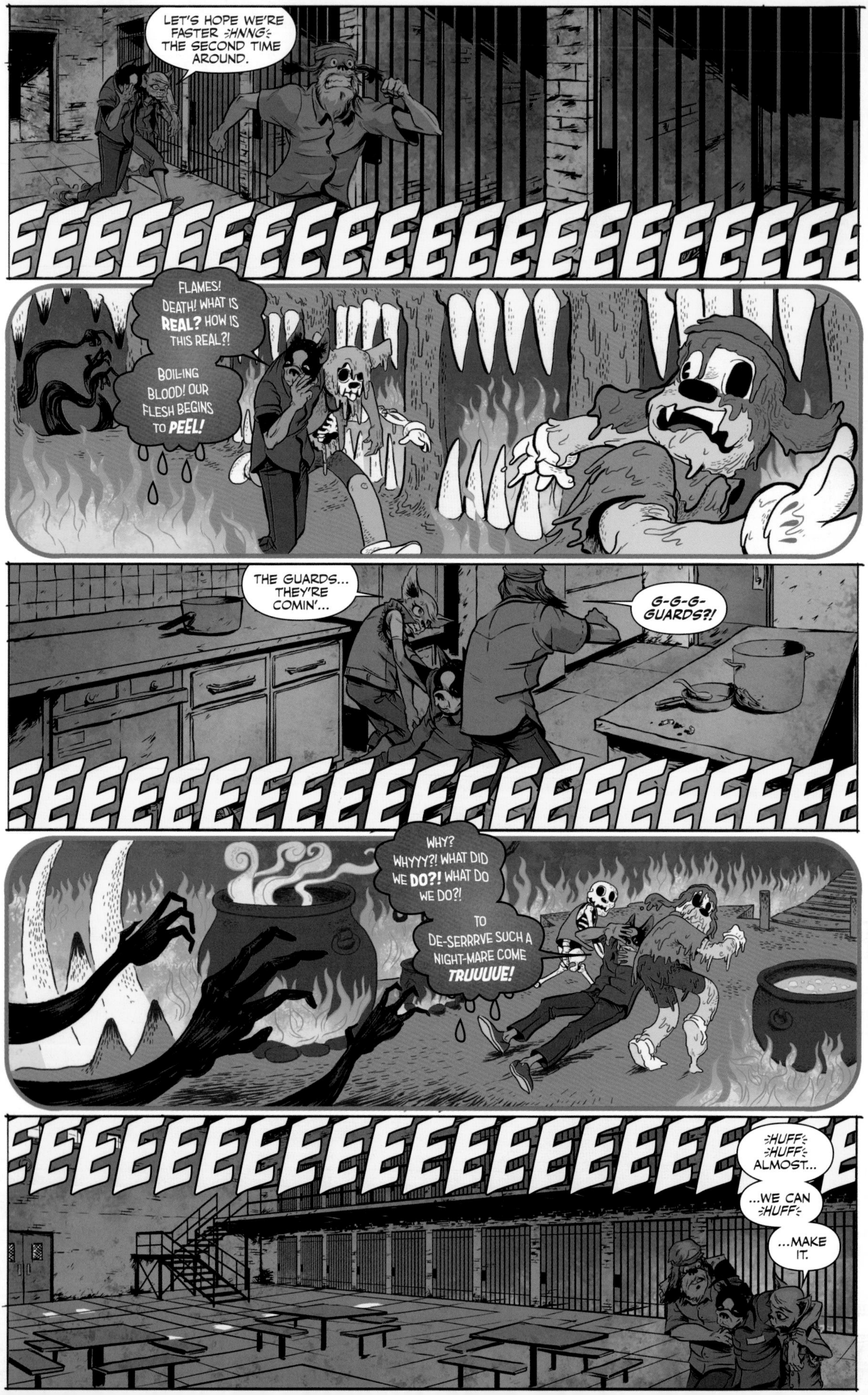

LET'S HOPE WE'RE FASTER ⸗HNNG⸗ THE SECOND TIME AROUND.
EEEEEEEEEEEEEEEEEE
FLAMES! DEATH! WHAT IS **REAL?** HOW IS THIS REAL?!
BOIL-ING BLOOD! OUR FLESH BEGINS TO ***PEEL!***
THE GUARDS... THEY'RE COMIN'...
G-G-G-GUARDS?!
EEEEEEEEEEEEEEEEEE
WHY? WHYYY?! WHAT DID WE **DO?!** WHAT DO WE DO?!
TO DE-SERRRVE SUCH A NIGHT-MARE COME ***TRUUUUE!***
EEEEEEEEEEEEEEEEE
⸗HUFF⸗ ⸗HUFF⸗ ALMOST...
...WE CAN ⸗HUFF⸗
...MAKE IT.

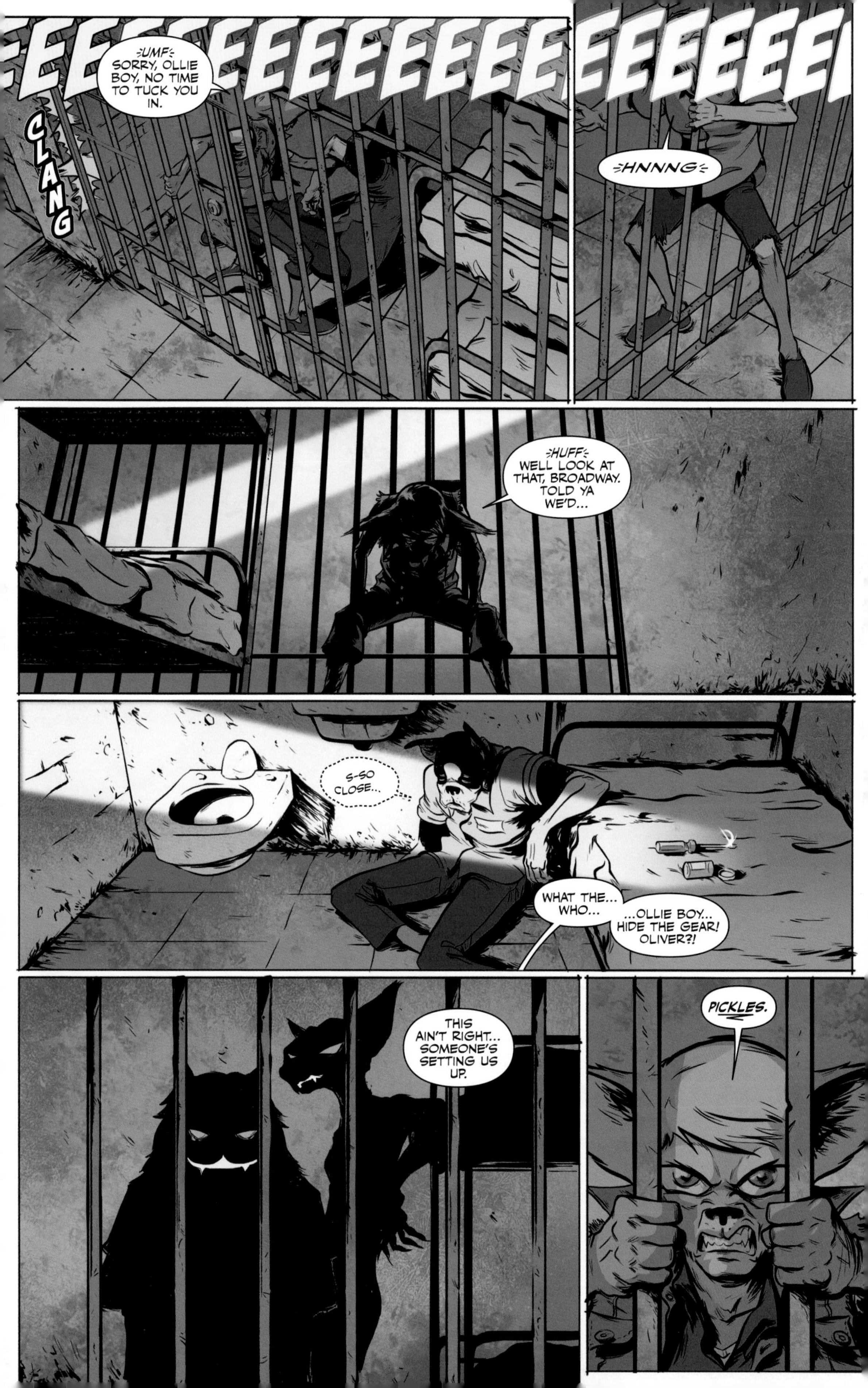
EEEEEEEEEEEEEEEEEEEEEEE
-UMF- SORRY, OLLIE BOY, NO TIME TO TUCK YOU IN.
CLANG
-HNNNG-
-HUFF- WELL LOOK AT THAT, BROADWAY. TOLD YA WE'D...
S-SO CLOSE...
WHAT THE... WHO...
...OLLIE BOY... HIDE THE GEAR! OLIVER?!
THIS AIN'T RIGHT... SOMEONE'S SETTING US UP.
PICKLES.

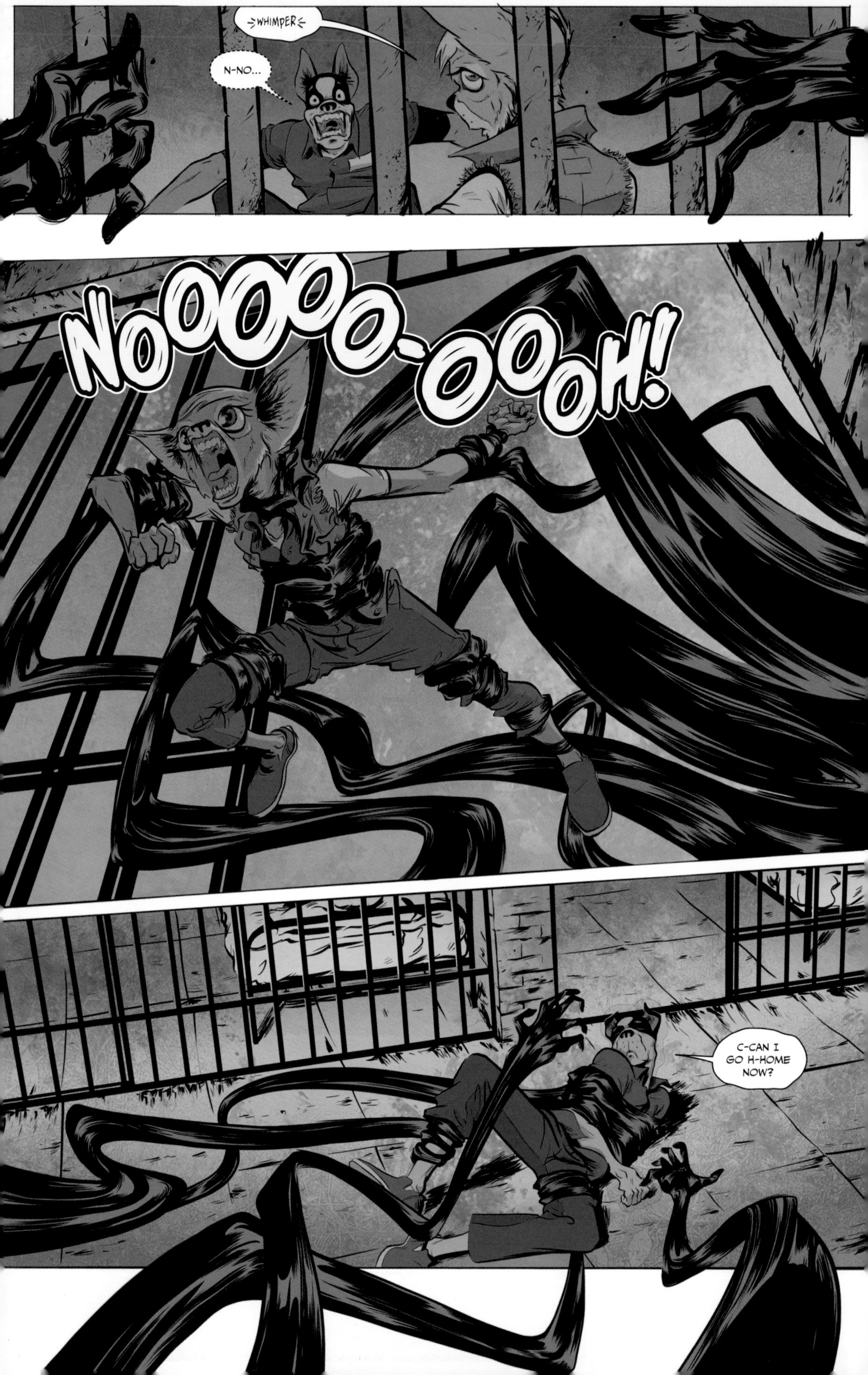
WHIMPER
N-NO...
NOOOOO-OOOOH!
C-CAN I GO H-HOME NOW?

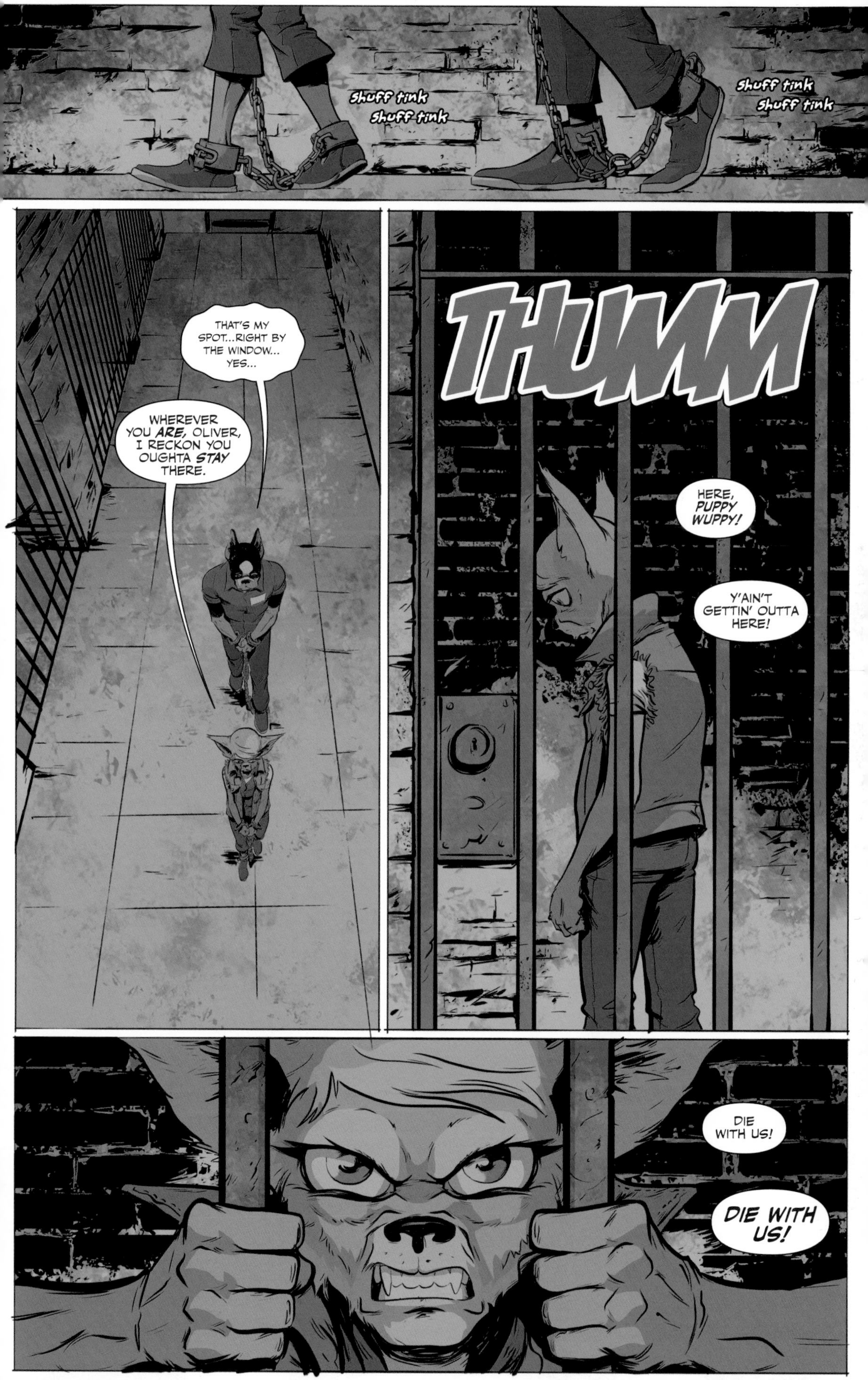
Shuff tink
Shuff tink
Shuff tink
Shuff tink
THAT'S MY SPOT...RIGHT BY THE WINDOW... YES...
WHEREVER YOU ARE, OLIVER, I RECKON YOU OUGHTA STAY THERE.
THUMM
HERE, PUPPY WUPPY!
Y'AIN'T GETTIN' OUTTA HERE!
DIE WITH US!
DIE WITH US!

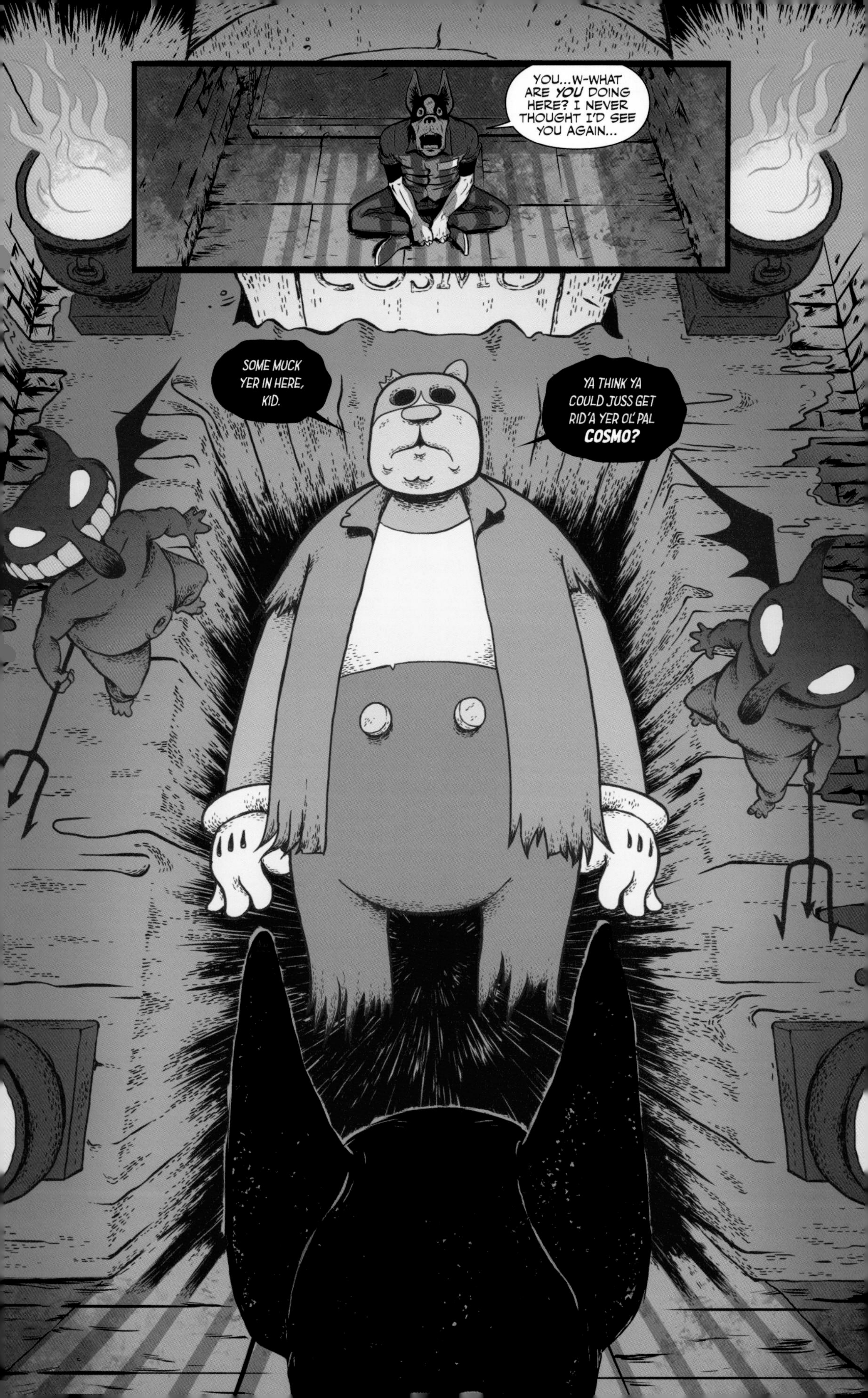
YOU...W-WHAT ARE YOU DOING HERE? I NEVER THOUGHT I'D SEE YOU AGAIN...
COSMO
SOME MUCK YER IN HERE, KID.
YA THINK YA COULD JUSS GET RID'A YER OL' PAL COSMO?

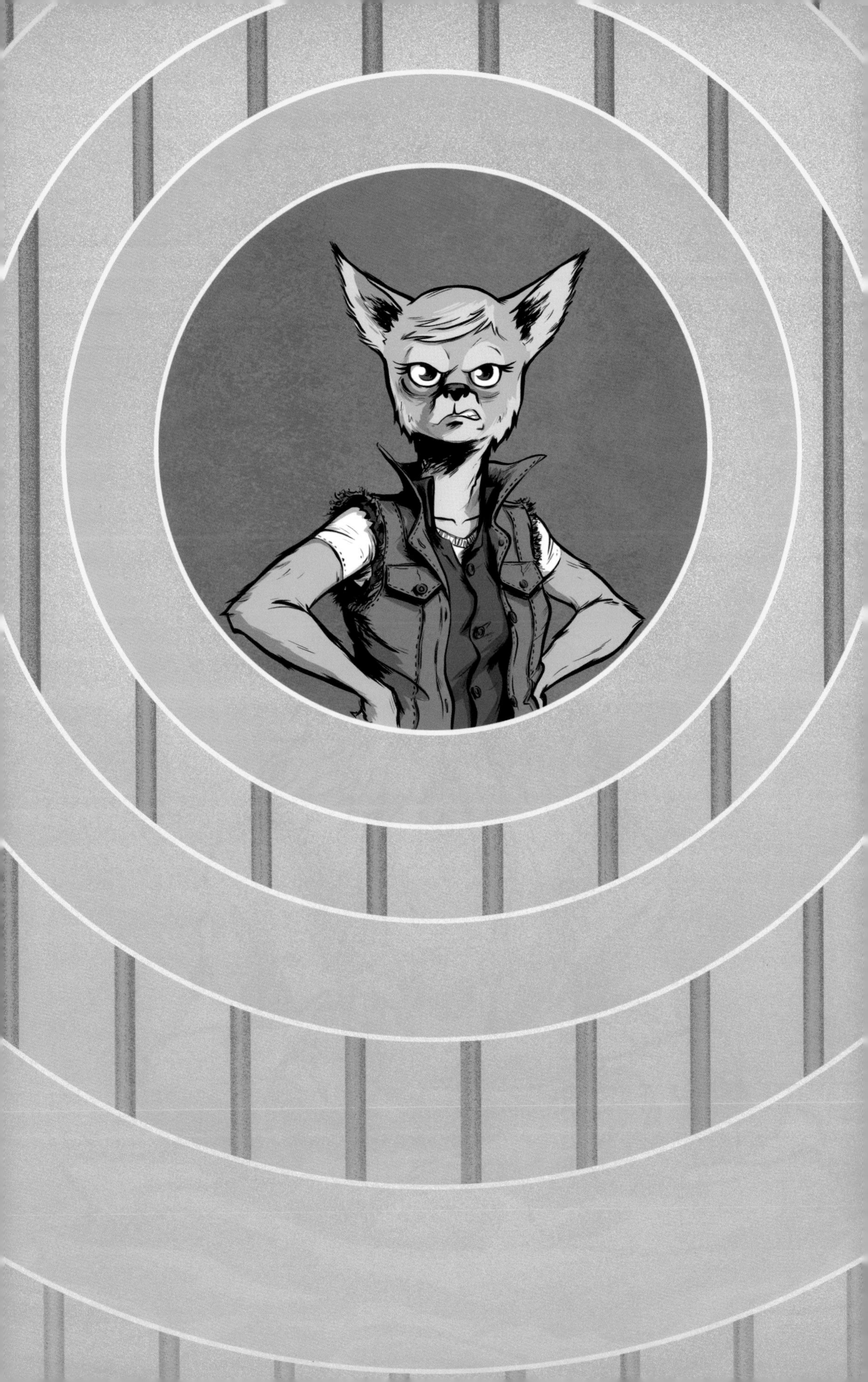

Chapter Three

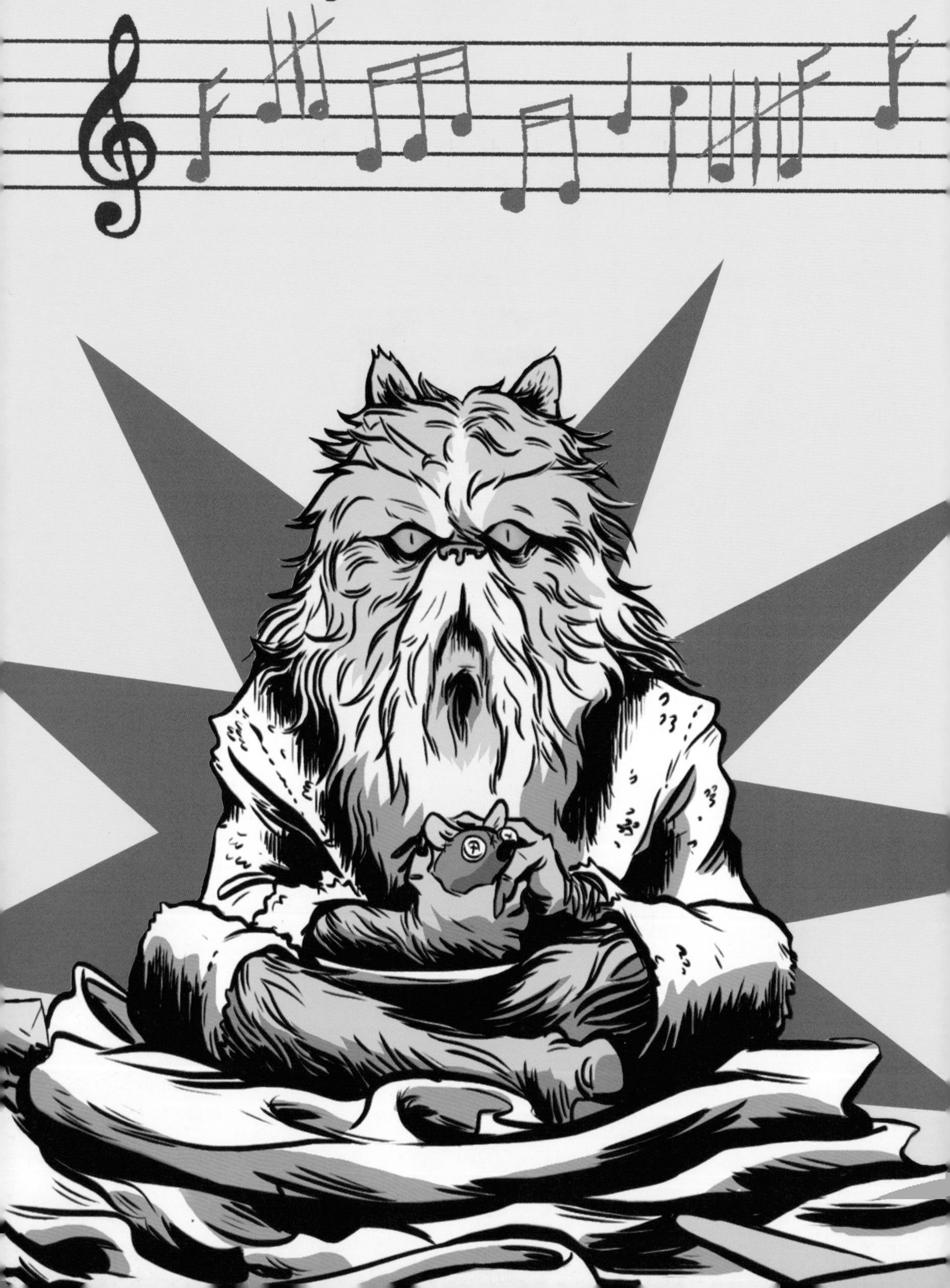

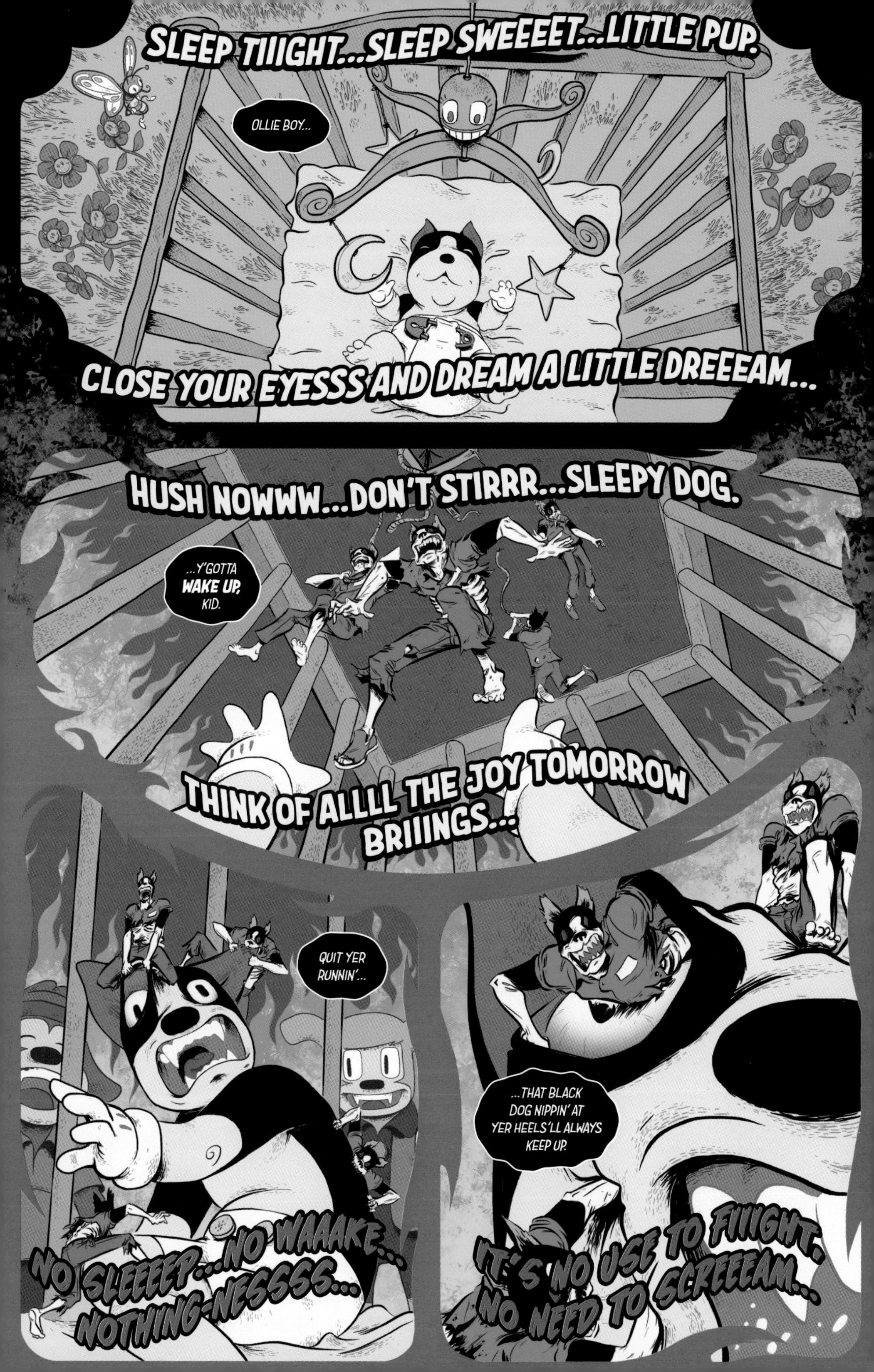
SLEEP TIIIGHT...SLEEP SWEEEET...LITTLE PUP.
OLLIE BOY...
CLOSE YOUR EYESSS AND DREAM A LITTLE DREEEAM...
HUSH NOWWW...DON'T STIRRR...SLEEPY DOG.
...Y'GOTTA WAKE UP, KID.
THINK OF ALLLL THE JOY TOMORROW BRIIINGS...
QUIT YER RUNNIN'...
NO SLEEEEP...NO WAAAKE... NOTHING-NESSSS...
...THAT BLACK DOG NIPPIN' AT YER HEELS'LL ALWAYS KEEP UP.
IT'S NO USE TO FIIIGHT. NO NEED TO SCREEEAM...

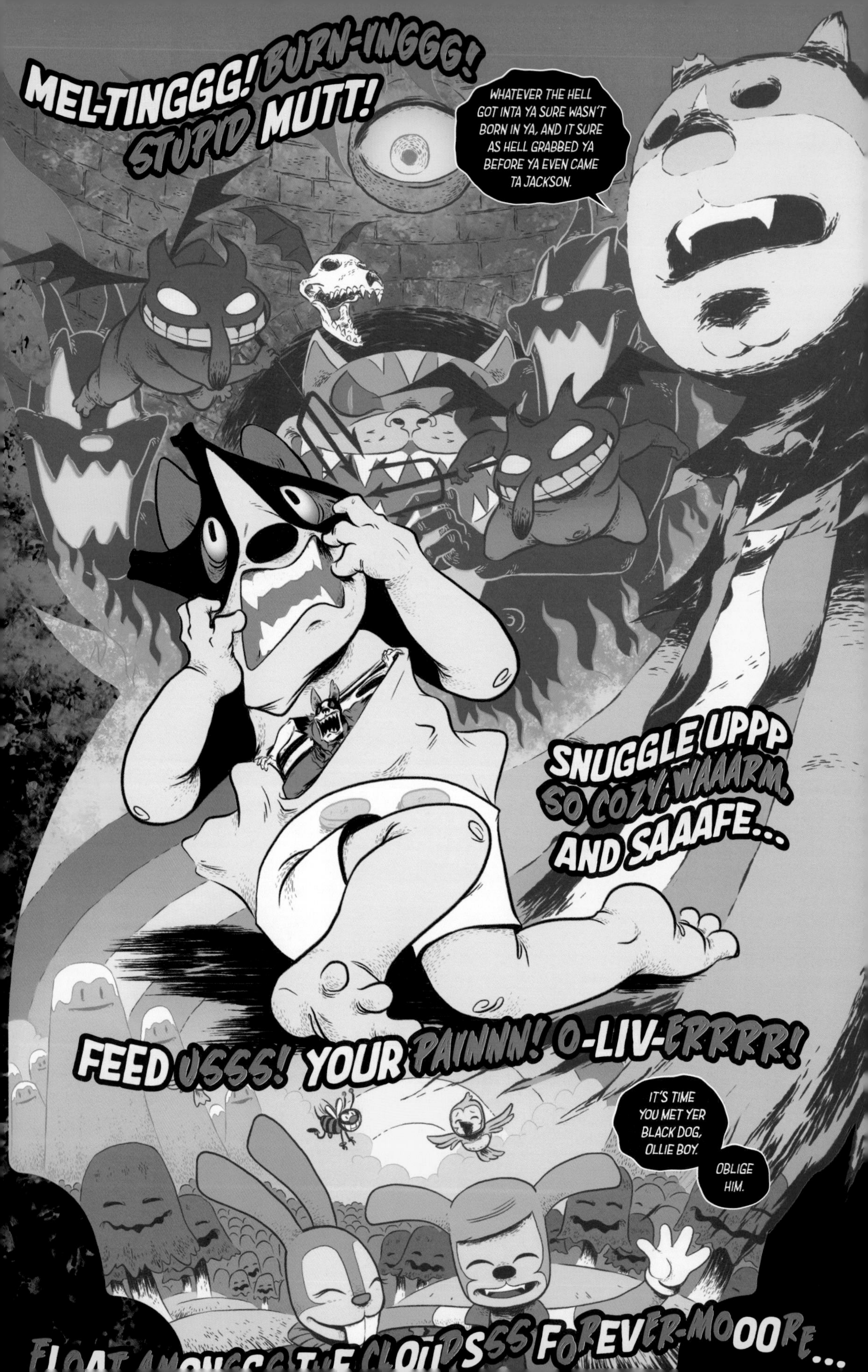
MEL-TINGGG! BURN-INGGG! STUPID MUTT!
WHATEVER THE HELL GOT INTA YA SURE WASN'T BORN IN YA, AND IT SURE AS HELL GRABBED YA BEFORE YA EVEN CAME TA JACKSON.
SNUGGLE UPPP SO COZY, WAAARM, AND SAAAFE...
FEED USSS! YOUR PAINNN! O-LIV-ERRRR!
IT'S TIME YOU MET YER BLACK DOG, OLLIE BOY.
OBLIGE HIM.

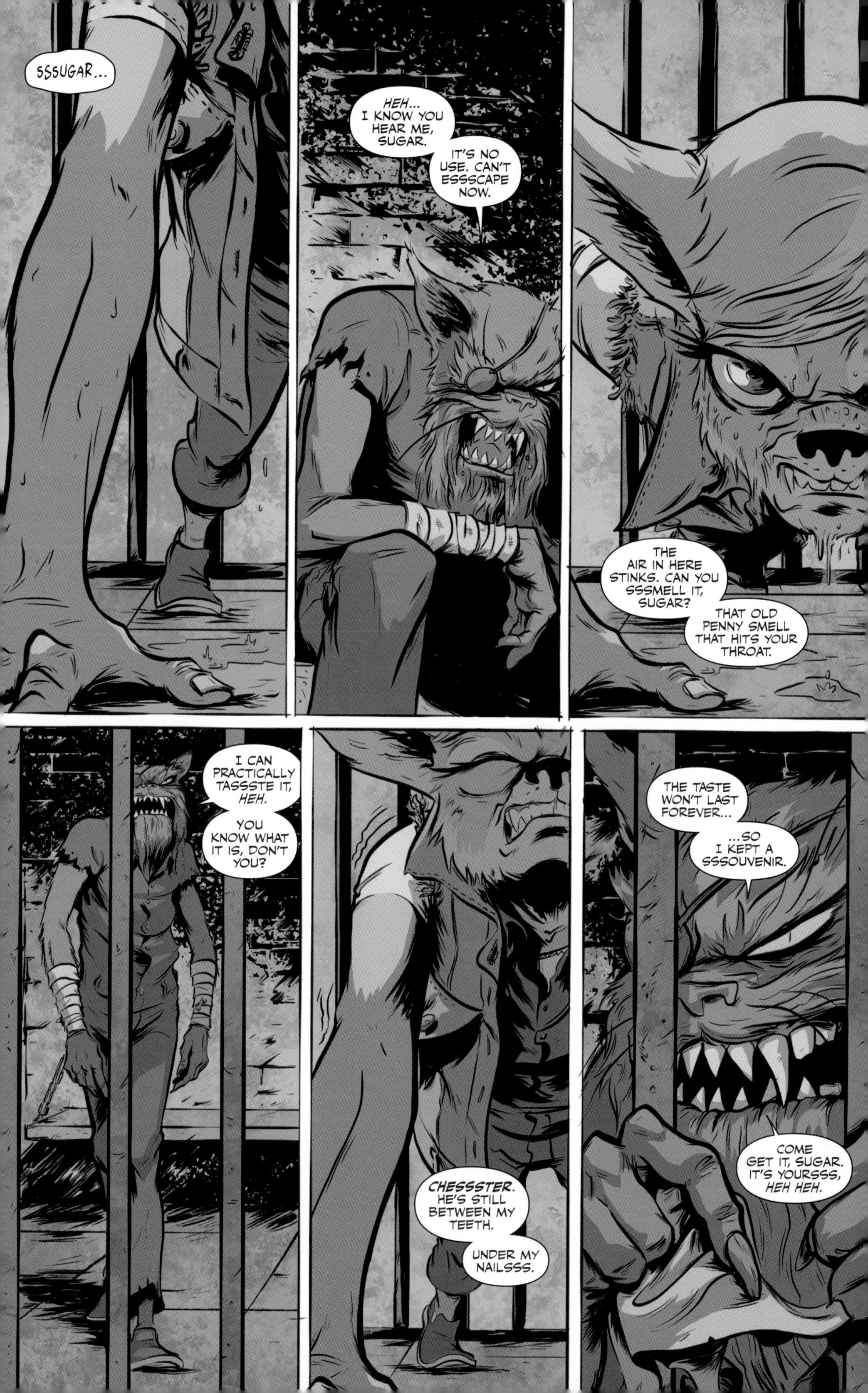
SSSUGAR...
HEH... I KNOW YOU HEAR ME, SUGAR.
IT'S NO USE. CAN'T ESSSCAPE NOW.
THE AIR IN HERE STINKS. CAN YOU SSSMELL IT, SUGAR?
THAT OLD PENNY SMELL THAT HITS YOUR THROAT.
I CAN PRACTICALLY TASSSTE IT, *HEH.*
YOU KNOW WHAT IT IS, DON'T YOU?
CHESSSTER. HE'S STILL BETWEEN MY TEETH.
UNDER MY NAILSSS.
THE TASTE WON'T LAST FOREVER...
...SO I KEPT A SSSOUVENIR.
COME GET IT, SUGAR. IT'S YOURSSS, *HEH HEH.*

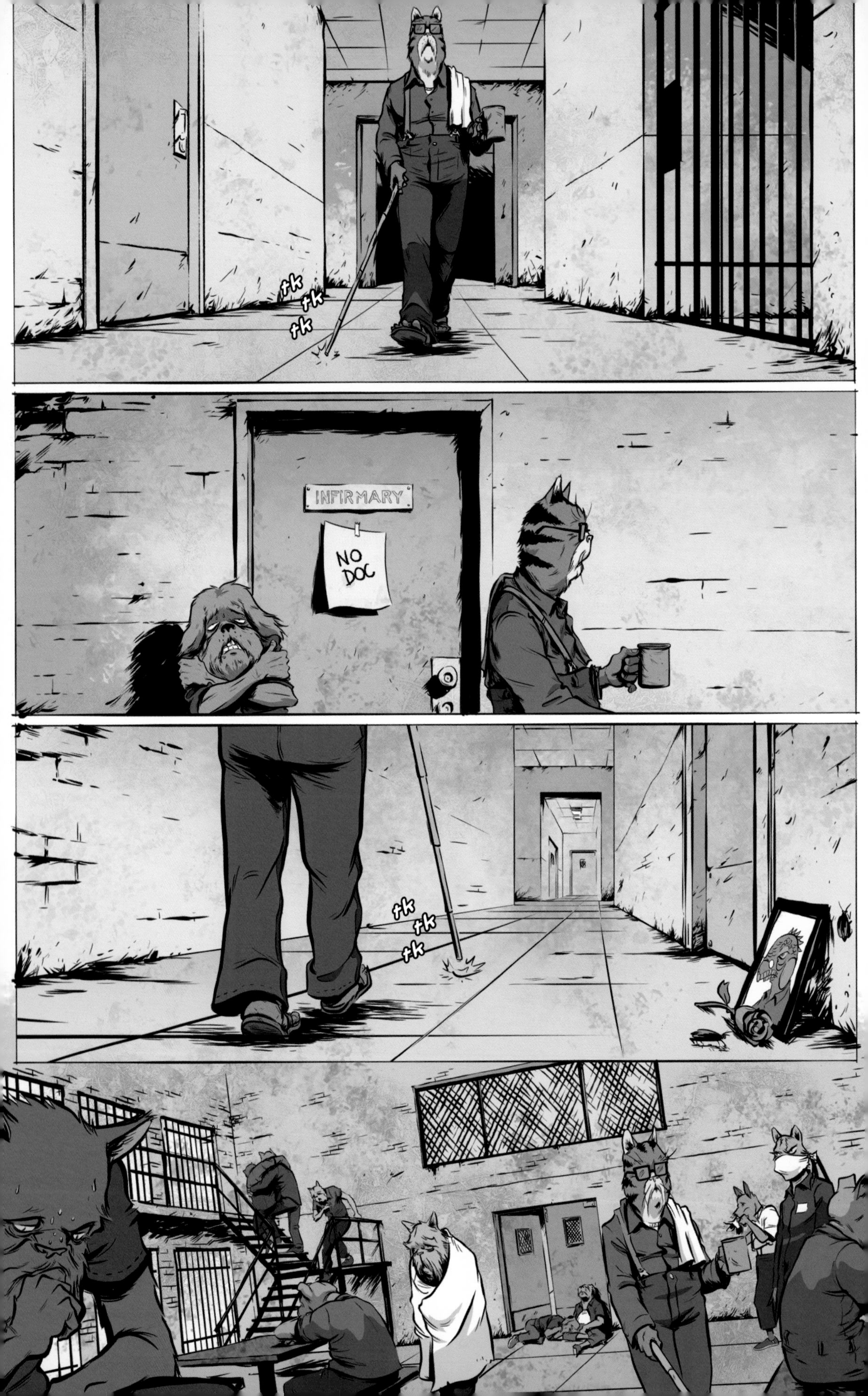
tk
tk
tk
INFIRMARY
NO DOC
tk
tk
tk

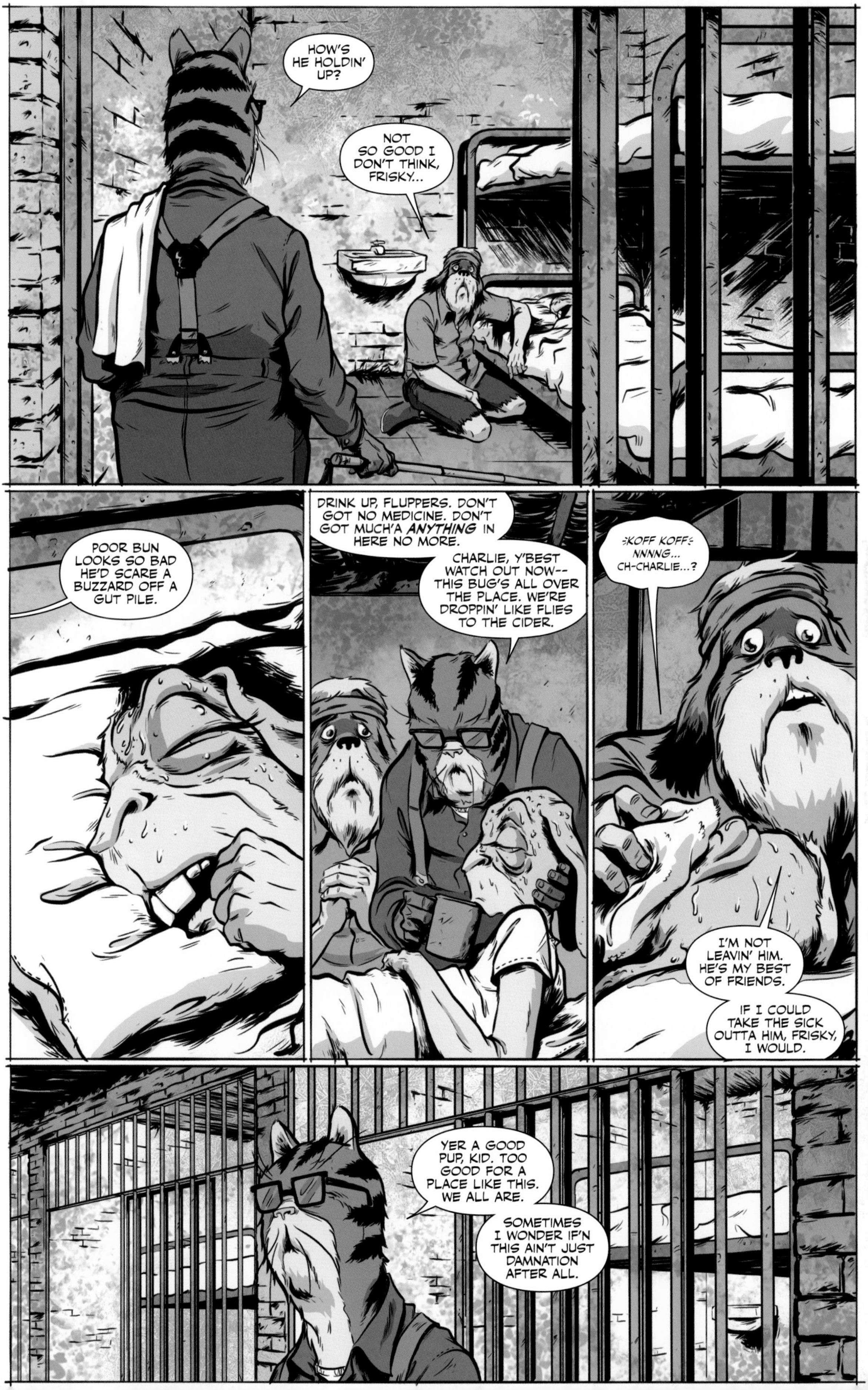
HOW'S HE HOLDIN' UP?
NOT SO GOOD I DON'T THINK, FRISKY...
POOR BUN LOOKS SO BAD HE'D SCARE A BUZZARD OFF A GUT PILE.
DRINK UP, FLUPPERS. DON'T GOT NO MEDICINE. DON'T GOT MUCH'A *ANYTHING* IN HERE NO MORE.
CHARLIE, Y'BEST WATCH OUT NOW-- THIS BUG'S ALL OVER THE PLACE. WE'RE DROPPIN' LIKE FLIES TO THE CIDER.
KOFF KOFF NNNNG... CH-CHARLIE...?
I'M NOT LEAVIN' HIM. HE'S MY BEST OF FRIENDS.
IF I COULD TAKE THE SICK OUTTA HIM, FRISKY, I WOULD.
YER A GOOD PUP, KID. TOO GOOD FOR A PLACE LIKE THIS. WE ALL ARE.
SOMETIMES I WONDER IF'N THIS AIN'T JUST DAMNATION AFTER ALL.

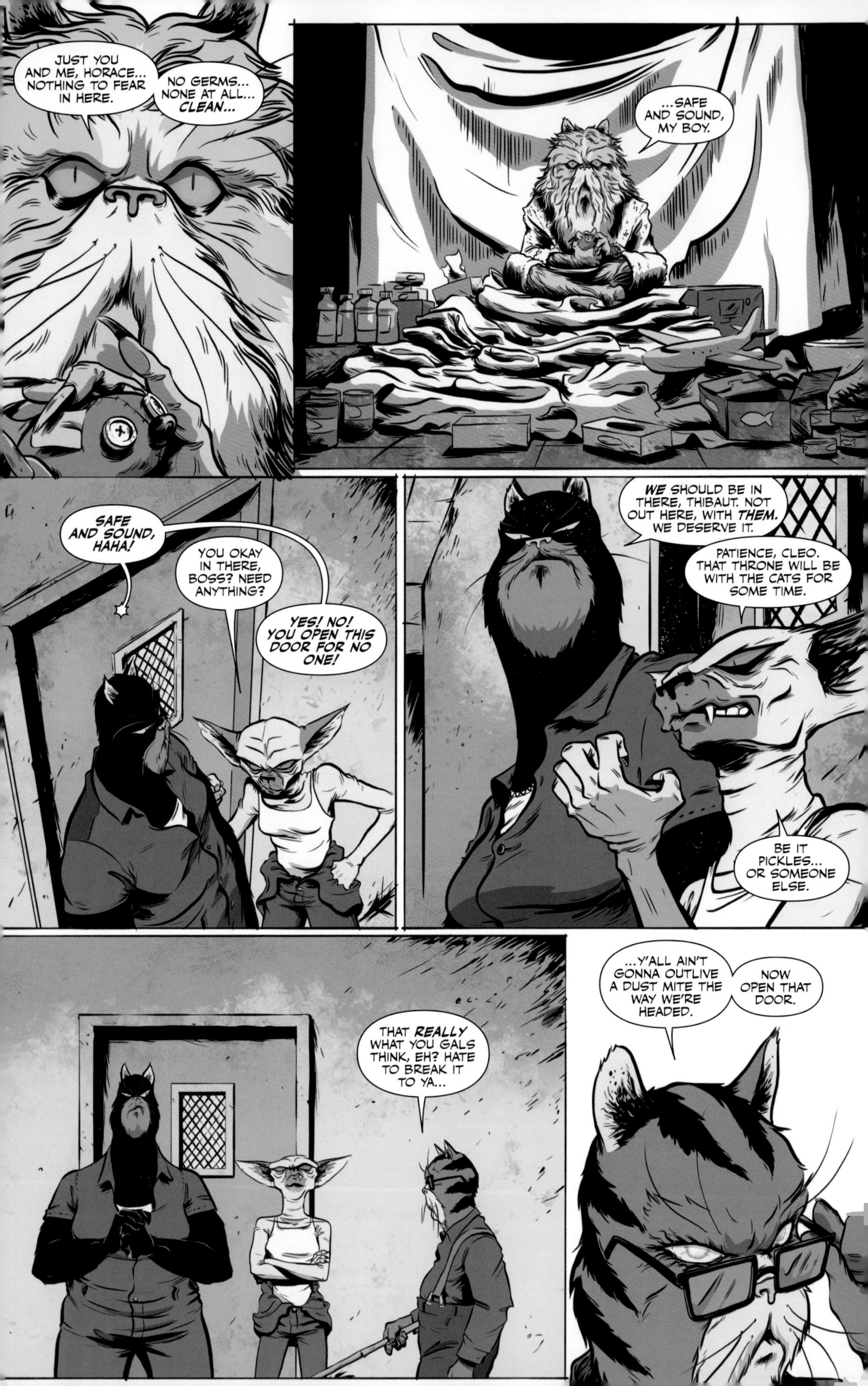
JUST YOU AND ME, HORACE... NOTHING TO FEAR IN HERE.
NO GERMS... NONE AT ALL... *CLEAN...*
...SAFE AND SOUND, MY BOY.
SAFE AND SOUND, HAHA!
YOU OKAY IN THERE, BOSS? NEED ANYTHING?
YES! NO! YOU OPEN THIS DOOR FOR NO ONE!
WE SHOULD BE IN THERE, THIBAUT. NOT OUT HERE, WITH *THEM.* WE DESERVE IT.
PATIENCE, CLEO. THAT THRONE WILL BE WITH THE CATS FOR SOME TIME.
BE IT PICKLES... OR SOMEONE ELSE.
THAT *REALLY* WHAT YOU GALS THINK, EH? HATE TO BREAK IT TO YA...
...Y'ALL AIN'T GONNA OUTLIVE A DUST MITE THE WAY WE'RE HEADED.
NOW OPEN THAT DOOR.

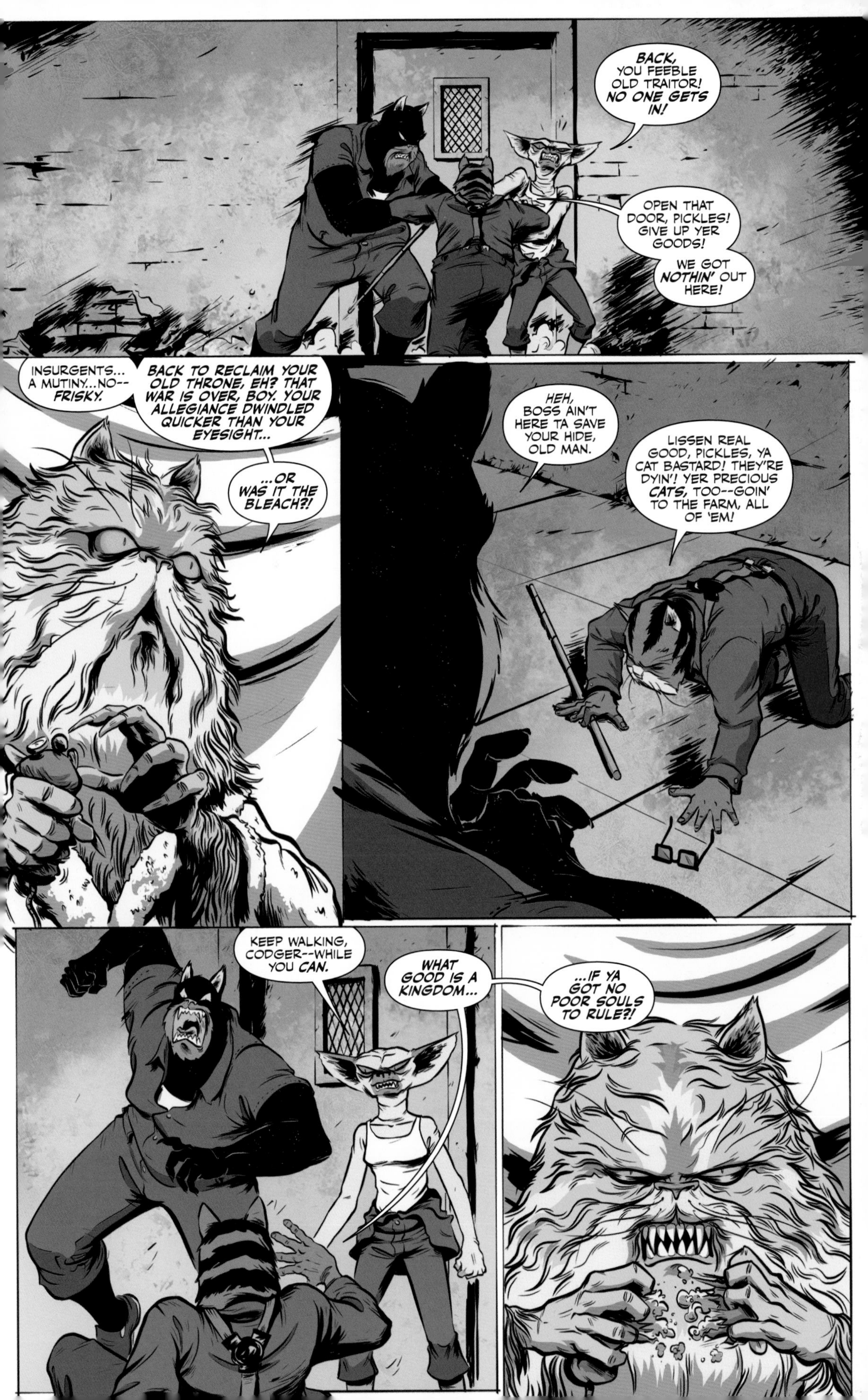
BACK, YOU FEEBLE OLD TRAITOR! NO ONE GETS IN!
OPEN THAT DOOR, PICKLES! GIVE UP YER GOODS!
WE GOT NOTHIN' OUT HERE!
INSURGENTS... A MUTINY...NO-- FRISKY.
BACK TO RECLAIM YOUR OLD THRONE, EH? THAT WAR IS OVER, BOY. YOUR ALLEGIANCE DWINDLED QUICKER THAN YOUR EYESIGHT...
...OR WAS IT THE BLEACH?!
HEH, BOSS AIN'T HERE TA SAVE YOUR HIDE, OLD MAN.
LISSEN REAL GOOD, PICKLES, YA CAT BASTARD! THEY'RE DYIN'! YER PRECIOUS CATS, TOO--GOIN' TO THE FARM, ALL OF 'EM!
KEEP WALKING, CODGER--WHILE YOU CAN.
WHAT GOOD IS A KINGDOM...
...IF YA GOT NO POOR SOULS TO RULE?!

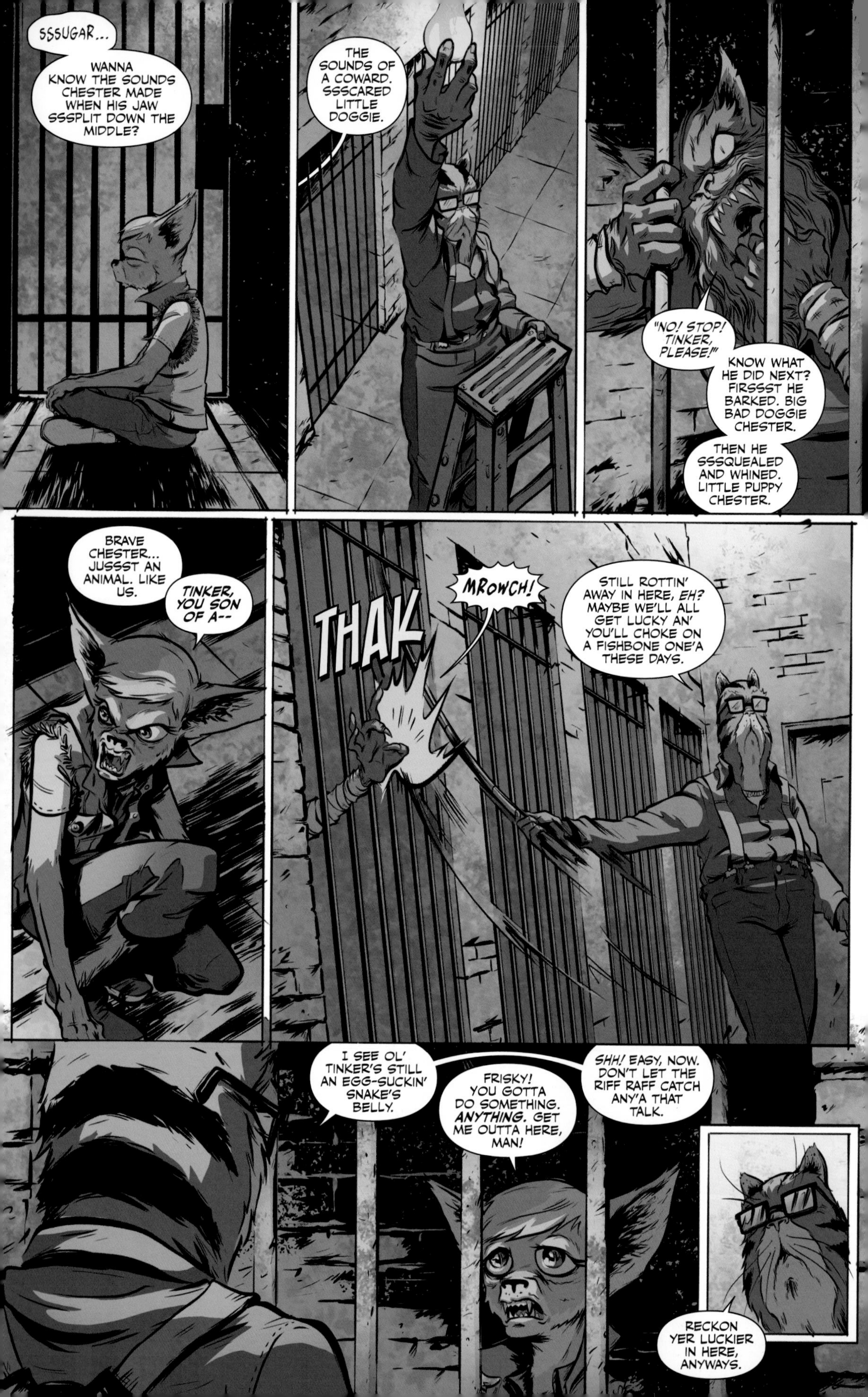
SSSUGAR...
WANNA KNOW THE SOUNDS CHESTER MADE WHEN HIS JAW SSSPLIT DOWN THE MIDDLE?
THE SOUNDS OF A COWARD. SSSCARED LITTLE DOGGIE.
"NO! STOP! TINKER, PLEASE!"
KNOW WHAT HE DID NEXT? FIRSSST HE BARKED. BIG BAD DOGGIE CHESTER.
THEN HE SSSQUEALED AND WHINED. LITTLE PUPPY CHESTER.
BRAVE CHESTER... JUSSST AN ANIMAL. LIKE US.
TINKER, YOU SON OF A--
THAK
MROWCH!
STILL ROTTIN' AWAY IN HERE, EH? MAYBE WE'LL ALL GET LUCKY AN' YOU'LL CHOKE ON A FISHBONE ONE'A THESE DAYS.
I SEE OL' TINKER'S STILL AN EGG-SUCKIN' SNAKE'S BELLY.
FRISKY! YOU GOTTA DO SOMETHING. ANYTHING. GET ME OUTTA HERE, MAN!
SHH! EASY, NOW. DON'T LET THE RIFF RAFF CATCH ANY'A THAT TALK.
RECKON YER LUCKIER IN HERE, ANYWAYS.

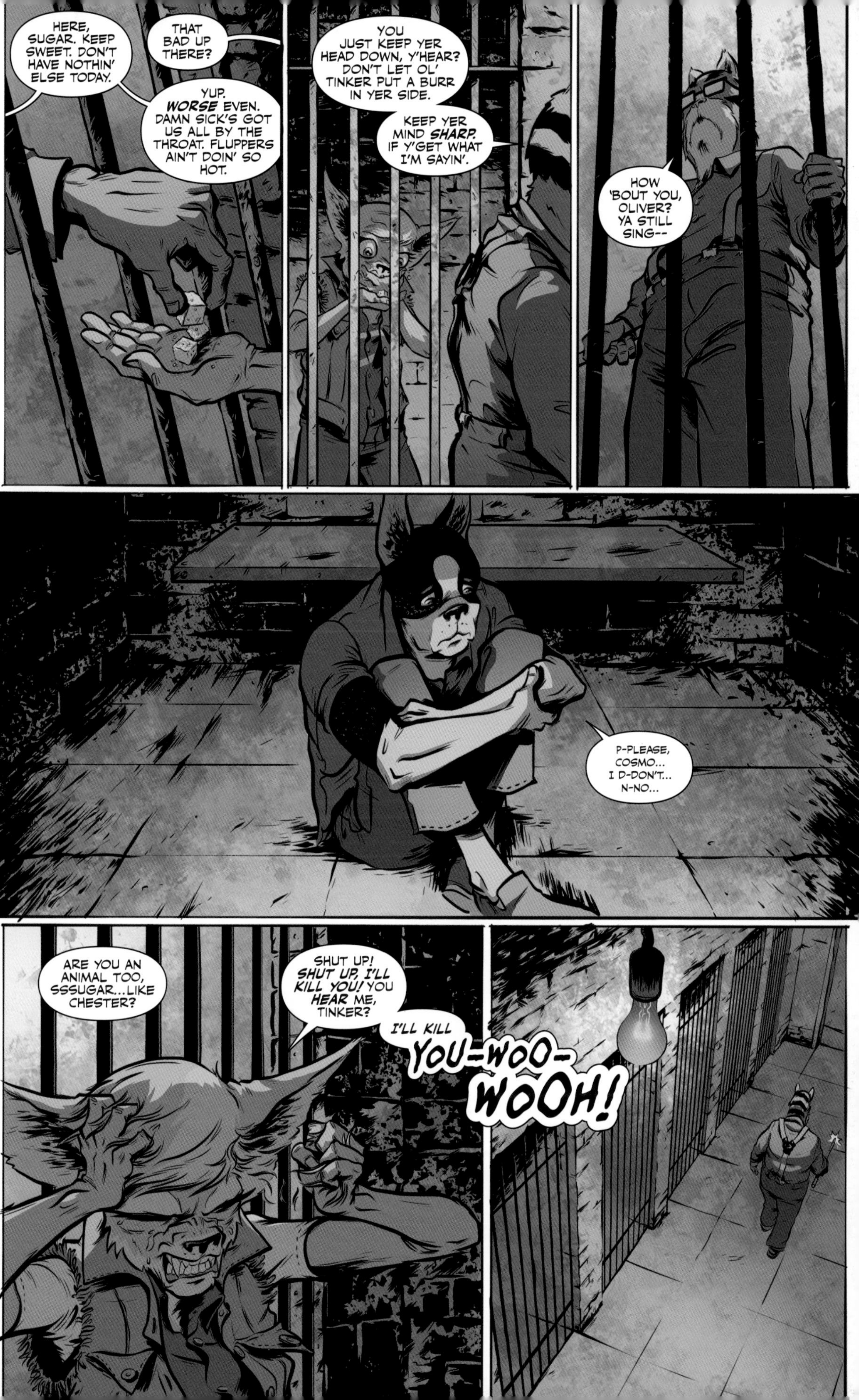
HERE, SUGAR. KEEP SWEET. DON'T HAVE NOTHIN' ELSE TODAY.
THAT BAD UP THERE?
YUP. WORSE EVEN. DAMN SICK'S GOT US ALL BY THE THROAT. FLUPPERS AIN'T DOIN' SO HOT.
YOU JUST KEEP YER HEAD DOWN, Y'HEAR? DON'T LET OL' TINKER PUT A BURR IN YER SIDE.
KEEP YER MIND SHARP. IF Y'GET WHAT I'M SAYIN'.
HOW 'BOUT YOU, OLIVER? YA STILL SING--
P-PLEASE, COSMO... I D-DON'T... N-NO...
ARE YOU AN ANIMAL TOO, SSSUGAR...LIKE CHESTER?
SHUT UP! SHUT UP, I'LL KILL YOU! YOU HEAR ME, TINKER?
I'LL KILL YOU-WOO-WOOH!

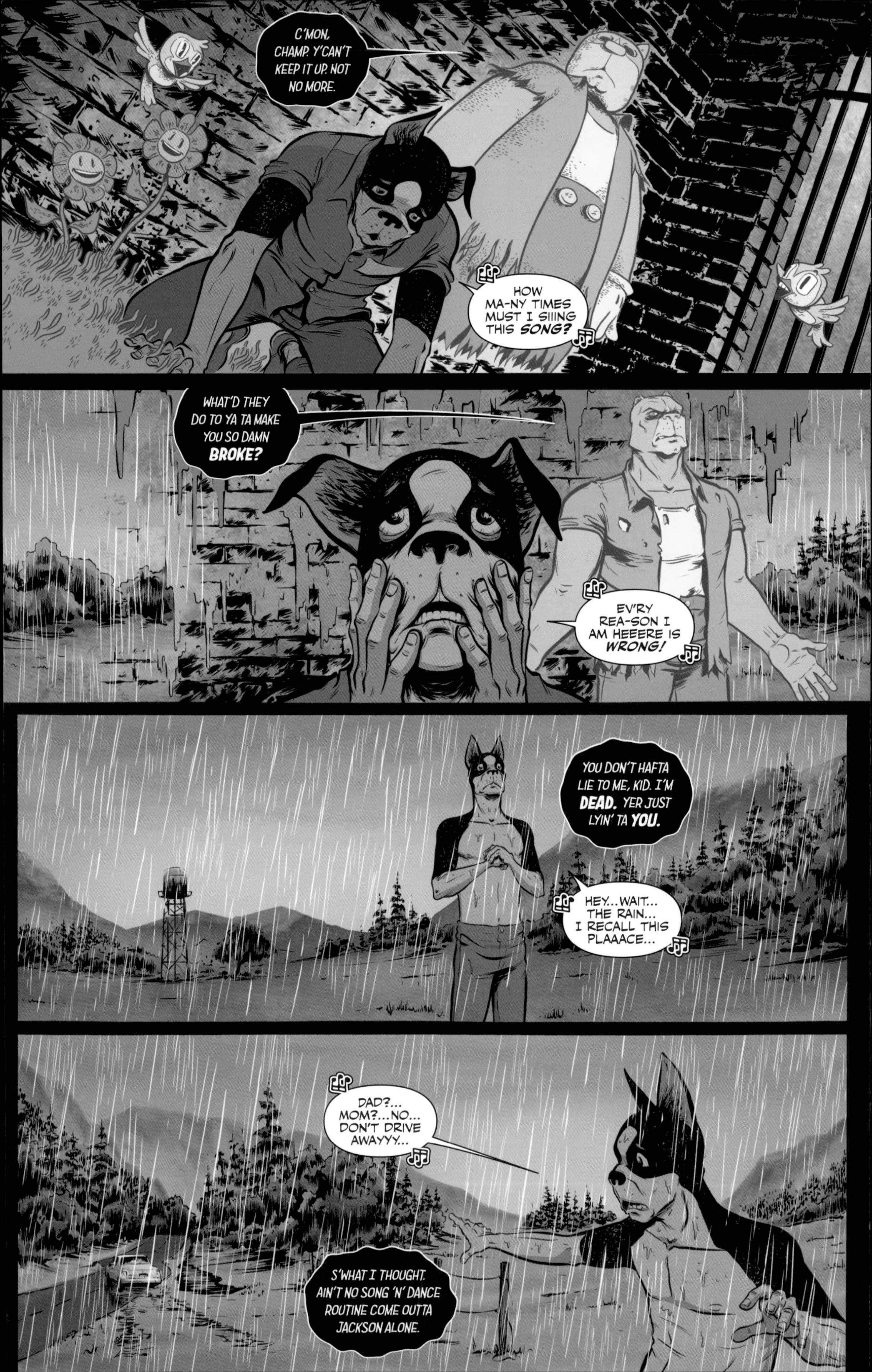
C'MON, CHAMP. Y'CAN'T KEEP IT UP. NOT NO MORE.
HOW MA-NY TIMES MUST I SIIING THIS SONG?
WHAT'D THEY DO TO YA TA MAKE YOU SO DAMN BROKE?
EV'RY REA-SON I AM HEEERE IS WRONG!
YOU DON'T HAFTA LIE TO ME, KID. I'M DEAD. YER JUST LYIN' TA YOU.
HEY...WAIT... THE RAIN... I RECALL THIS PLAAACE...
DAD?... MOM?...NO... DON'T DRIVE AWAYYY...
S'WHAT I THOUGHT. AIN'T NO SONG 'N' DANCE ROUTINE COME OUTTA JACKSON ALONE.

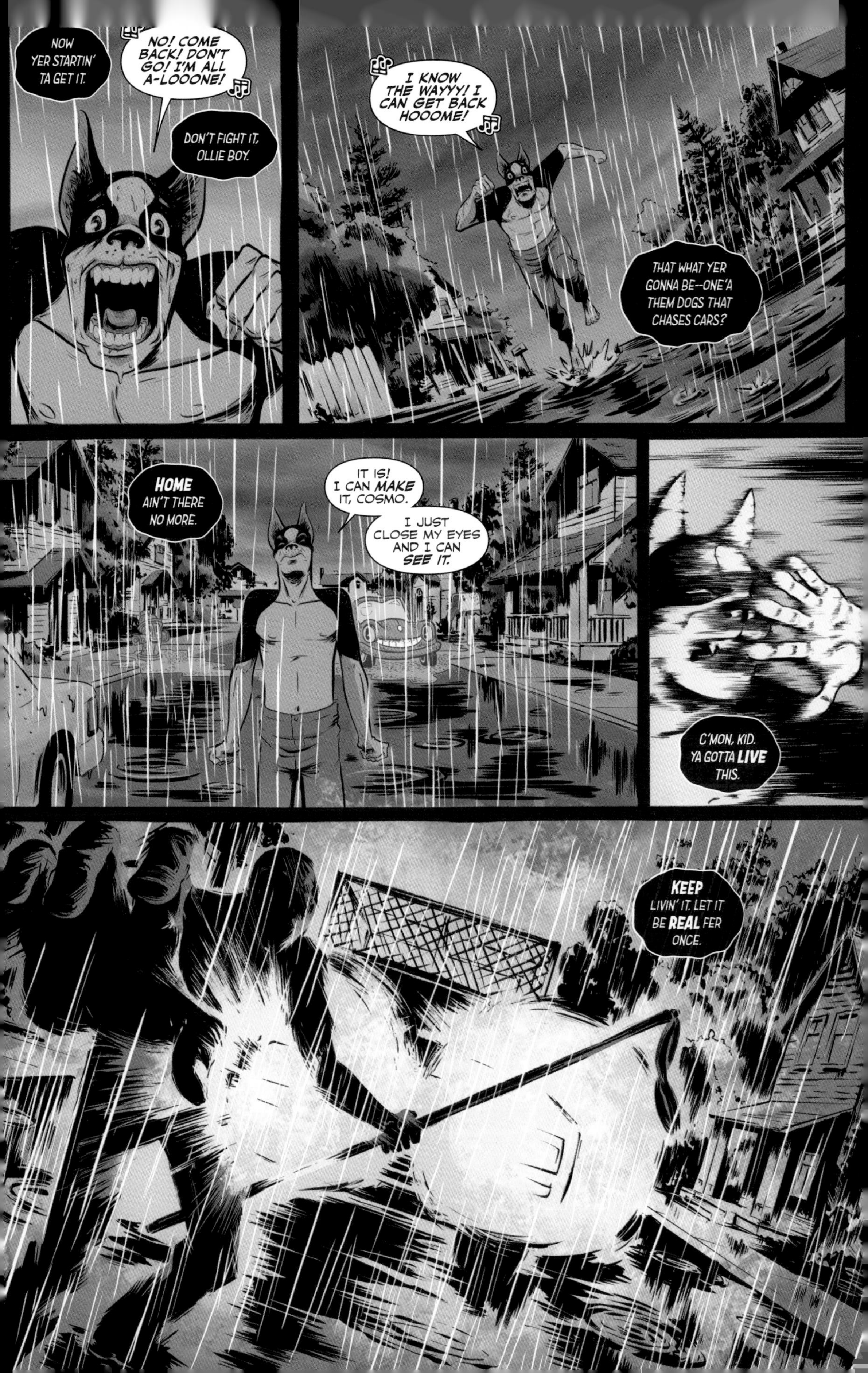
NOW YER STARTIN' TA GET IT.
NO! COME BACK! DON'T GO! I'M ALL A-LOOONE!
DON'T FIGHT IT, OLLIE BOY.
I KNOW THE WAYYY! I CAN GET BACK HOOOME!
THAT WHAT YER GONNA BE--ONE'A THEM DOGS THAT CHASES CARS?
HOME AIN'T THERE NO MORE.
IT IS! I CAN MAKE IT, COSMO.
I JUST CLOSE MY EYES AND I CAN SEE IT.
C'MON, KID. YA GOTTA LIVE THIS.
KEEP LIVIN' IT. LET IT BE REAL FER ONCE.

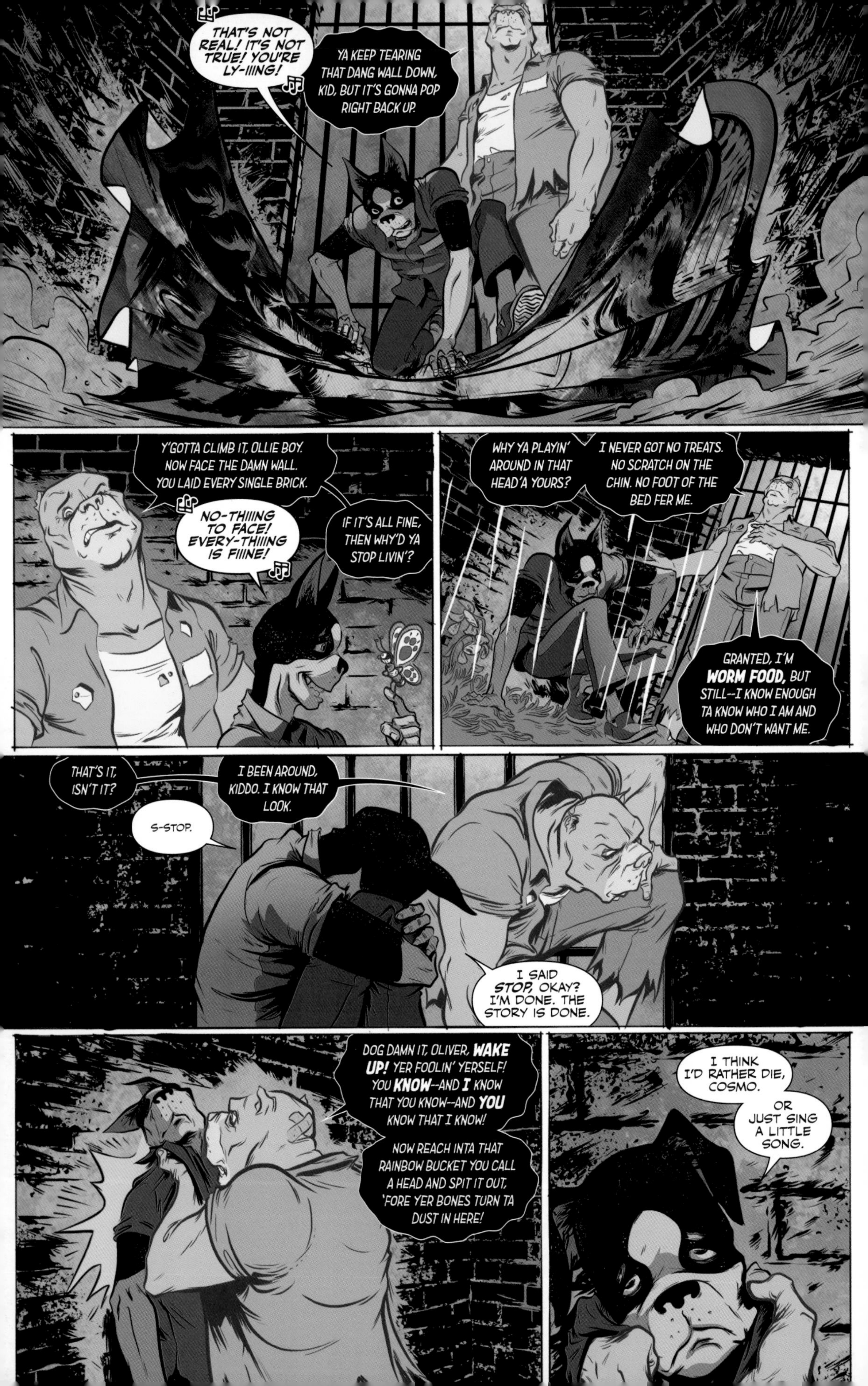
THAT'S NOT REAL! IT'S NOT TRUE! YOU'RE LY-IIING!
YA KEEP TEARING THAT DANG WALL DOWN, KID, BUT IT'S GONNA POP RIGHT BACK UP.
Y'GOTTA CLIMB IT, OLLIE BOY. NOW FACE THE DAMN WALL. YOU LAID EVERY SINGLE BRICK.
NO-THIIING TO FACE! EVERY-THIIING IS FIIINE!
IF IT'S ALL FINE, THEN WHY'D YA STOP LIVIN'?
WHY YA PLAYIN' AROUND IN THAT HEAD'A YOURS?
I NEVER GOT NO TREATS. NO SCRATCH ON THE CHIN. NO FOOT OF THE BED FER ME.
GRANTED, I'M **WORM FOOD,** BUT STILL--I KNOW ENOUGH TA KNOW WHO I AM AND WHO DON'T WANT ME.
THAT'S IT, ISN'T IT?
I BEEN AROUND, KIDDO. I KNOW THAT LOOK.
S-STOP.
I SAID ***STOP,*** OKAY? I'M DONE. THE STORY IS DONE.
DOG DAMN IT, OLIVER, **WAKE UP!** YER FOOLIN' YERSELF! YOU **KNOW**--AND **I** KNOW THAT YOU KNOW--AND **YOU** KNOW THAT I KNOW!
NOW REACH INTA THAT RAINBOW BUCKET YOU CALL A HEAD AND SPIT IT OUT, 'FORE YER BONES TURN TA DUST IN HERE!
I THINK I'D RATHER DIE, COSMO.
OR JUST SING A LITTLE SONG.

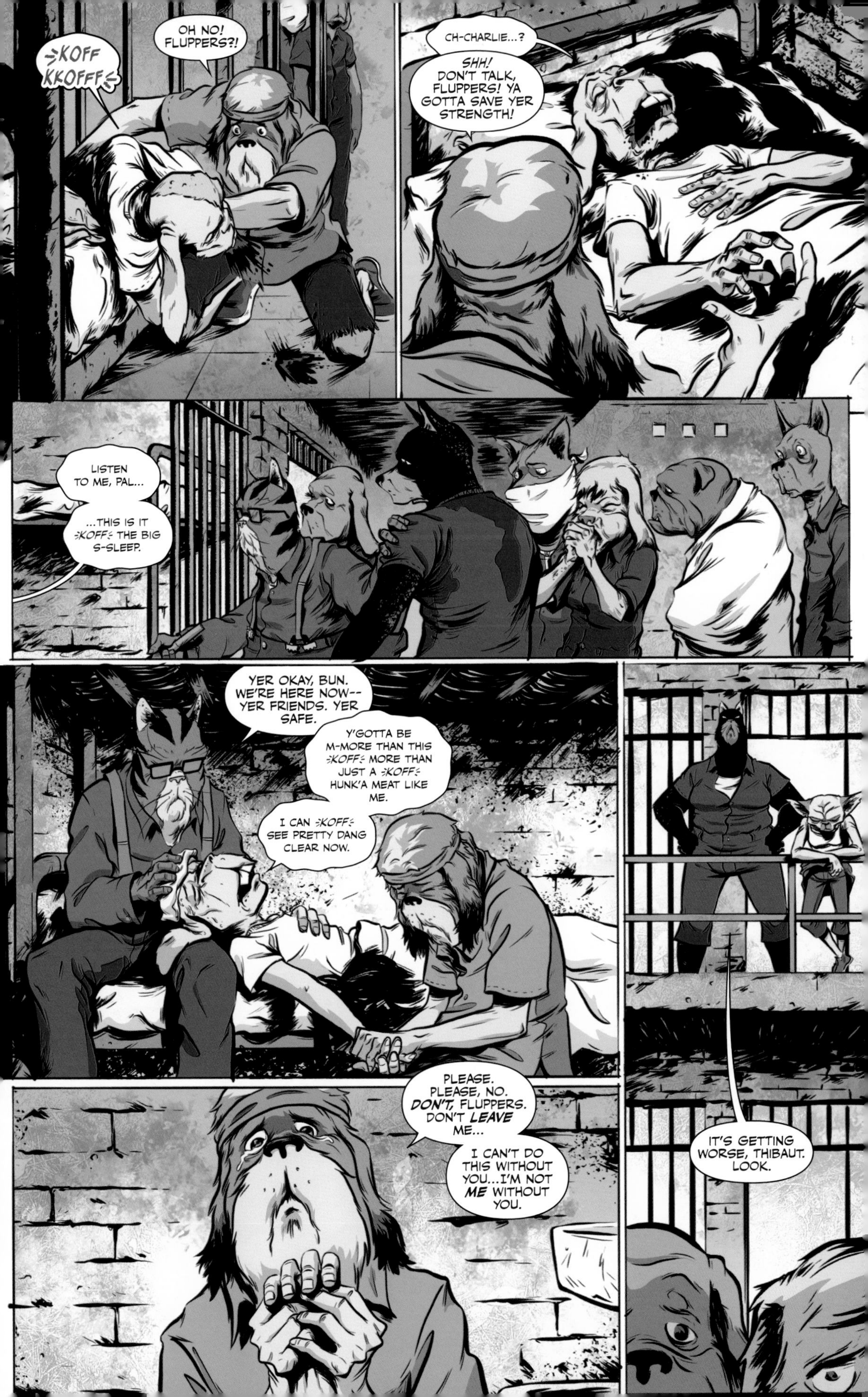

OH NO! FLUPPERS?!
KOFF KKOFFF
CH-CHARLIE...?
SHH! DON'T TALK, FLUPPERS! YA GOTTA SAVE YER STRENGTH!
LISTEN TO ME, PAL...
...THIS IS IT KOFF THE BIG S-SLEEP.
YER OKAY, BUN. WE'RE HERE NOW-- YER FRIENDS. YER SAFE.
Y'GOTTA BE M-MORE THAN THIS KOFF MORE THAN JUST A KOFF HUNK'A MEAT LIKE ME.
I CAN KOFF SEE PRETTY DANG CLEAR NOW.
PLEASE. PLEASE, NO. DON'T, FLUPPERS. DON'T LEAVE ME...
I CAN'T DO THIS WITHOUT YOU...I'M NOT ME WITHOUT YOU.
IT'S GETTING WORSE, THIBAUT. LOOK.

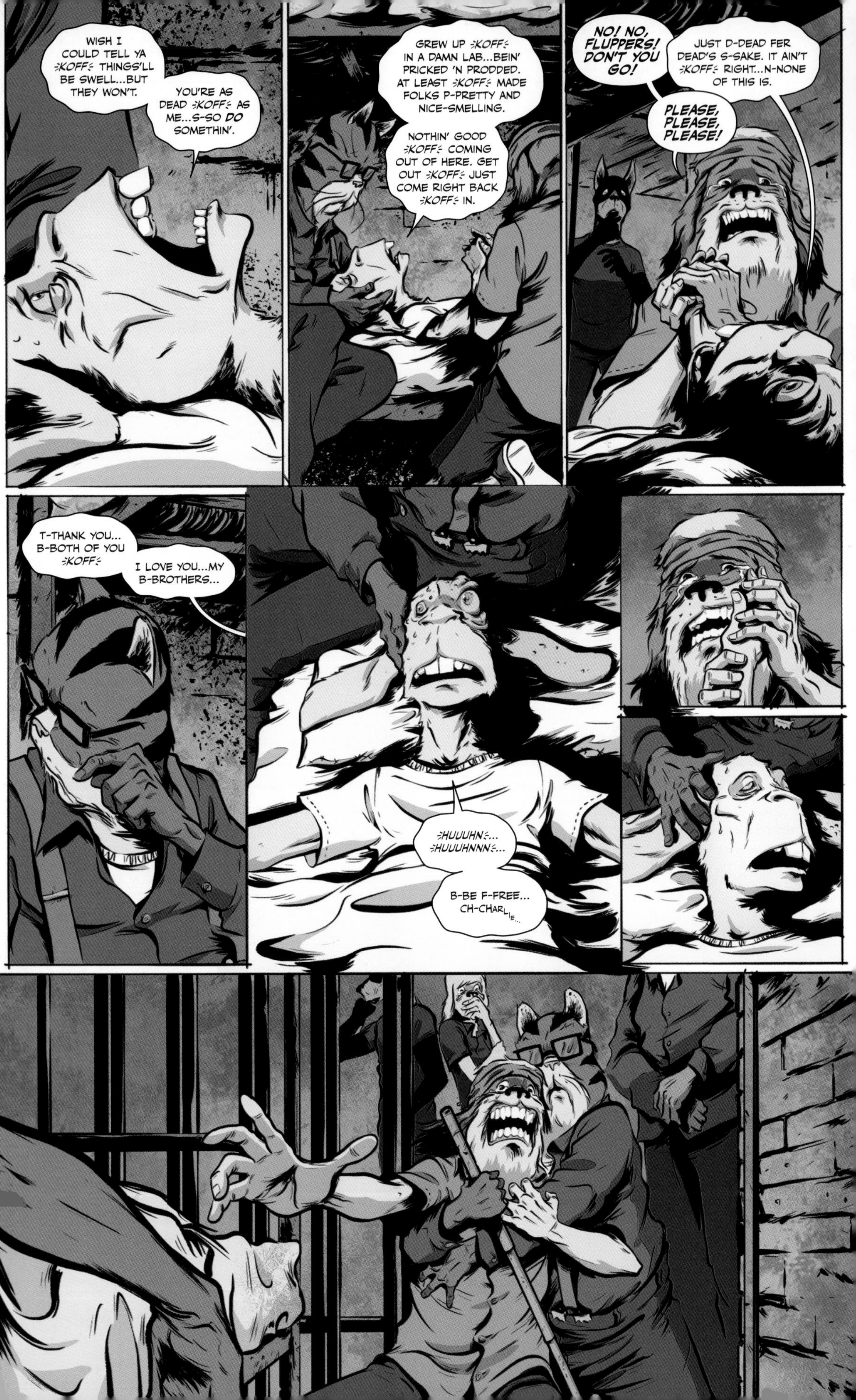
WISH I COULD TELL YA *KOFF* THINGS'LL BE SWELL...BUT THEY WON'T.
YOU'RE AS DEAD *KOFF* AS ME...S-SO *DO* SOMETHIN'.
GREW UP *KOFF* IN A DAMN LAB...BEIN' PRICKED 'N PRODDED. AT LEAST *KOFF* MADE FOLKS P-PRETTY AND NICE-SMELLING.
NOTHIN' GOOD *KOFF* COMING OUT OF HERE. GET OUT *KOFF* JUST COME RIGHT BACK *KOFF* IN.
NO! NO, FLUPPERS! DON'T YOU GO!
JUST D-DEAD FER DEAD'S S-SAKE. IT AIN'T *KOFF* RIGHT...N-NONE OF THIS IS.
PLEASE, PLEASE, PLEASE!
T-THANK YOU... B-BOTH OF YOU *KOFF*
I LOVE YOU...MY B-BROTHERS...
HUUUHN... *HUUUHNNN*...
B-BE F-FREE... CH-CHARLIE...

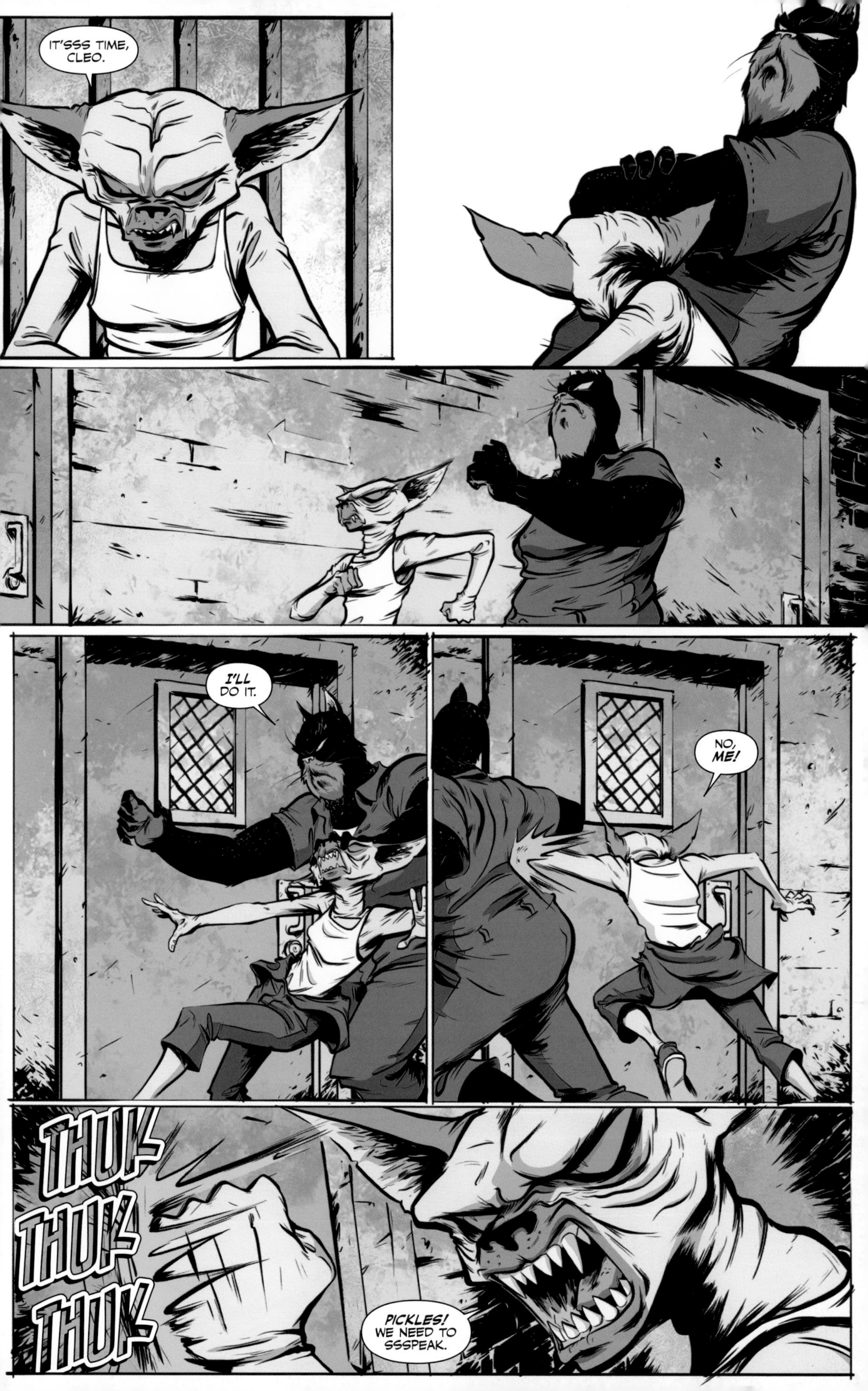
IT'SSS TIME, CLEO.
I'LL DO IT.
NO, ME!
THUK
THUK
THUK
PICKLES! WE NEED TO SSSPEAK.

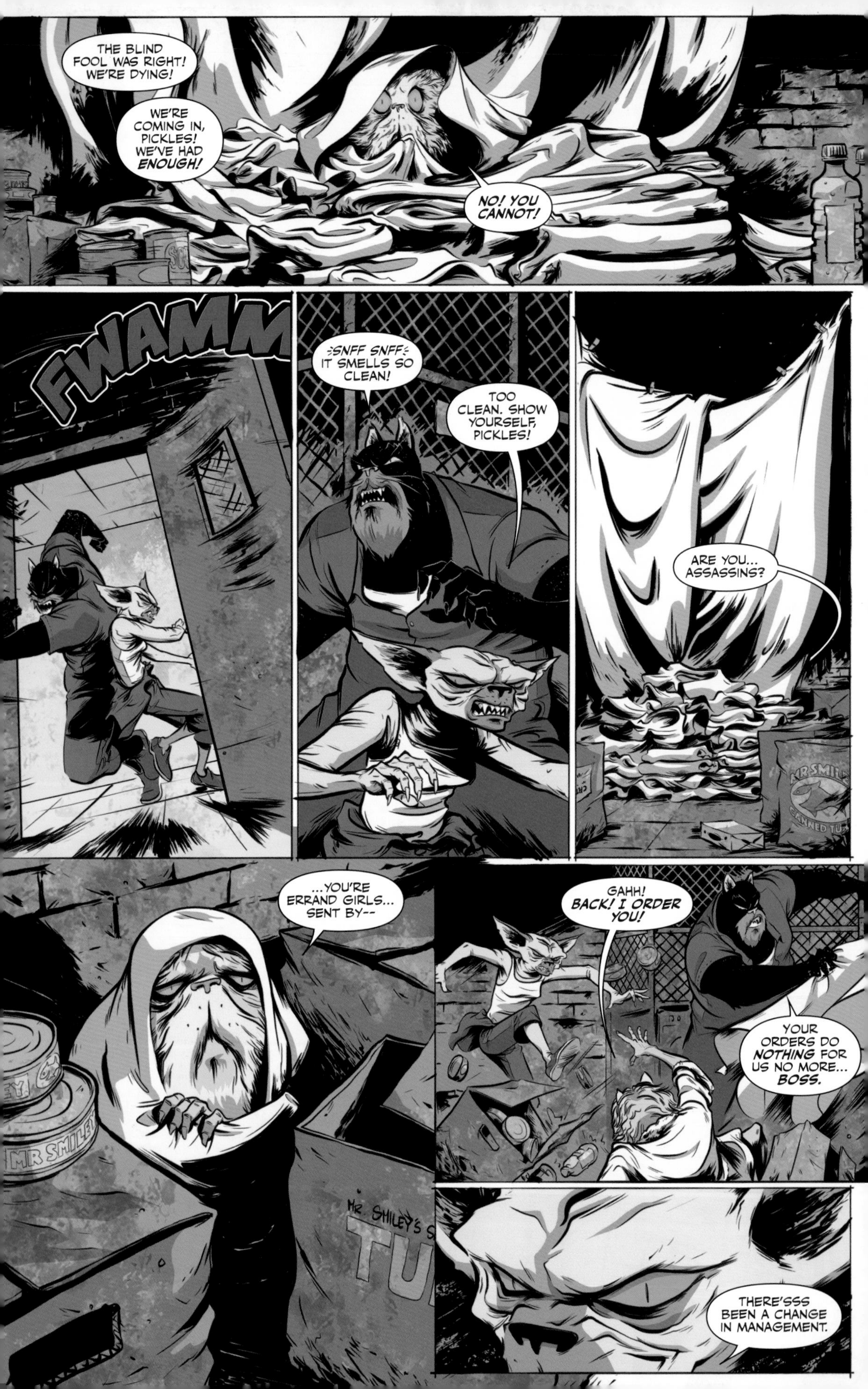
THE BLIND FOOL WAS RIGHT! WE'RE DYING!
WE'RE COMING IN, PICKLES! WE'VE HAD *ENOUGH!*
NO! YOU CANNOT!
FWAMM
SNFF SNFF IT SMELLS SO CLEAN!
TOO CLEAN. SHOW YOURSELF, PICKLES!
ARE YOU... ASSASSINS?
MR SMILEY'S CANNED TUNA
...YOU'RE ERRAND GIRLS... SENT BY--
MR SMILEY
MR. SMILEY'S TU
GAHH! *BACK! I ORDER YOU!*
YOUR ORDERS DO *NOTHING* FOR US NO MORE... *BOSS.*
THERE'SSS BEEN A CHANGE IN MANAGEMENT.

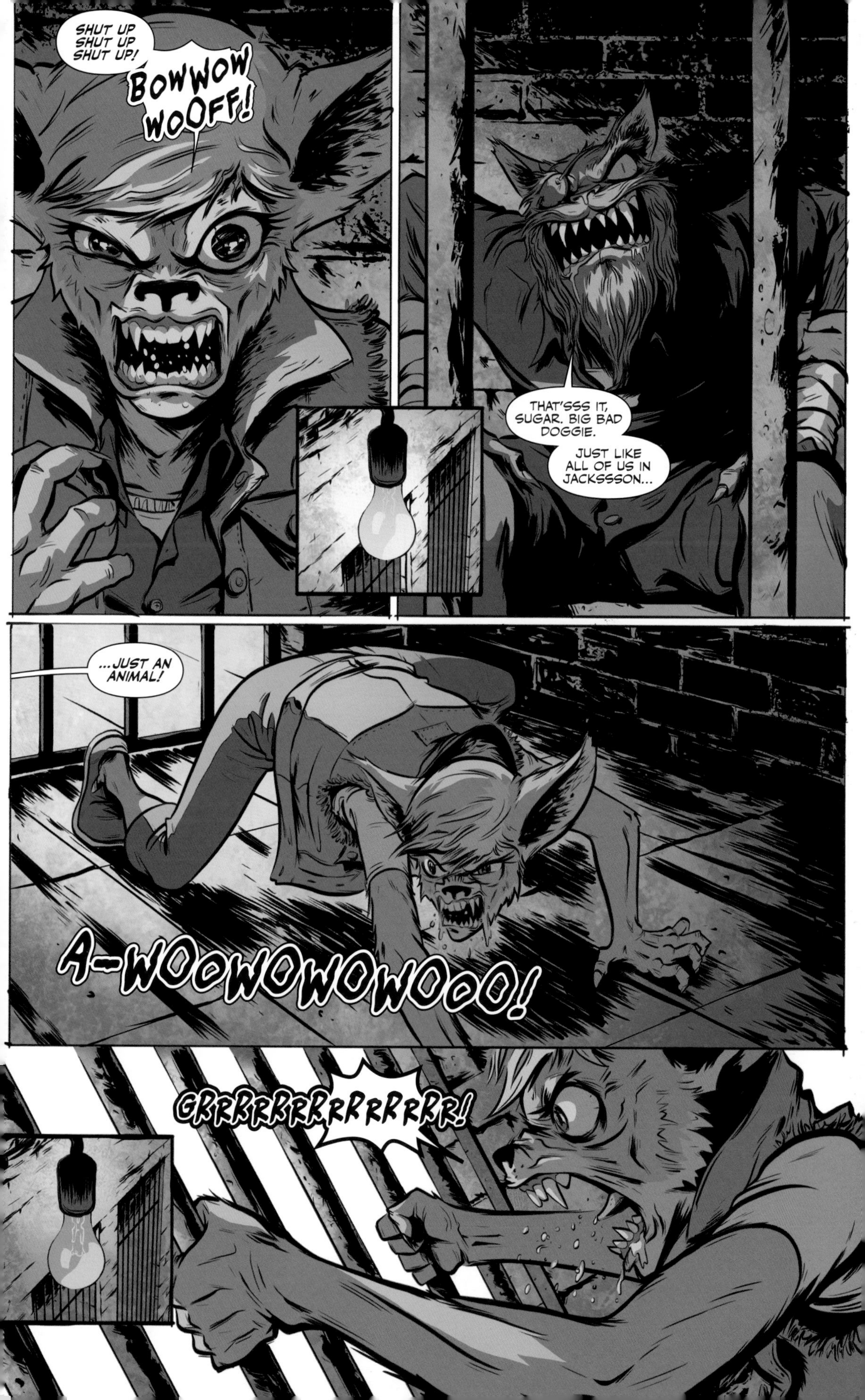
SHUT UP
SHUT UP
SHUT UP!
BOWWOW WOOFF!
THAT'SSS IT, SUGAR. BIG BAD DOGGIE.
JUST LIKE ALL OF US IN JACKSSSON...
...JUST AN ANIMAL!
A-WOOWOWOWOWOOOO!
GRRRRRRRRRRRRRRR!

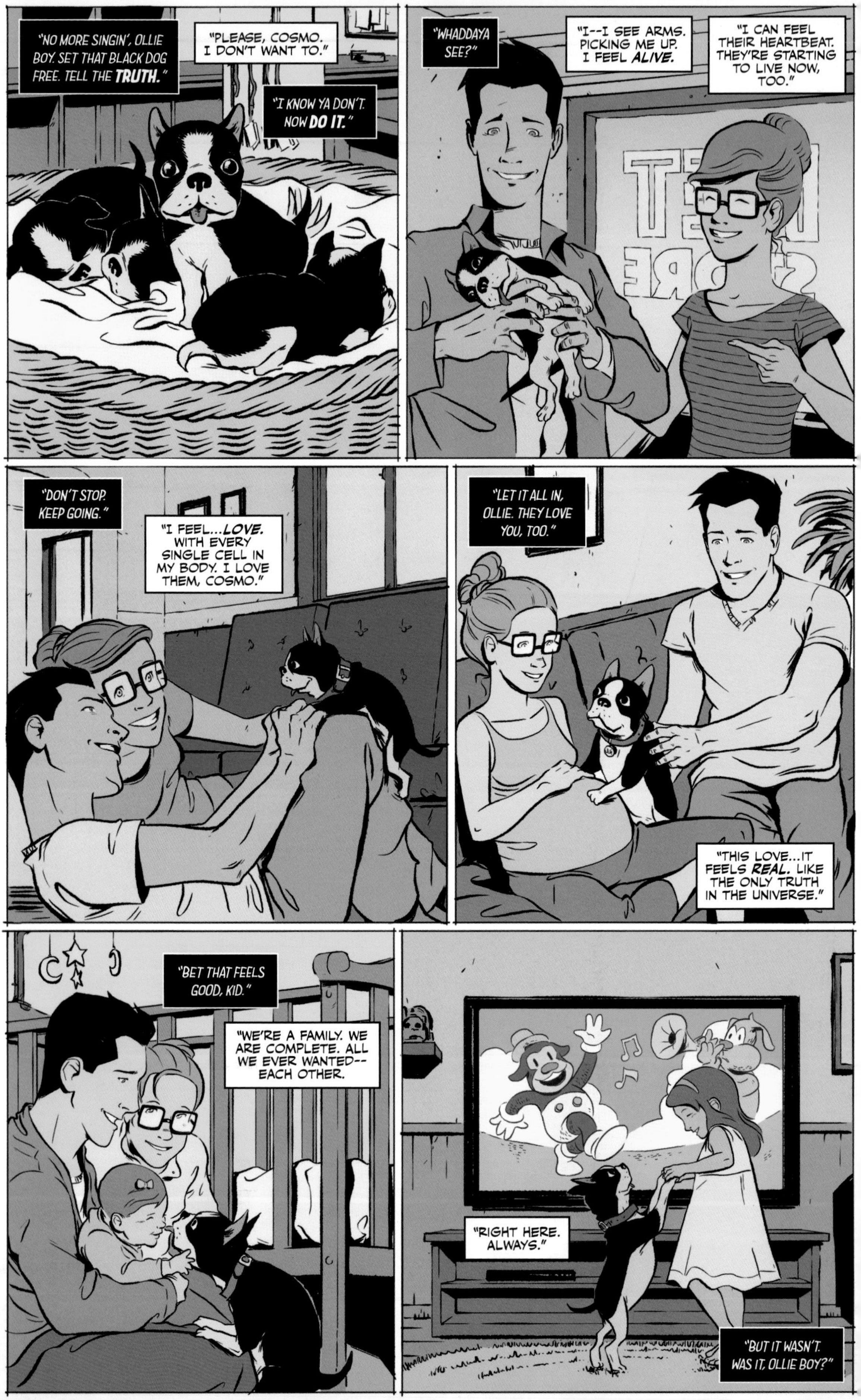
"NO MORE SINGIN', OLLIE BOY. SET THAT BLACK DOG FREE. TELL THE TRUTH."
"PLEASE, COSMO. I DON'T WANT TO."
"I KNOW YA DON'T. NOW DO IT."
"WHADDAYA SEE?"
"I--I SEE ARMS. PICKING ME UP. I FEEL ALIVE.
"I CAN FEEL THEIR HEARTBEAT. THEY'RE STARTING TO LIVE NOW, TOO."
"DON'T STOP. KEEP GOING."
"I FEEL...LOVE. WITH EVERY SINGLE CELL IN MY BODY. I LOVE THEM, COSMO."
"LET IT ALL IN, OLLIE. THEY LOVE YOU, TOO."
"THIS LOVE...IT FEELS REAL. LIKE THE ONLY TRUTH IN THE UNIVERSE."
"BET THAT FEELS GOOD, KID."
"WE'RE A FAMILY. WE ARE COMPLETE. ALL WE EVER WANTED-- EACH OTHER.
"RIGHT HERE. ALWAYS."
"BUT IT WASN'T. WAS IT, OLLIE BOY?"

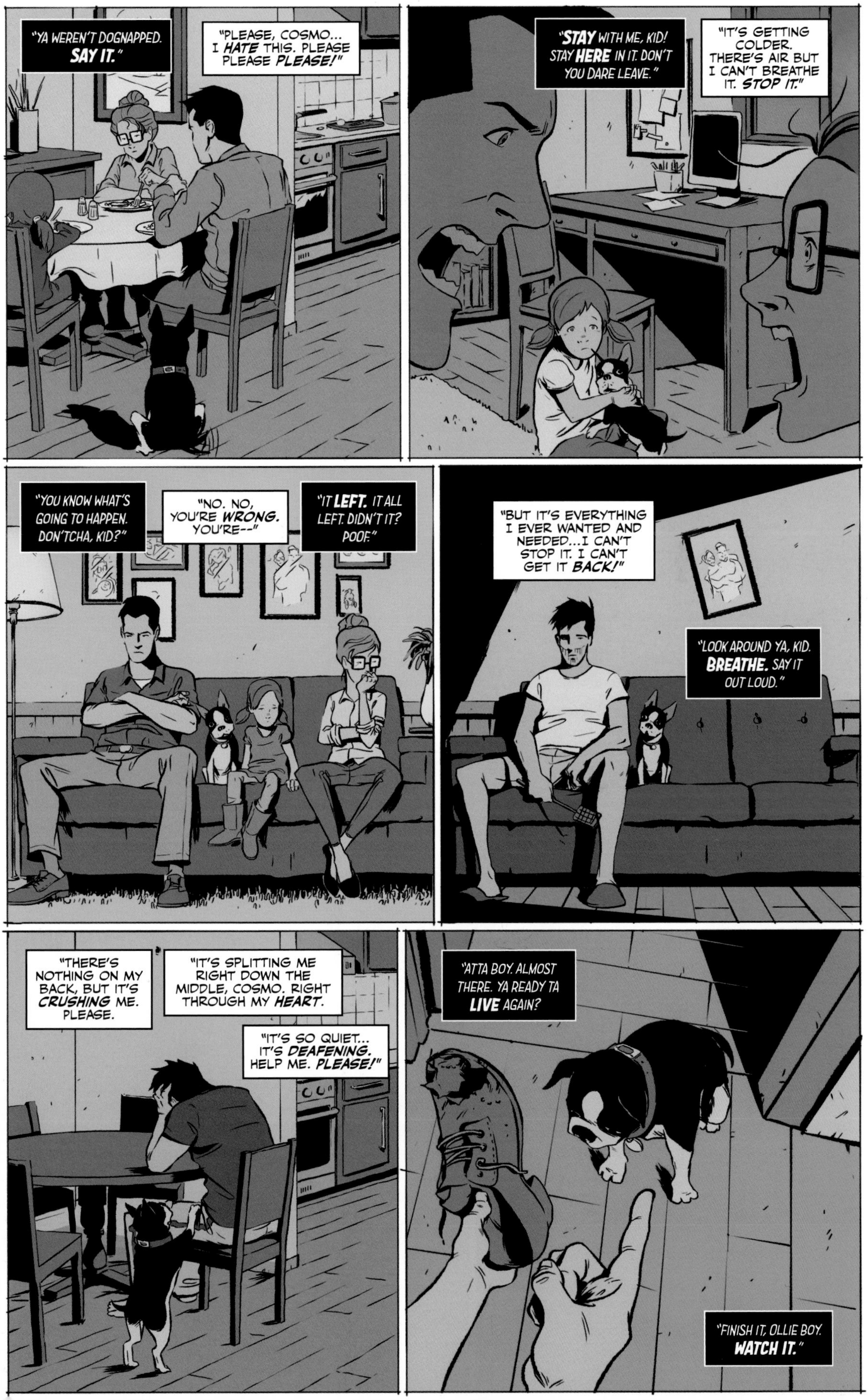
"YA WEREN'T DOGNAPPED. SAY IT."
"PLEASE, COSMO... I HATE THIS. PLEASE PLEASE PLEASE!"
"STAY WITH ME, KID! STAY HERE IN IT. DON'T YOU DARE LEAVE."
"IT'S GETTING COLDER. THERE'S AIR BUT I CAN'T BREATHE IT. STOP IT."
"YOU KNOW WHAT'S GOING TO HAPPEN. DON'TCHA, KID?"
"NO. NO, YOU'RE WRONG. YOU'RE--"
"IT LEFT. IT ALL LEFT. DIDN'T IT? POOF."
"BUT IT'S EVERYTHING I EVER WANTED AND NEEDED...I CAN'T STOP IT. I CAN'T GET IT BACK!"
"LOOK AROUND YA, KID. BREATHE. SAY IT OUT LOUD."
"THERE'S NOTHING ON MY BACK, BUT IT'S CRUSHING ME. PLEASE.
"IT'S SPLITTING ME RIGHT DOWN THE MIDDLE, COSMO. RIGHT THROUGH MY HEART.
"IT'S SO QUIET... IT'S DEAFENING. HELP ME. PLEASE!"
"ATTA BOY. ALMOST THERE. YA READY TA LIVE AGAIN?
"FINISH IT, OLLIE BOY. WATCH IT."

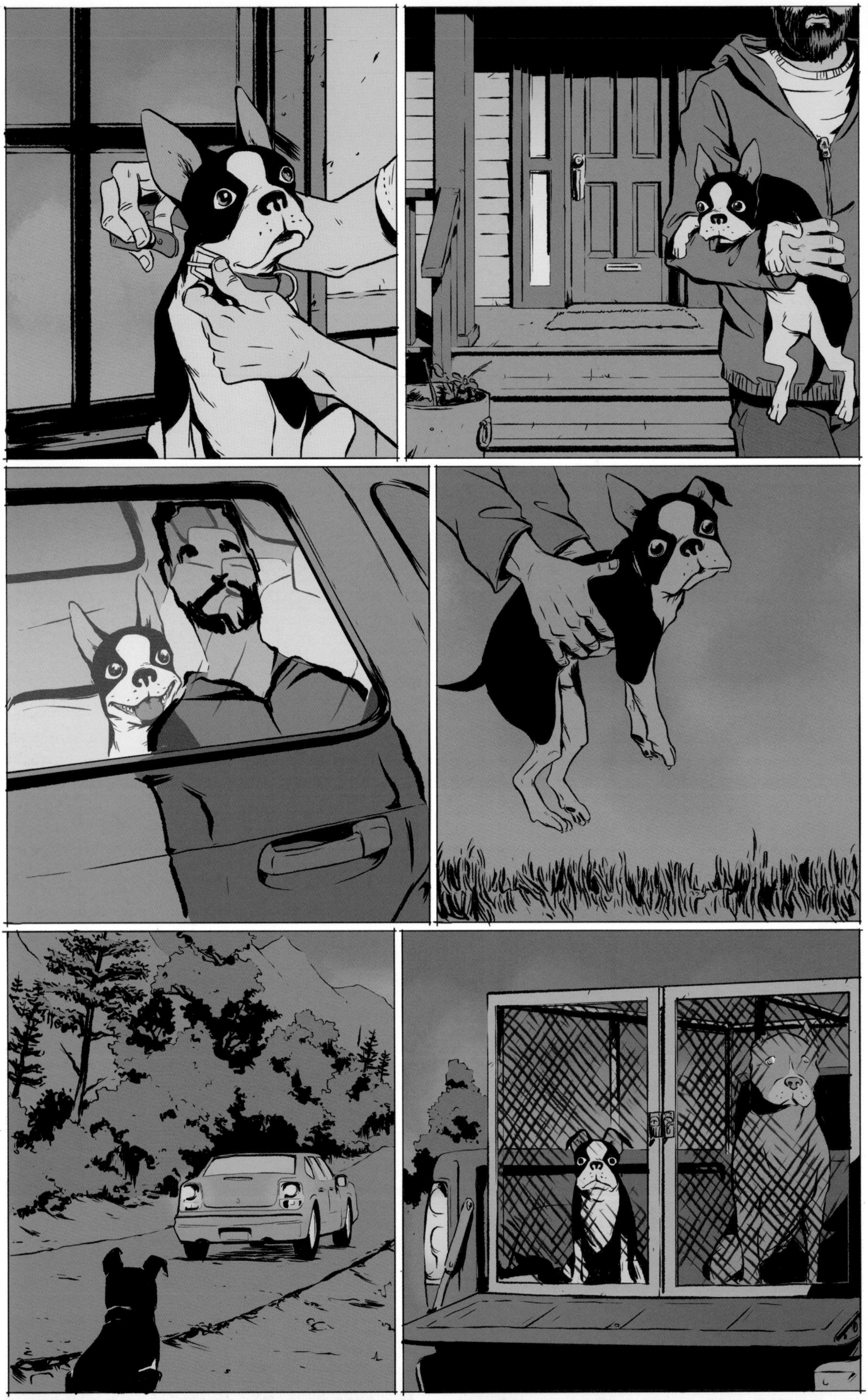

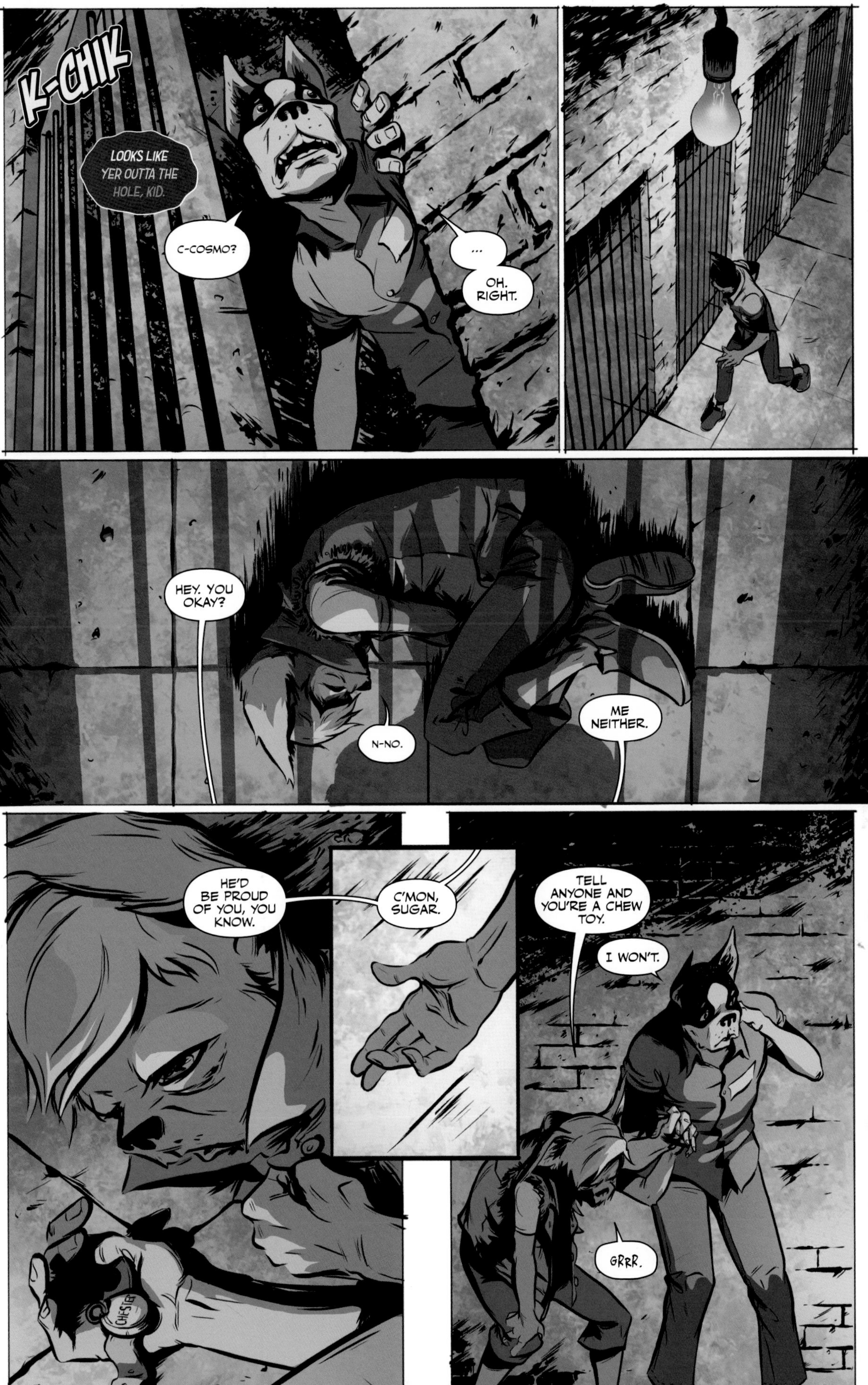
K-CHIK
LOOKS LIKE YER OUTTA THE HOLE, KID.
C-COSMO?
...
OH. RIGHT.
HEY. YOU OKAY?
N-NO.
ME NEITHER.
HE'D BE PROUD OF YOU, YOU KNOW.
C'MON, SUGAR.
TELL ANYONE AND YOU'RE A CHEW TOY.
I WON'T.
GRRR.
CHESTER

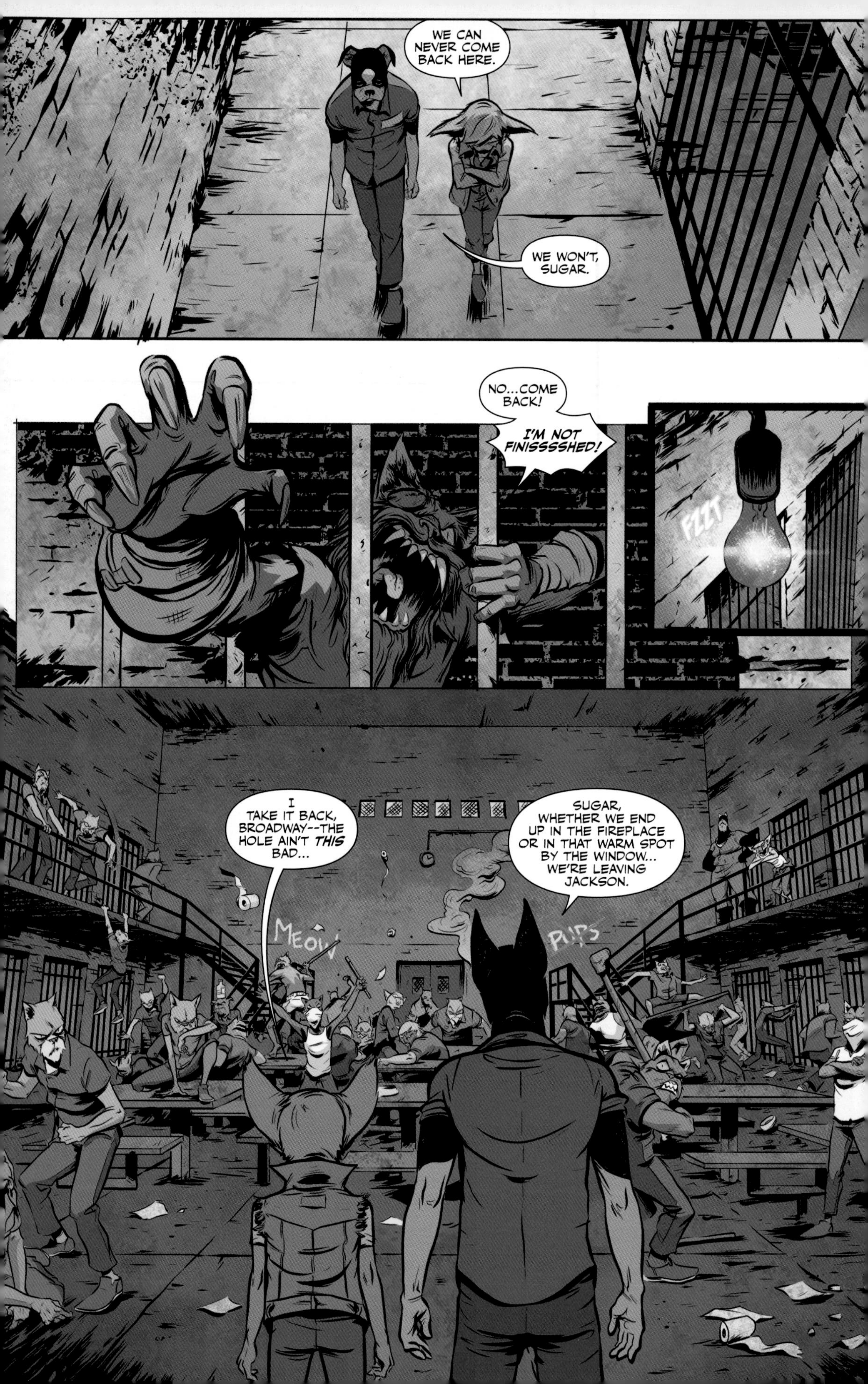
WE CAN NEVER COME BACK HERE.
WE WON'T, SUGAR.
NO...COME BACK!
I'M NOT FINISSSSHED!
FZZT
I TAKE IT BACK, BROADWAY--THE HOLE AIN'T *THIS* BAD...
SUGAR, WHETHER WE END UP IN THE FIREPLACE OR IN THAT WARM SPOT BY THE WINDOW... WE'RE LEAVING JACKSON.
MEOW
PUPS

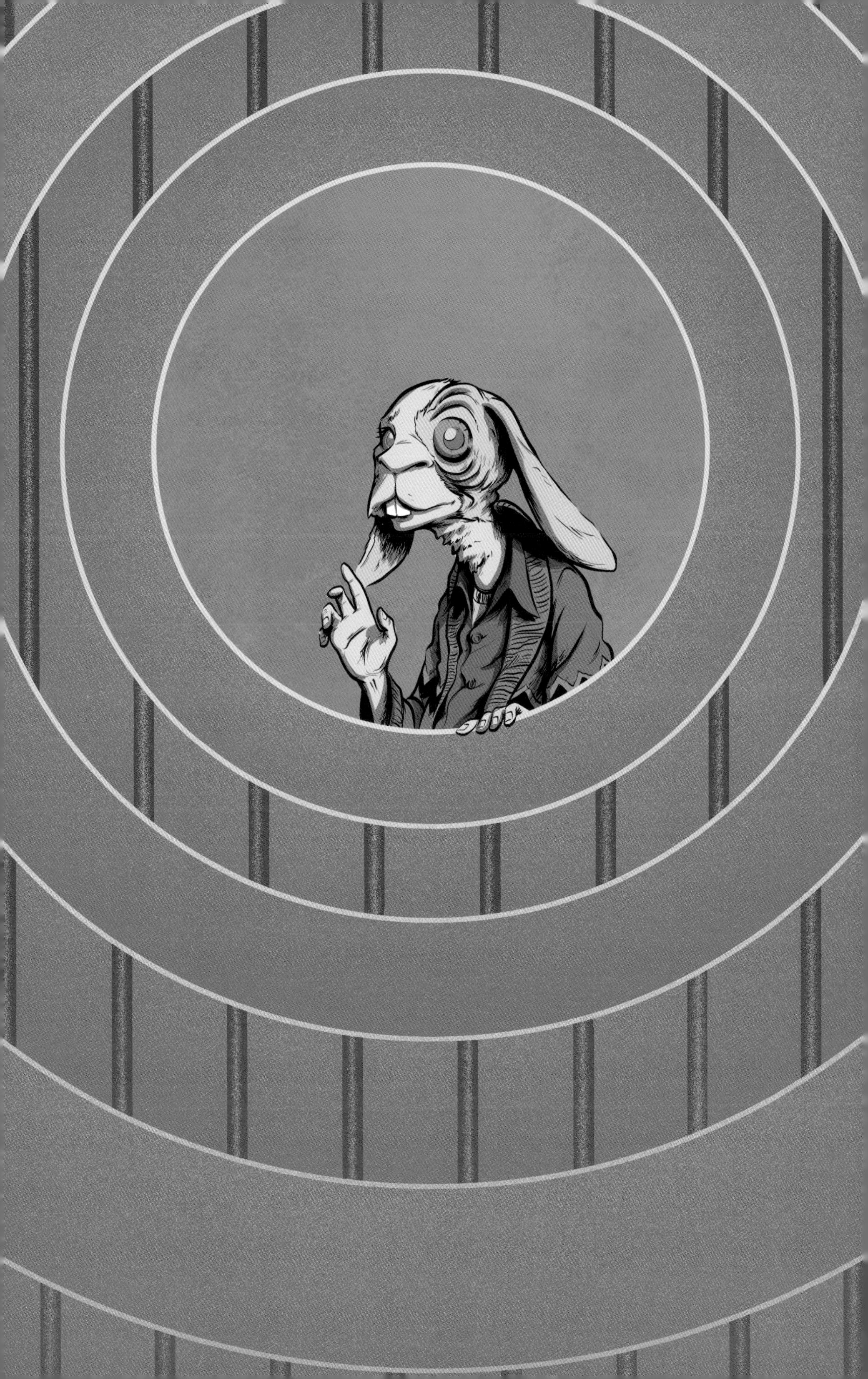

Chapter Four

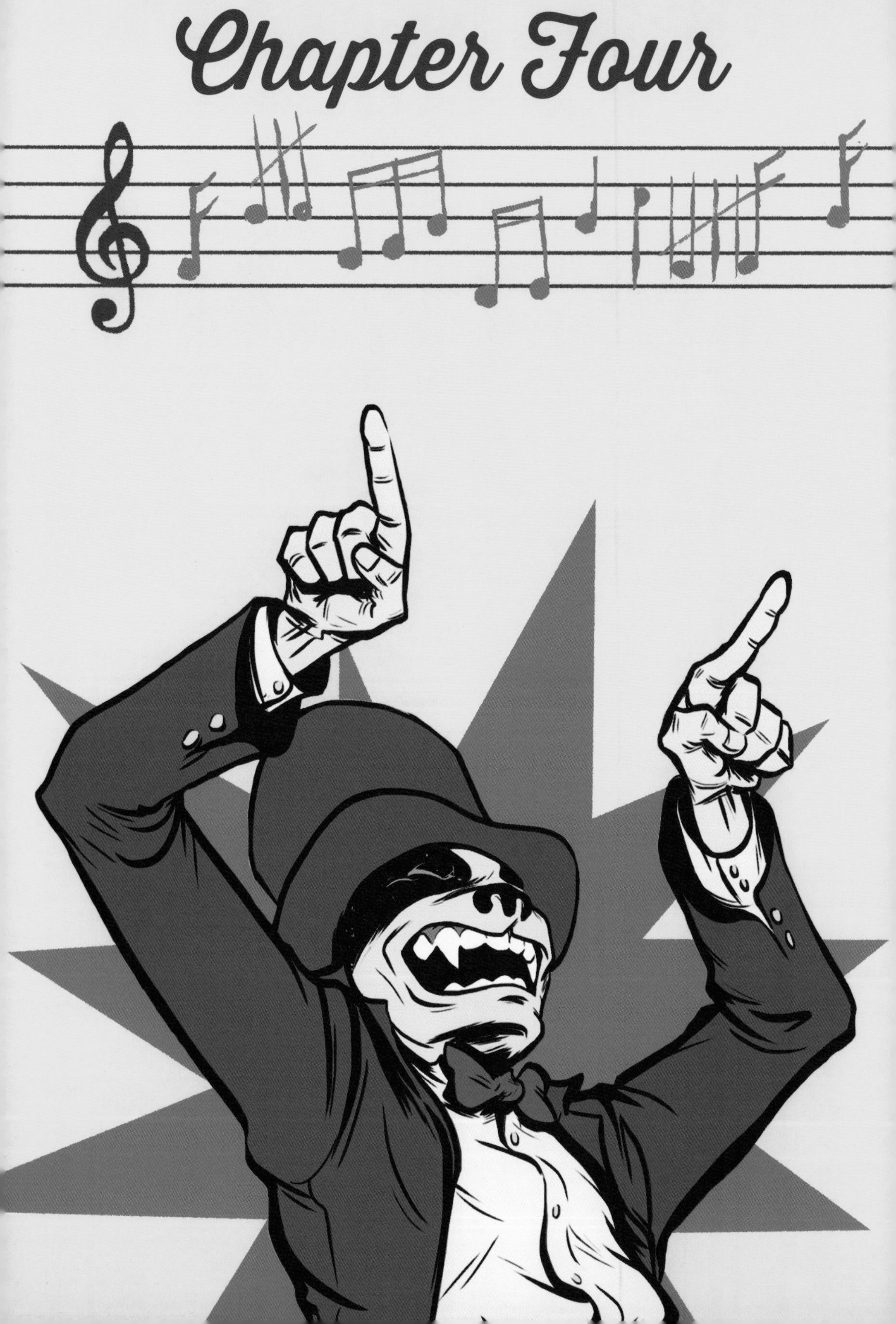

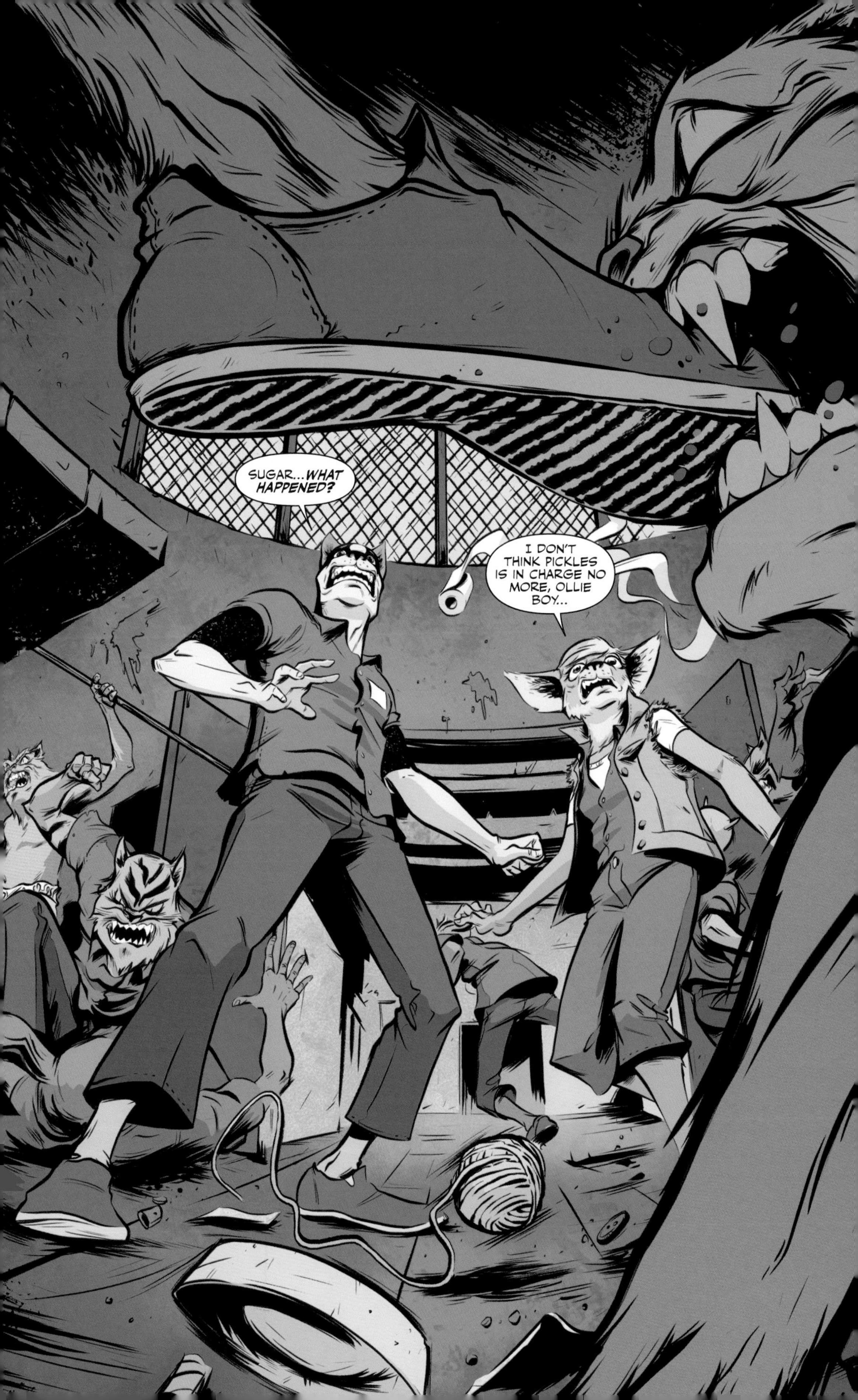
SUGAR...WHAT HAPPENED?
I DON'T THINK PICKLES IS IN CHARGE NO MORE, OLLIE BOY...

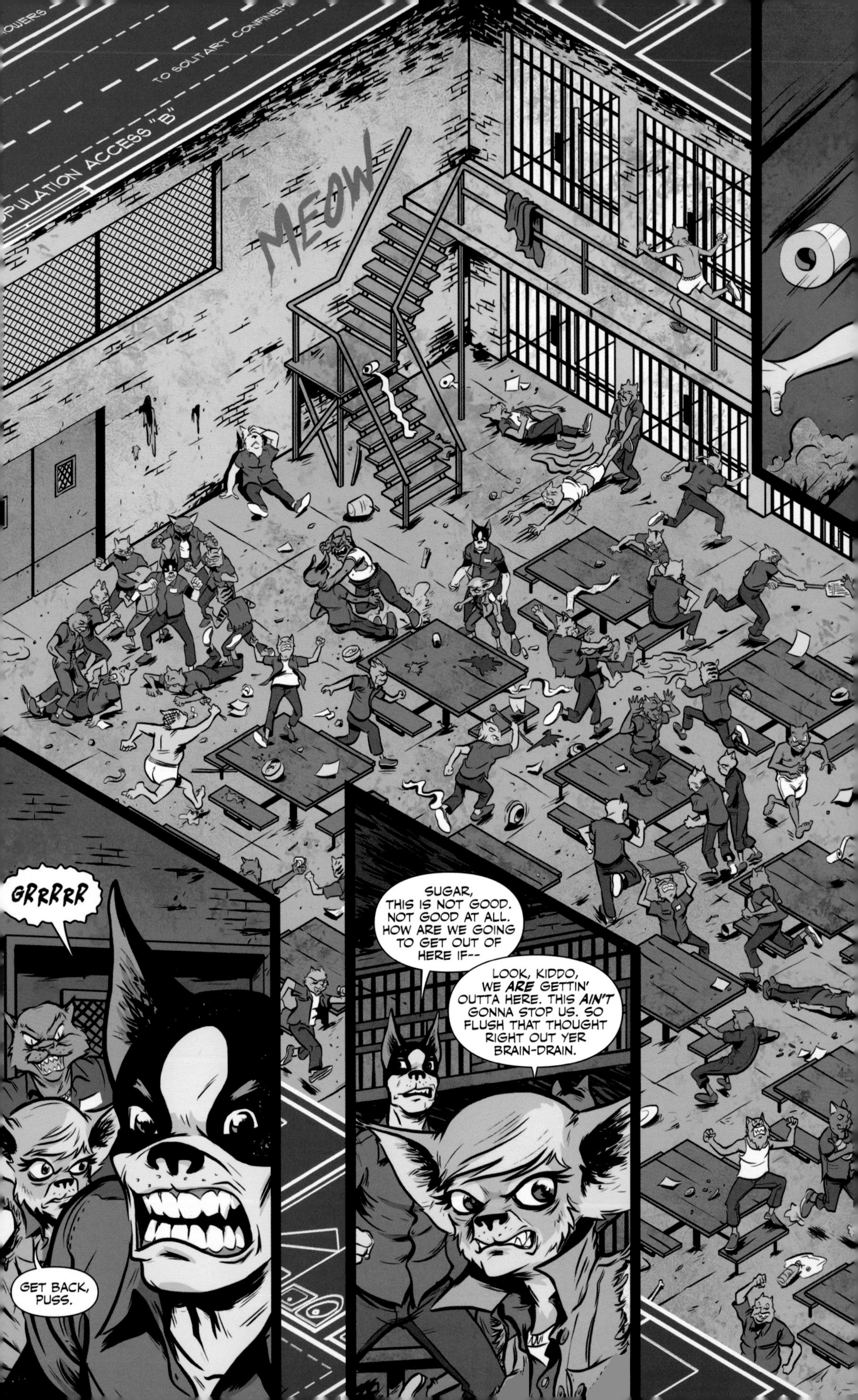
MEOW
GRRRRR
GET BACK, PUSS.
SUGAR, THIS IS NOT GOOD. NOT GOOD AT ALL. HOW ARE WE GOING TO GET OUT OF HERE IF--
LOOK, KIDDO, WE *ARE* GETTIN' OUTTA HERE. THIS *AIN'T* GONNA STOP US. SO FLUSH THAT THOUGHT RIGHT OUT YER BRAIN-DRAIN.

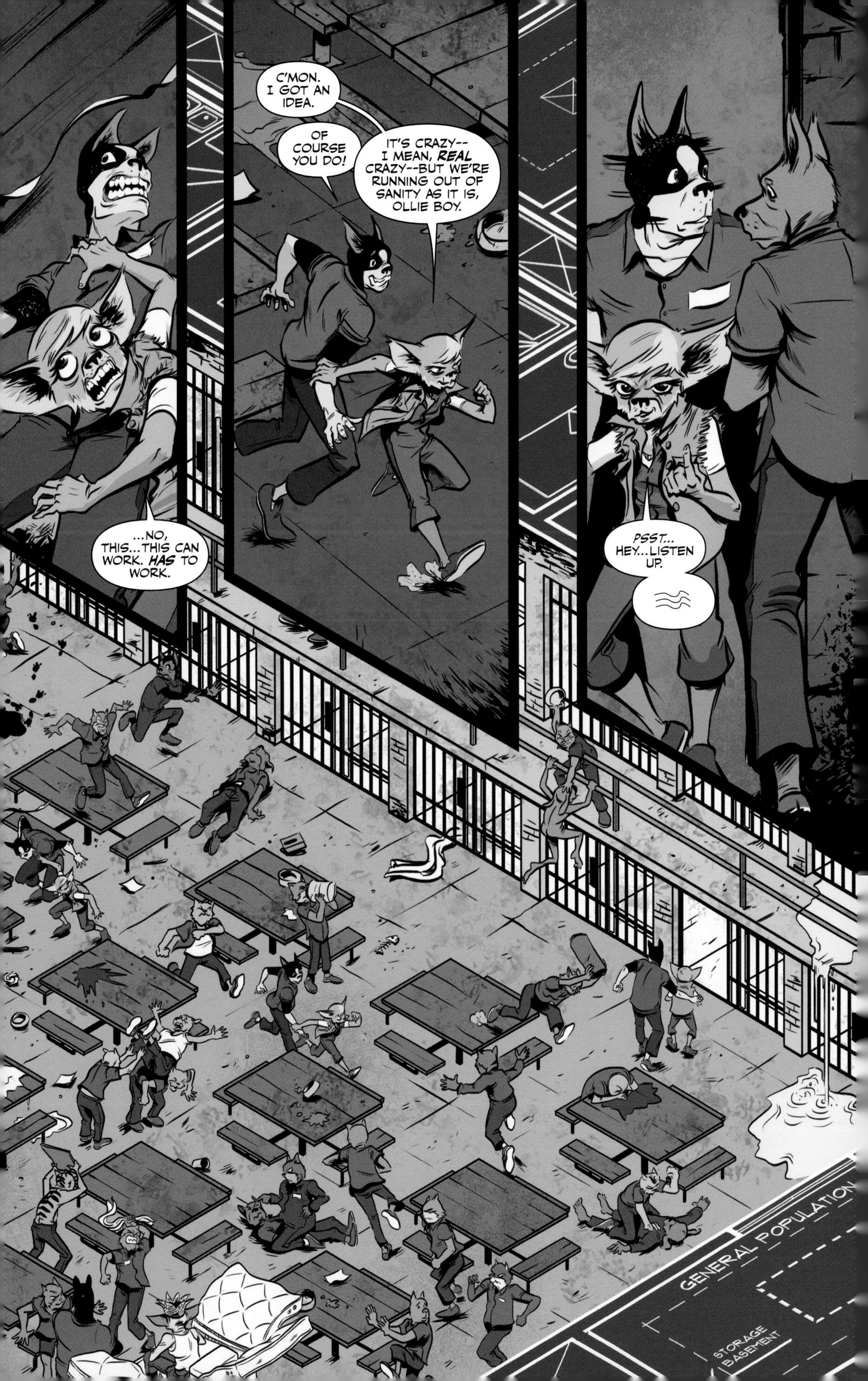
...NO, THIS...THIS CAN WORK. HAS TO WORK.
C'MON. I GOT AN IDEA.
OF COURSE YOU DO!
IT'S CRAZY-- I MEAN, REAL CRAZY--BUT WE'RE RUNNING OUT OF SANITY AS IT IS, OLLIE BOY.
PSST... HEY...LISTEN UP.
GENERAL POPULATION
STORAGE BASEMENT

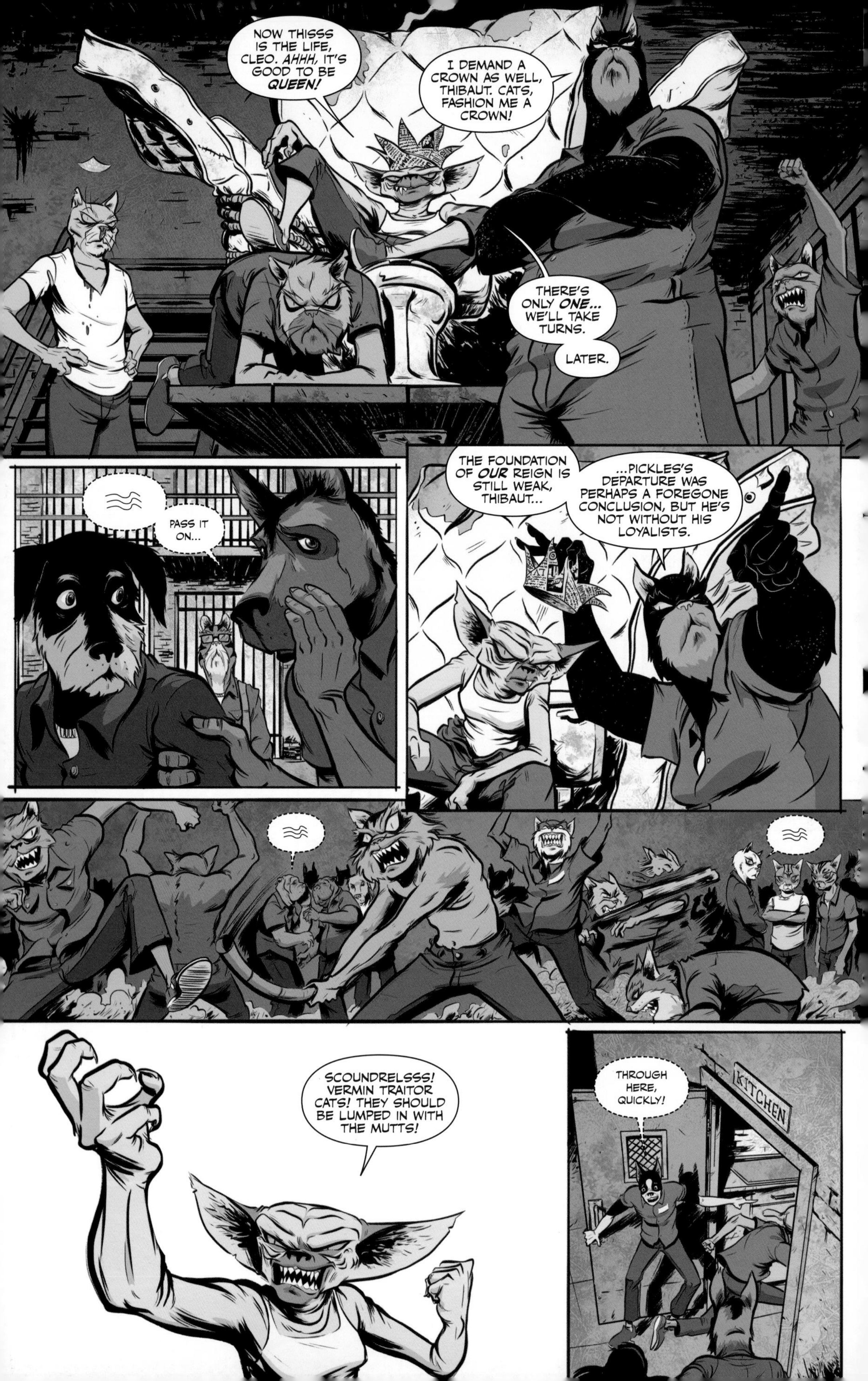

NOW THISSS IS THE LIFE, CLEO. AHHH, IT'S GOOD TO BE QUEEN!
I DEMAND A CROWN AS WELL, THIBAUT. CATS, FASHION ME A CROWN!
THERE'S ONLY ONE... WE'LL TAKE TURNS.
LATER.
PASS IT ON...
THE FOUNDATION OF OUR REIGN IS STILL WEAK, THIBAUT...
...PICKLES'S DEPARTURE WAS PERHAPS A FOREGONE CONCLUSION, BUT HE'S NOT WITHOUT HIS LOYALISTS.
SCOUNDRELSSS! VERMIN TRAITOR CATS! THEY SHOULD BE LUMPED IN WITH THE MUTTS!
THROUGH HERE, QUICKLY!
KITCHEN

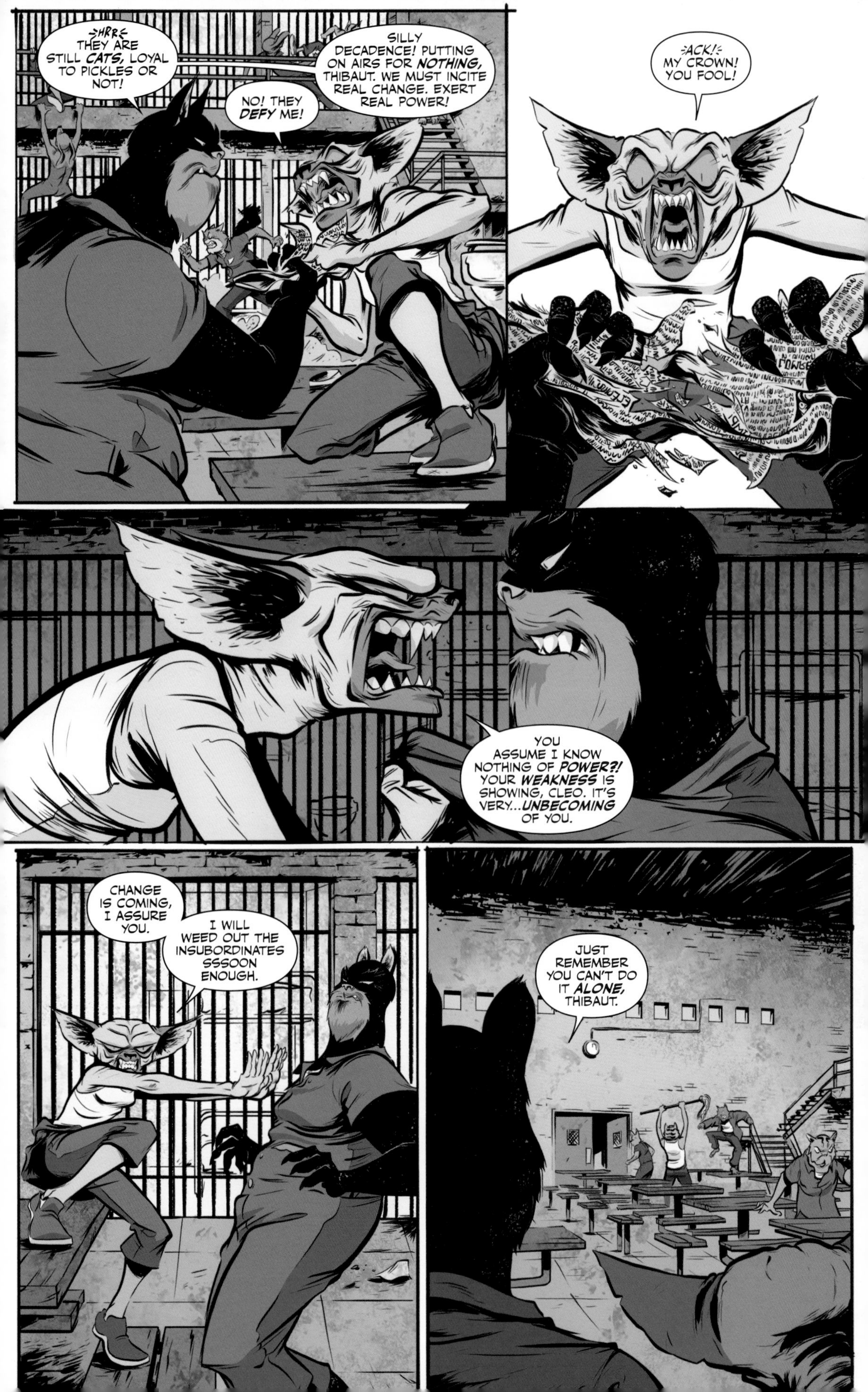

SHRR THEY ARE STILL CATS, LOYAL TO PICKLES OR NOT!
NO! THEY DEFY ME!
SILLY DECADENCE! PUTTING ON AIRS FOR NOTHING, THIBAUT. WE MUST INCITE REAL CHANGE. EXERT REAL POWER!
ACK! MY CROWN! YOU FOOL!
YOU ASSUME I KNOW NOTHING OF POWER?! YOUR WEAKNESS IS SHOWING, CLEO. IT'S VERY...UNBECOMING OF YOU.
CHANGE IS COMING, I ASSURE YOU.
I WILL WEED OUT THE INSUBORDINATES SSSOON ENOUGH.
JUST REMEMBER YOU CAN'T DO IT ALONE, THIBAUT.

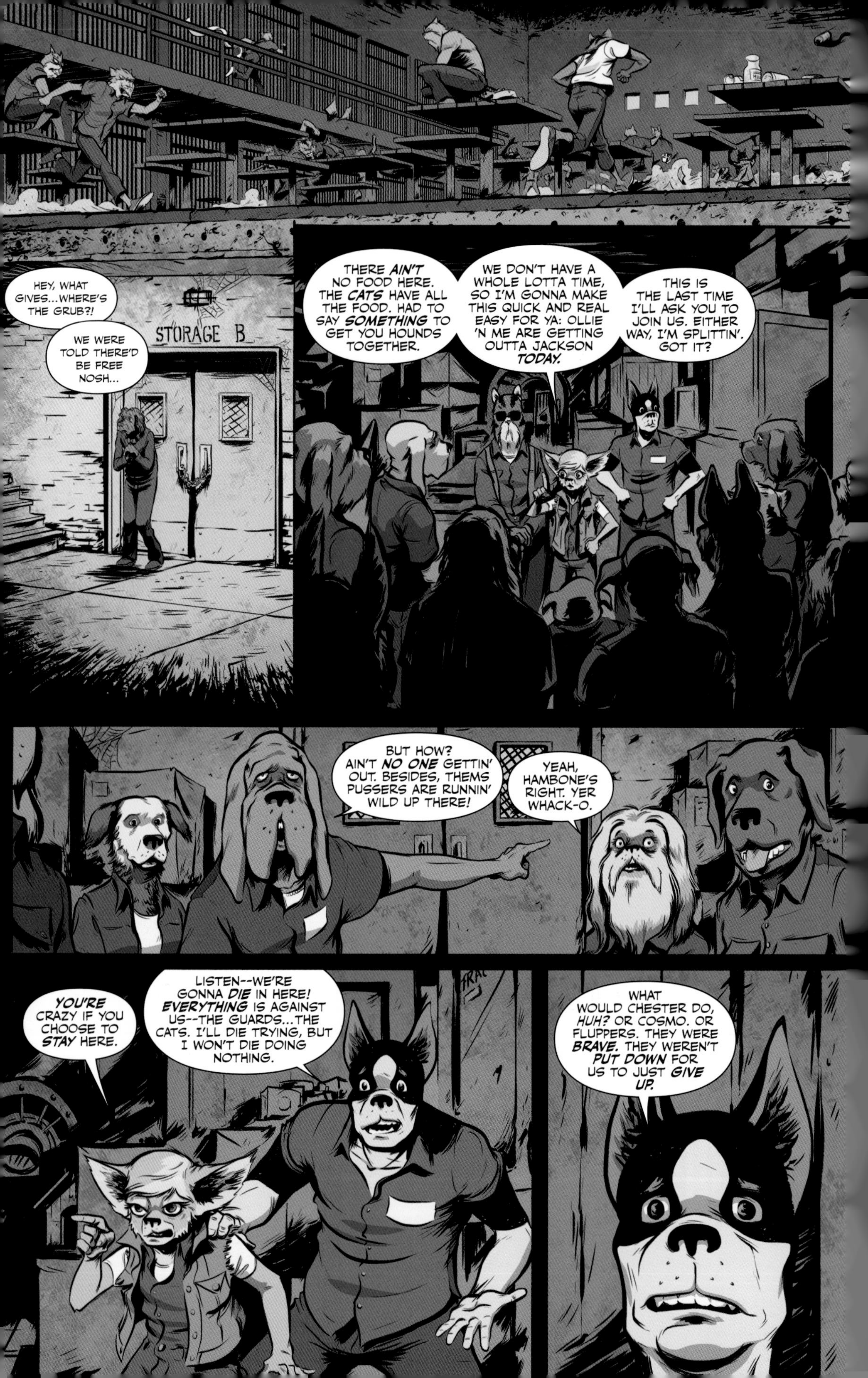

HEY, WHAT GIVES...WHERE'S THE GRUB?!
WE WERE TOLD THERE'D BE FREE NOSH...
STORAGE B
THERE AIN'T NO FOOD HERE. THE CATS HAVE ALL THE FOOD. HAD TO SAY SOMETHING TO GET YOU HOUNDS TOGETHER.
WE DON'T HAVE A WHOLE LOTTA TIME, SO I'M GONNA MAKE THIS QUICK AND REAL EASY FOR YA: OLLIE 'N ME ARE GETTING OUTTA JACKSON TODAY.
THIS IS THE LAST TIME I'LL ASK YOU TO JOIN US. EITHER WAY, I'M SPLITTIN'. GOT IT?
BUT HOW? AIN'T NO ONE GETTIN' OUT. BESIDES, THEMS PUSSERS ARE RUNNIN' WILD UP THERE!
YEAH, HAMBONE'S RIGHT. YER WHACK-O.
YOU'RE CRAZY IF YOU CHOOSE TO STAY HERE.
LISTEN--WE'RE GONNA DIE IN HERE! EVERYTHING IS AGAINST US--THE GUARDS...THE CATS. I'LL DIE TRYING, BUT I WON'T DIE DOING NOTHING.
WHAT WOULD CHESTER DO, HUH? OR COSMO. OR FLUPPERS. THEY WERE BRAVE. THEY WEREN'T PUT DOWN FOR US TO JUST GIVE UP.

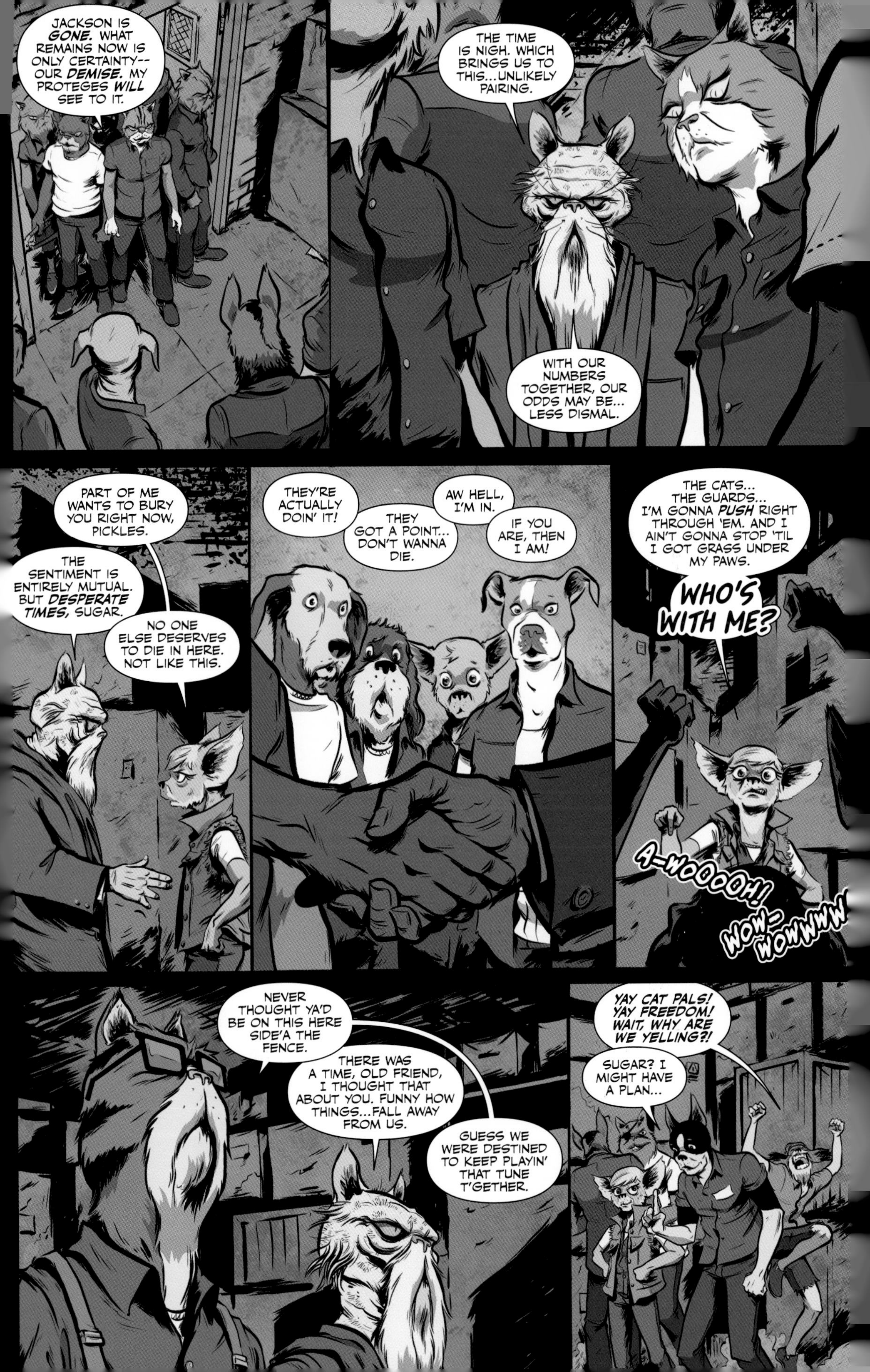
JACKSON IS GONE. WHAT REMAINS NOW IS ONLY CERTAINTY-- OUR DEMISE. MY PROTEGES WILL SEE TO IT.
THE TIME IS NIGH. WHICH BRINGS US TO THIS...UNLIKELY PAIRING.
WITH OUR NUMBERS TOGETHER, OUR ODDS MAY BE... LESS DISMAL.
PART OF ME WANTS TO BURY YOU RIGHT NOW, PICKLES.
THE SENTIMENT IS ENTIRELY MUTUAL. BUT DESPERATE TIMES, SUGAR.
NO ONE ELSE DESERVES TO DIE IN HERE. NOT LIKE THIS.
THEY'RE ACTUALLY DOIN' IT!
THEY GOT A POINT... DON'T WANNA DIE.
AW HELL, I'M IN.
IF YOU ARE, THEN I AM!
THE CATS... THE GUARDS... I'M GONNA PUSH RIGHT THROUGH 'EM. AND I AIN'T GONNA STOP 'TIL I GOT GRASS UNDER MY PAWS.
WHO'S WITH ME?
A-WOOOOOH!
WOW-WOWWWW
NEVER THOUGHT YA'D BE ON THIS HERE SIDE'A THE FENCE.
THERE WAS A TIME, OLD FRIEND, I THOUGHT THAT ABOUT YOU. FUNNY HOW THINGS...FALL AWAY FROM US.
GUESS WE WERE DESTINED TO KEEP PLAYIN' THAT TUNE T'GETHER.
YAY CAT PALS! YAY FREEDOM! WAIT, WHY ARE WE YELLING?!
SUGAR? I MIGHT HAVE A PLAN...

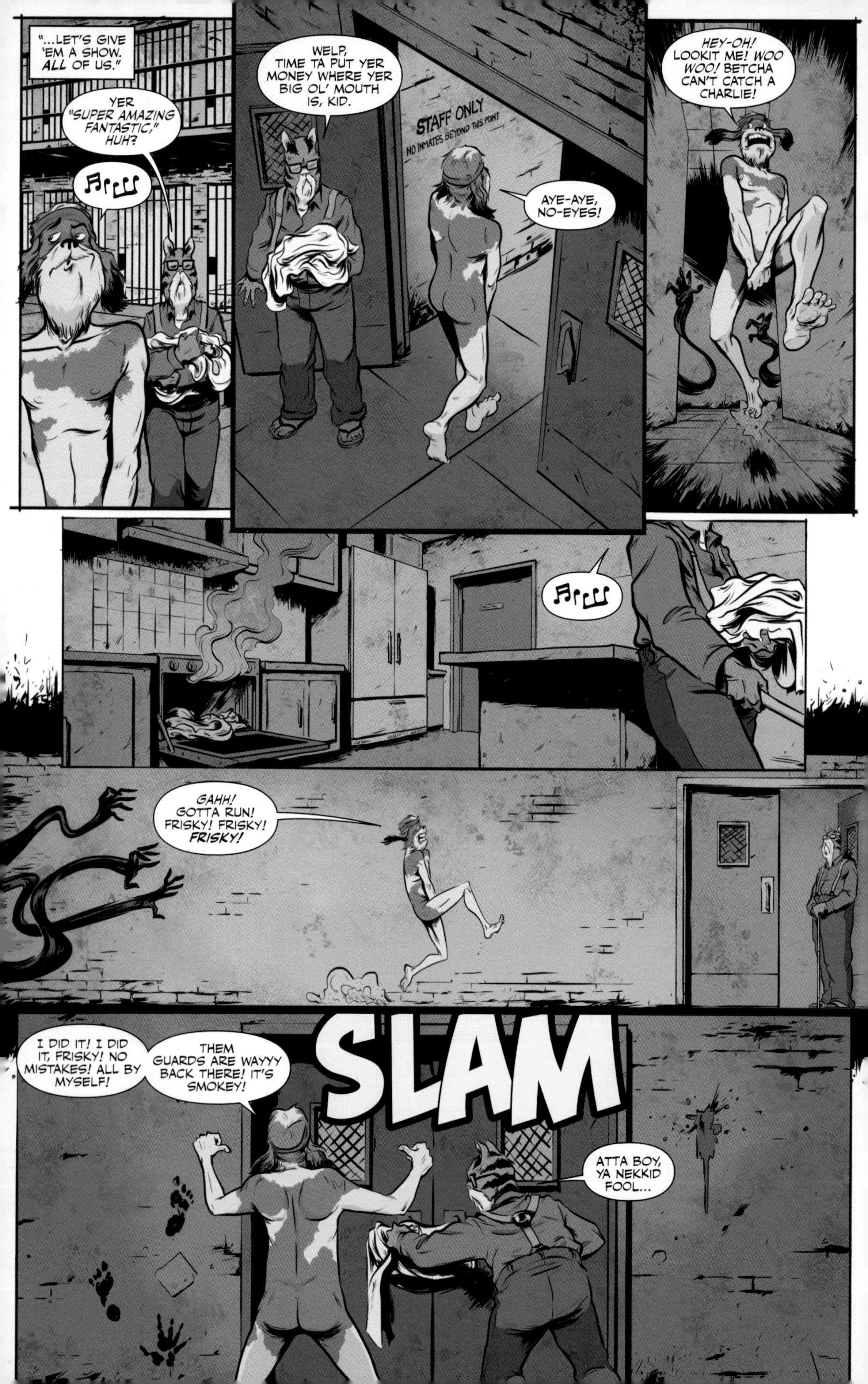
"...LET'S GIVE 'EM A SHOW. ALL OF US."
YER "SUPER AMAZING FANTASTIC," HUH?
WELP, TIME TA PUT YER MONEY WHERE YER BIG OL' MOUTH IS, KID.
STAFF ONLY
NO INMATES BEYOND THIS POINT
AYE-AYE, NO-EYES!
HEY-OH! LOOKIT ME! WOO WOO! BETCHA CAN'T CATCH A CHARLIE!
GAHH! GOTTA RUN! FRISKY! FRISKY! FRISKY!
SLAM
I DID IT! I DID IT, FRISKY! NO MISTAKES! ALL BY MYSELF!
THEM GUARDS ARE WAYYY BACK THERE! IT'S SMOKEY!
ATTA BOY, YA NEKKID FOOL...

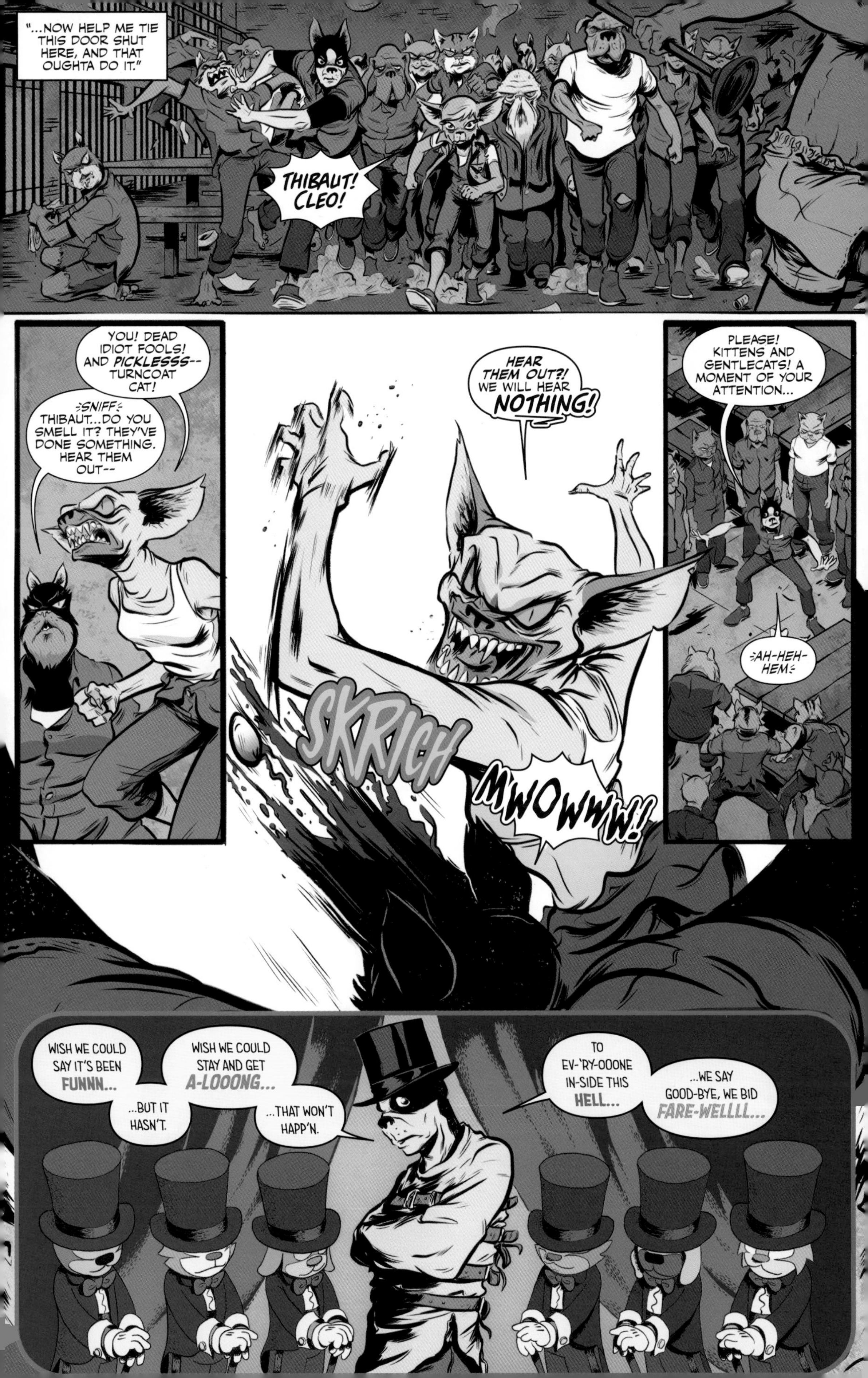
"...NOW HELP ME TIE THIS DOOR SHUT HERE, AND THAT OUGHTA DO IT."
THIBAUT! CLEO!
YOU! DEAD IDIOT FOOLS! AND PICKLESSS-- TURNCOAT CAT!
SNIFF THIBAUT...DO YOU SMELL IT? THEY'VE DONE SOMETHING. HEAR THEM OUT--
HEAR THEM OUT?! WE WILL HEAR NOTHING!
SKRICH
MWOWWW!
PLEASE! KITTENS AND GENTLECATS! A MOMENT OF YOUR ATTENTION...
AH-HEH-HEM
WISH WE COULD SAY IT'S BEEN FUNNN...
...BUT IT HASN'T.
WISH WE COULD STAY AND GET A-LOOONG...
...THAT WON'T HAPP'N.
TO EV-'RY-OOONE IN-SIDE THIS HELL...
...WE SAY GOOD-BYE, WE BID FARE-WELLLL...

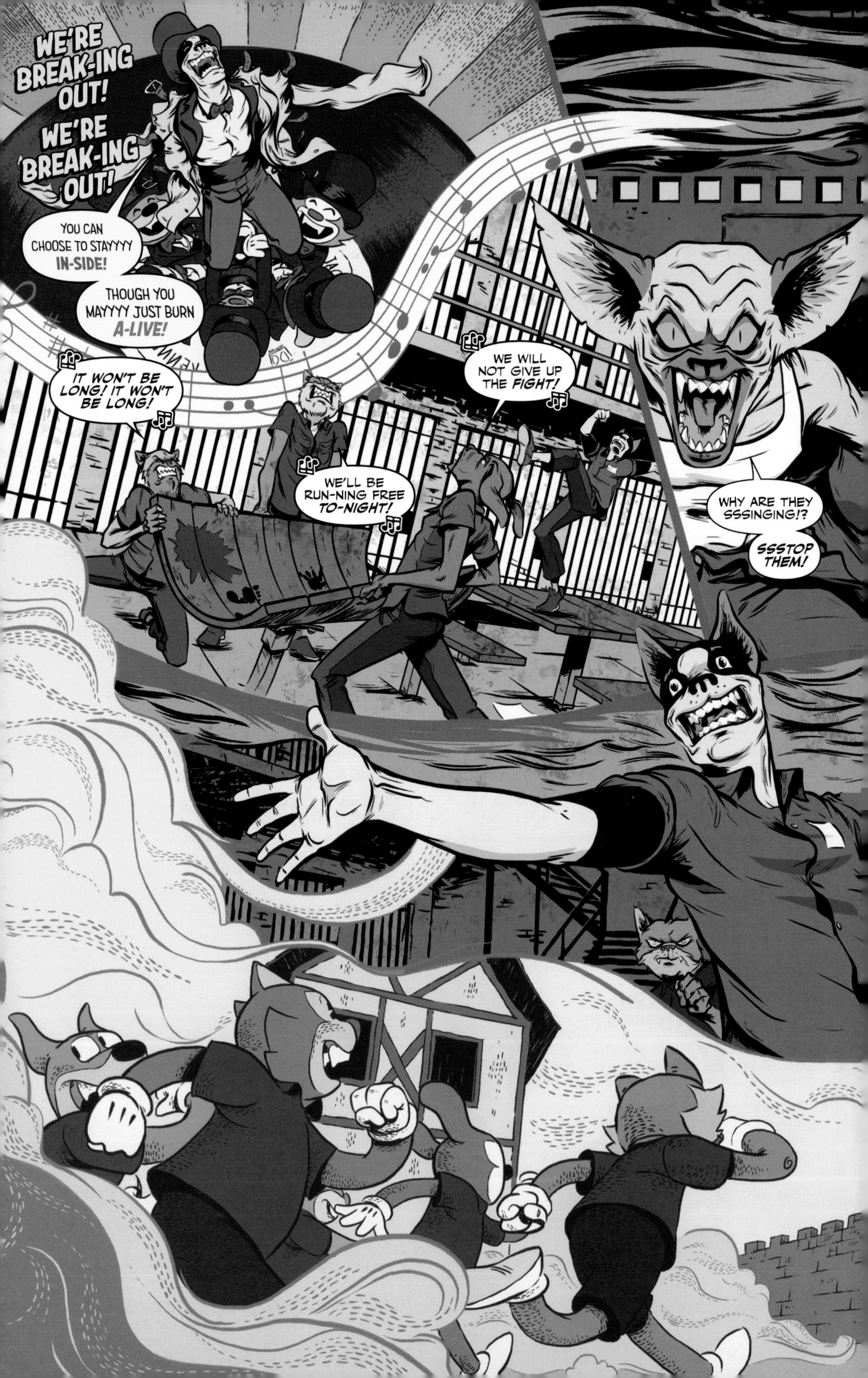
WE'RE BREAK-ING OUT! WE'RE BREAK-ING OUT!
YOU CAN CHOOSE TO STAYYYY IN-SIDE!
THOUGH YOU MAYYYY JUST BURN A-LIVE!
IT WON'T BE LONG! IT WON'T BE LONG!
WE'LL BE RUN-NING FREE TO-NIGHT!
WE WILL NOT GIVE UP THE FIGHT!
WHY ARE THEY SSSINGING!?
SSSTOP THEM!

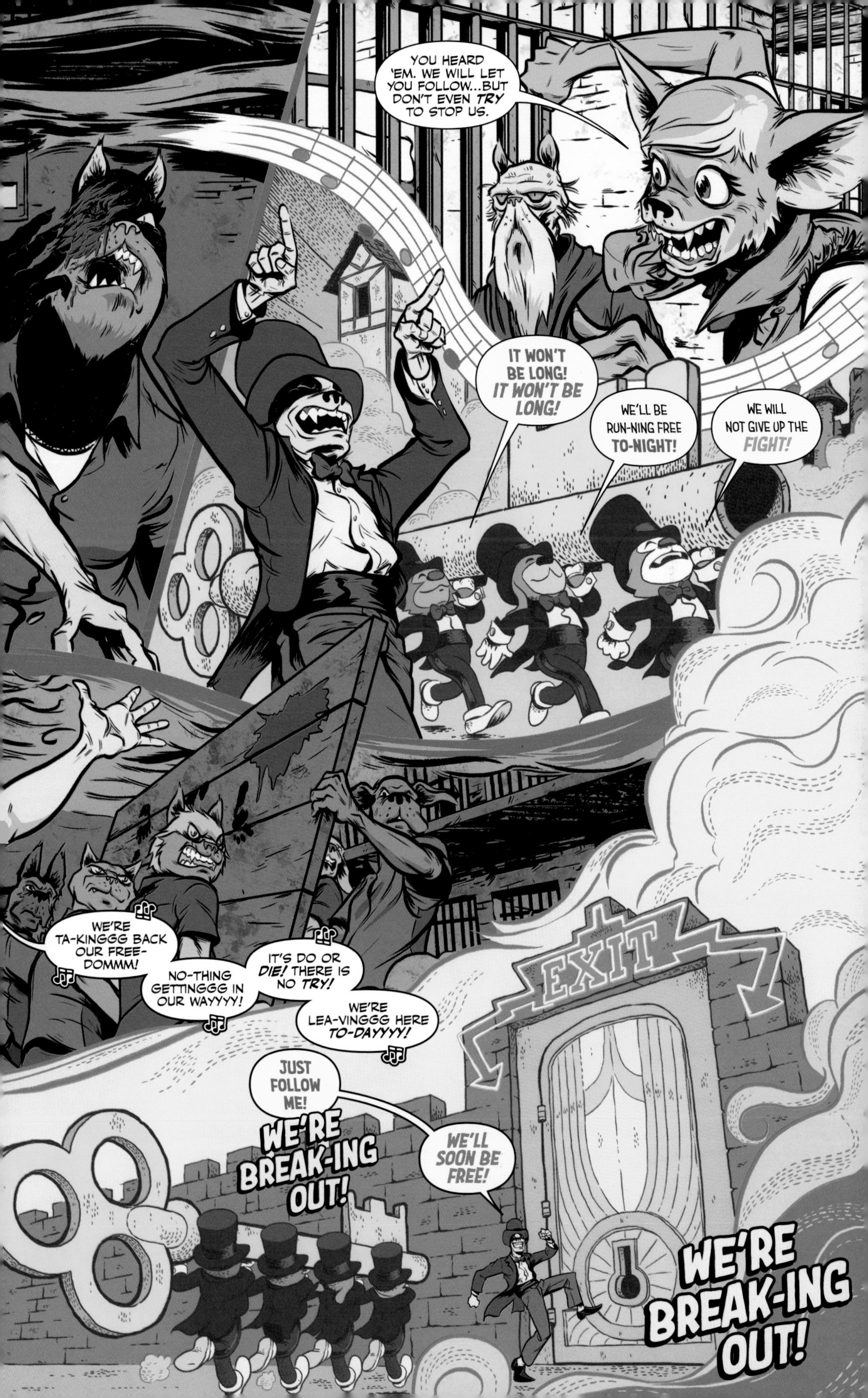
YOU HEARD 'EM. WE WILL LET YOU FOLLOW...BUT DON'T EVEN TRY TO STOP US.
IT WON'T BE LONG! IT WON'T BE LONG!
WE'LL BE RUN-NING FREE TO-NIGHT!
WE WILL NOT GIVE UP THE FIGHT!
WE'RE TA-KINGGG BACK OUR FREE-DOMMM!
NO-THING GETTINGGG IN OUR WAYYYY!
IT'S DO OR DIE! THERE IS NO TRY!
WE'RE LEA-VINGGG HERE TO-DAYYYY!
EXIT
JUST FOLLOW ME!
WE'RE BREAK-ING OUT!
WE'LL SOON BE FREE!
WE'RE BREAK-ING OUT!

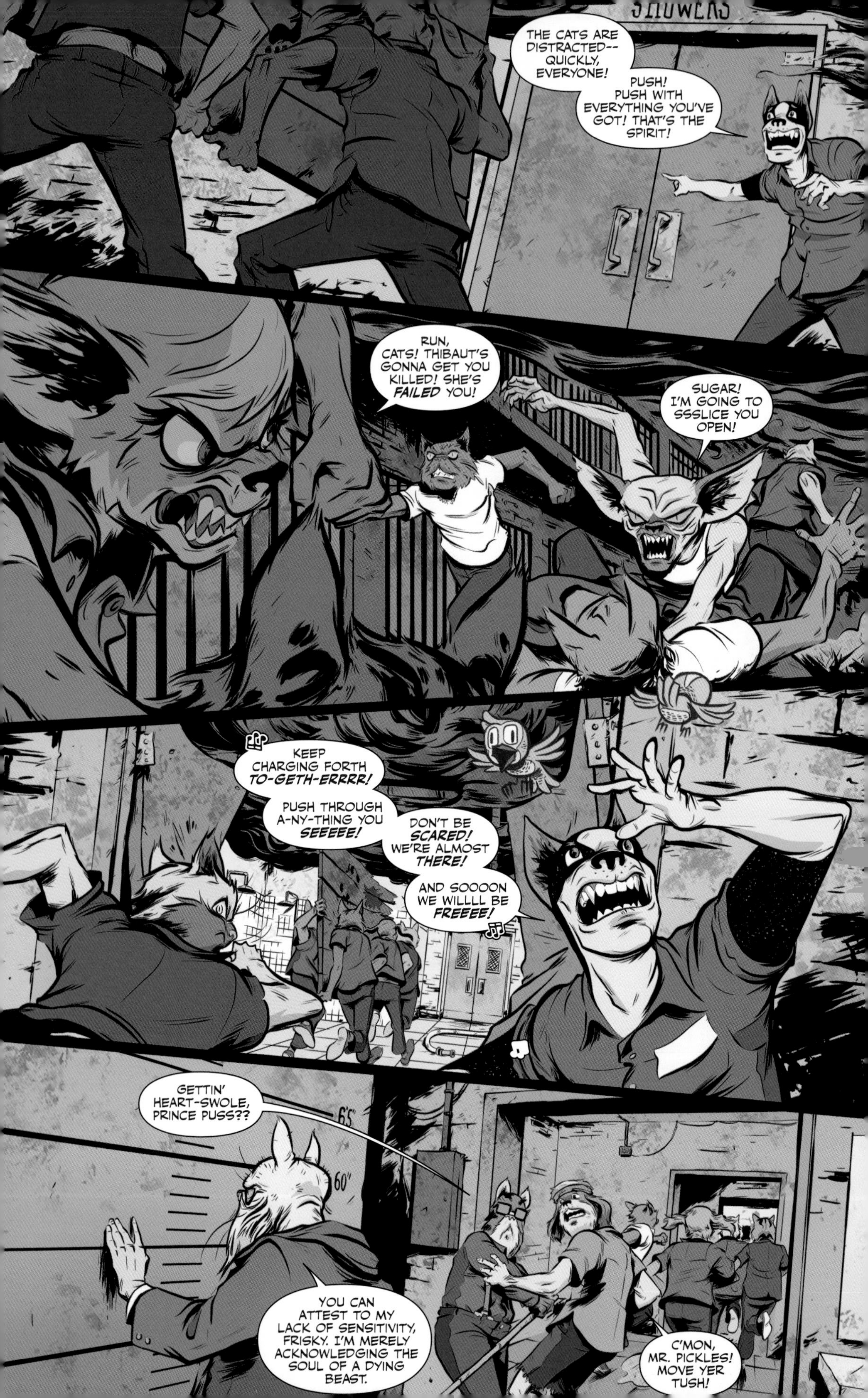
SHOWERS
THE CATS ARE DISTRACTED-- QUICKLY, EVERYONE!
PUSH! PUSH WITH EVERYTHING YOU'VE GOT! THAT'S THE SPIRIT!
RUN, CATS! THIBAUT'S GONNA GET YOU KILLED! SHE'S FAILED YOU!
SUGAR! I'M GOING TO SSSLICE YOU OPEN!
KEEP CHARGING FORTH TO-GETH-ERRRR!
PUSH THROUGH A-NY-THING YOU SEEEEE!
DON'T BE SCARED! WE'RE ALMOST THERE!
AND SOOOON WE WILLLL BE FREEEE!
GETTIN' HEART-SWOLE, PRINCE PUSS??
6'5"
60"
YOU CAN ATTEST TO MY LACK OF SENSITIVITY, FRISKY. I'M MERELY ACKNOWLEDGING THE SOUL OF A DYING BEAST.
C'MON, MR. PICKLES! MOVE YER TUSH!

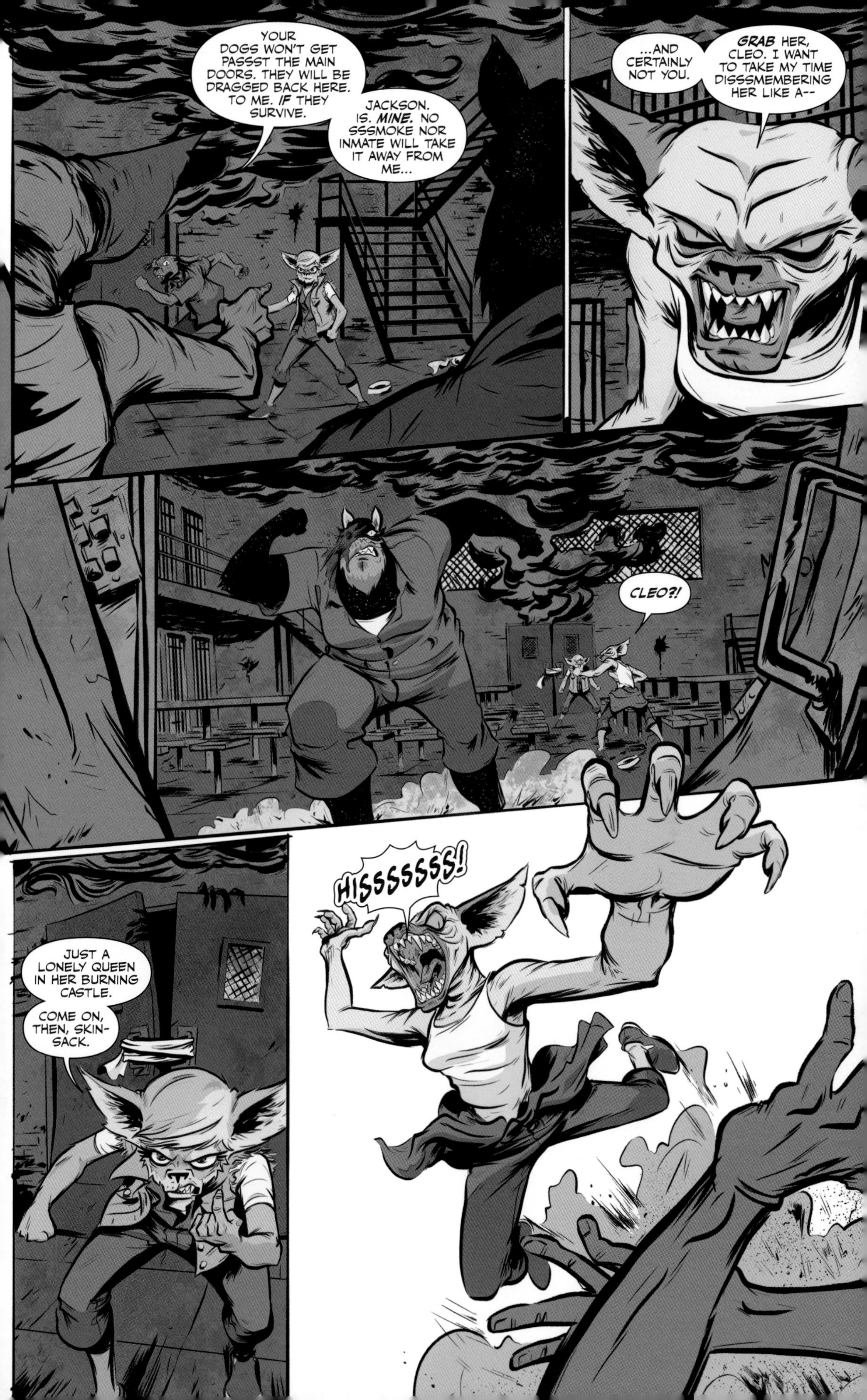
YOUR DOGS WON'T GET PASSST THE MAIN DOORS. THEY WILL BE DRAGGED BACK HERE. TO ME. IF THEY SURVIVE.
JACKSON. IS. MINE. NO SSSMOKE NOR INMATE WILL TAKE IT AWAY FROM ME...
...AND CERTAINLY NOT YOU.
GRAB HER, CLEO. I WANT TO TAKE MY TIME DISSSMEMBERING HER LIKE A--
CLEO?!
JUST A LONELY QUEEN IN HER BURNING CASTLE.
COME ON, THEN, SKIN-SACK.
HISSSSSSS!

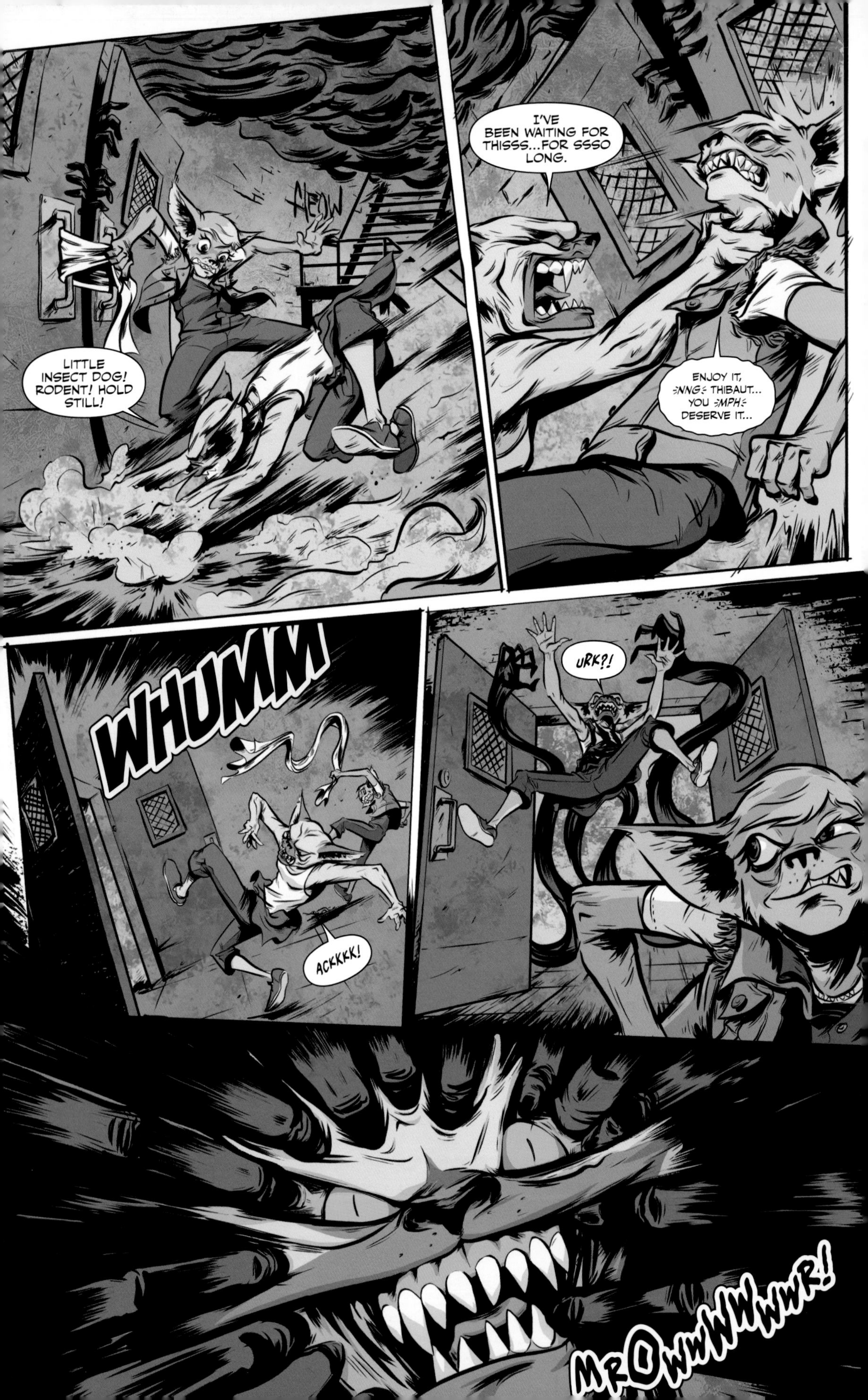
MEOW
LITTLE INSECT DOG! RODENT! HOLD STILL!
I'VE BEEN WAITING FOR THISSS...FOR SSSO LONG.
ENJOY IT, NNG THIBAUT... YOU MPH DESERVE IT...
WHUMM
ACKKKK!
URK?!
MROWWWWWWWR!

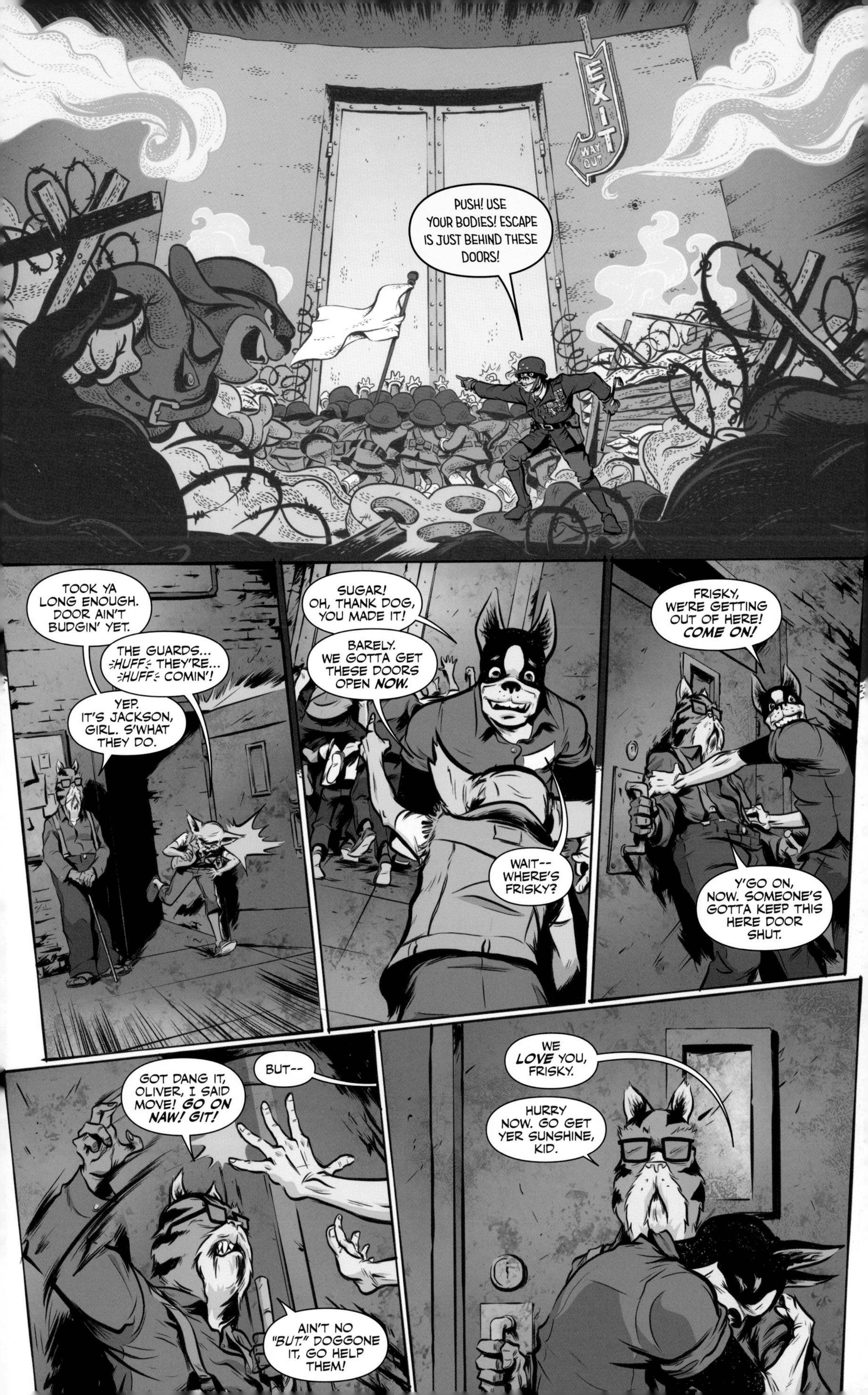
EXIT
WAY OUT
PUSH! USE YOUR BODIES! ESCAPE IS JUST BEHIND THESE DOORS!
TOOK YA LONG ENOUGH. DOOR AIN'T BUDGIN' YET.
THE GUARDS... *HUFF* THEY'RE... *HUFF* COMIN'!
YEP. IT'S JACKSON, GIRL. S'WHAT THEY DO.
SUGAR! OH, THANK DOG, YOU MADE IT!
BARELY. WE GOTTA GET THESE DOORS OPEN NOW.
WAIT-- WHERE'S FRISKY?
FRISKY, WE'RE GETTING OUT OF HERE! COME ON!
Y'GO ON, NOW. SOMEONE'S GOTTA KEEP THIS HERE DOOR SHUT.
GOT DANG IT, OLIVER, I SAID MOVE! GO ON NAW! GIT!
BUT--
AIN'T NO "BUT." DOGGONE IT, GO HELP THEM!
WE LOVE YOU, FRISKY.
HURRY NOW. GO GET YER SUNSHINE, KID.

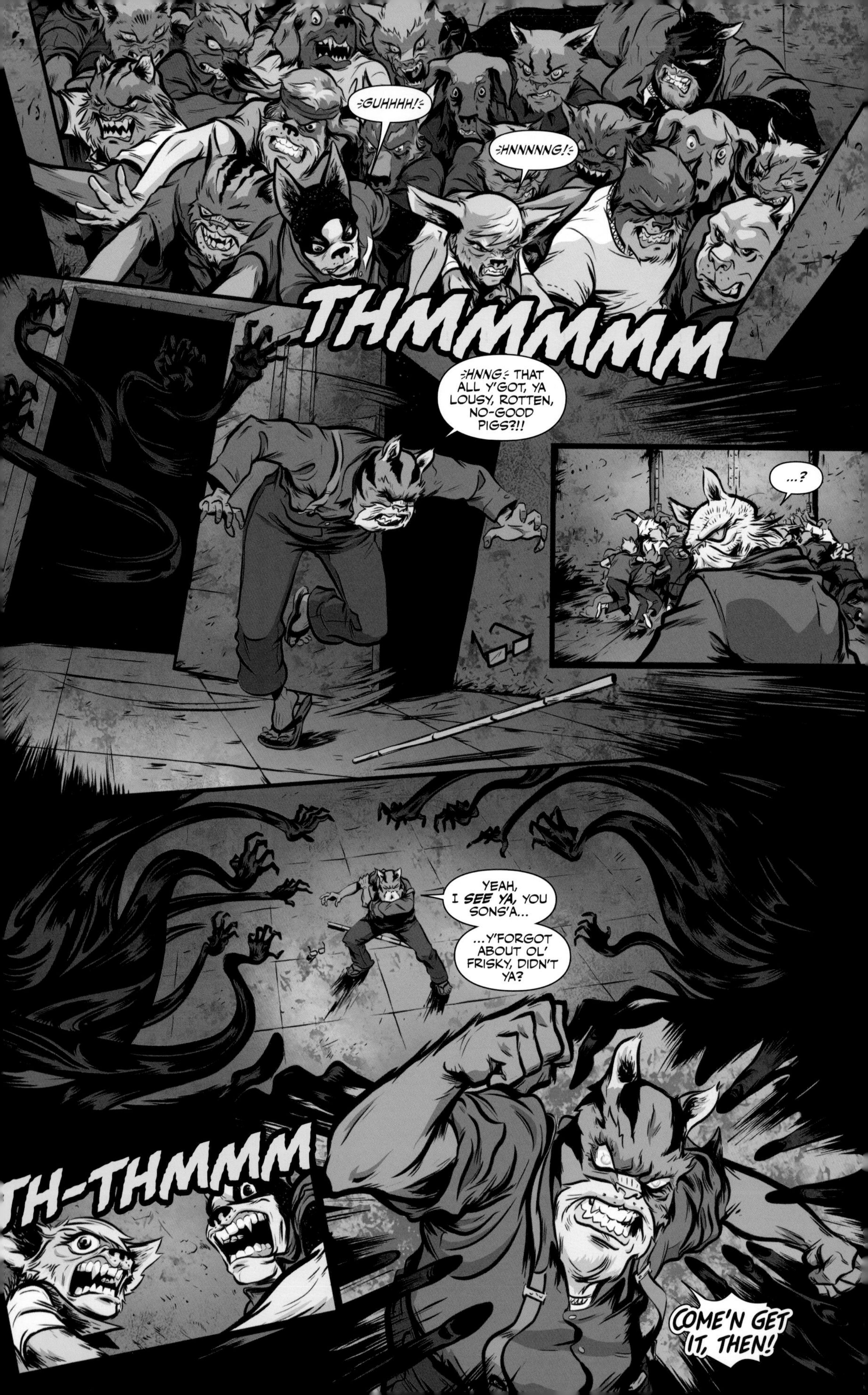
=GUHHHH!=
=HNNNNNG!=
THMMMMMM
=HNNG= THAT ALL Y'GOT, YA LOUSY, ROTTEN, NO-GOOD PIGS?!!
...?
YEAH, I SEE YA, YOU SONS'A...
...Y'FORGOT ABOUT OL' FRISKY, DIDN'T YA?
TH-THMMM
COME'N GET IT, THEN!

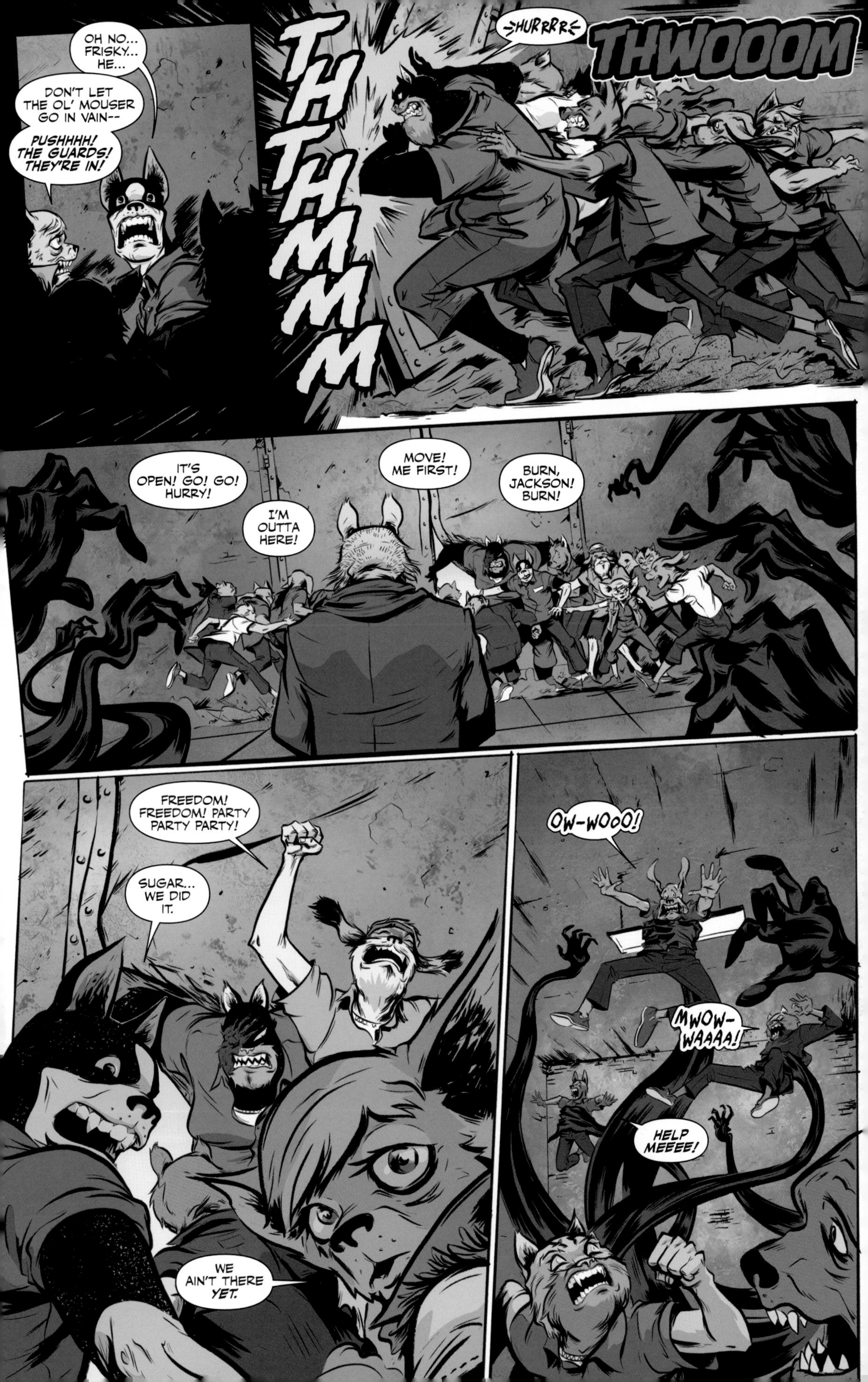

OH NO... FRISKY... HE...
DON'T LET THE OL' MOUSER GO IN VAIN--
PUSHHHH! THE GUARDS! THEY'RE IN!
THHMM
HURRRR
THWOOOM
IT'S OPEN! GO! GO! HURRY!
I'M OUTTA HERE!
MOVE! ME FIRST!
BURN, JACKSON! BURN!
FREEDOM! FREEDOM! PARTY PARTY PARTY!
SUGAR... WE DID IT.
WE AIN'T THERE YET.
OW-WOOO!
MWOW-WAAAA!
HELP MEEEE!

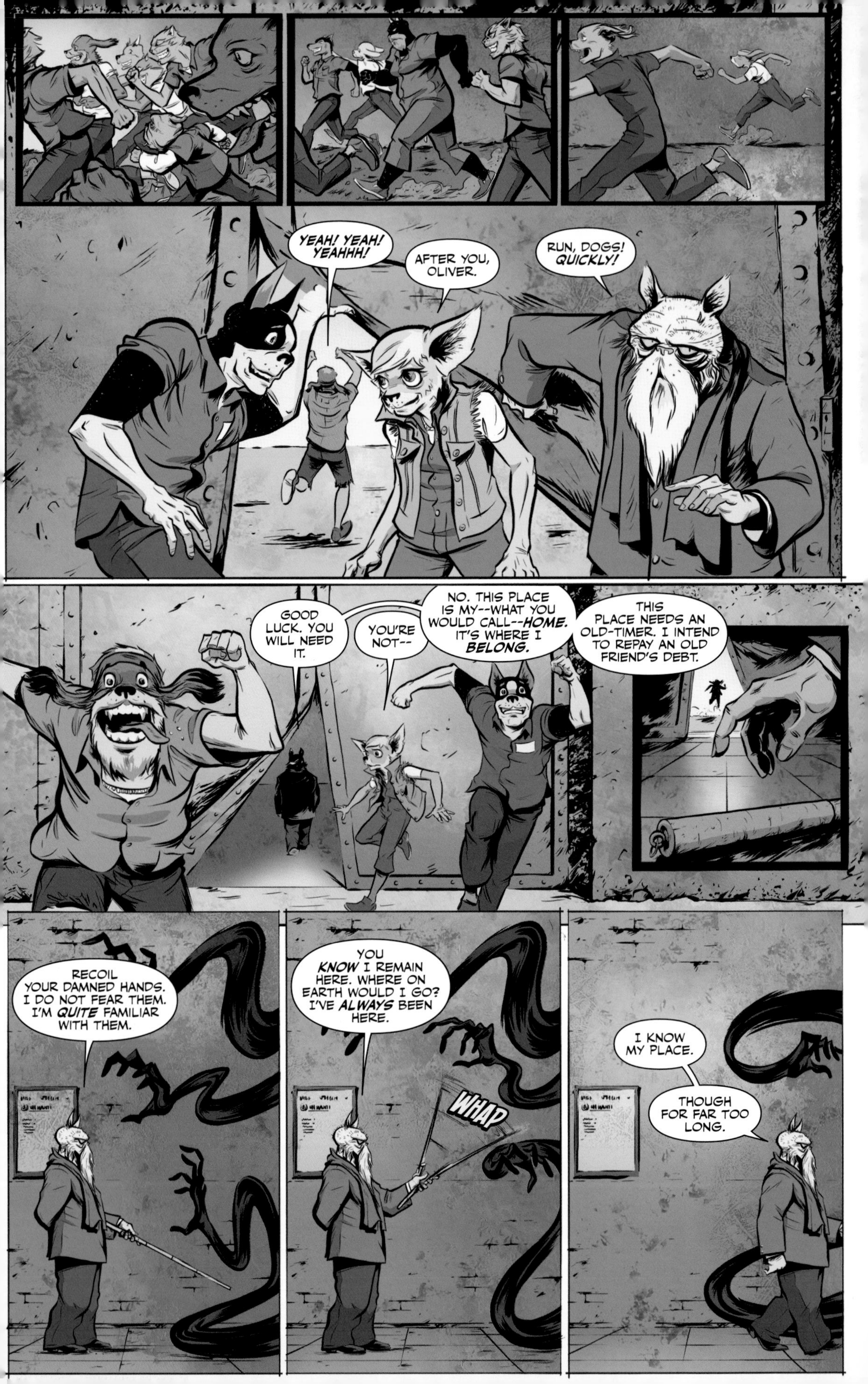
YEAH! YEAH! YEAHHH!
AFTER YOU, OLIVER.
RUN, DOGS! QUICKLY!
GOOD LUCK. YOU WILL NEED IT.
YOU'RE NOT--
NO. THIS PLACE IS MY--WHAT YOU WOULD CALL--HOME. IT'S WHERE I BELONG.
THIS PLACE NEEDS AN OLD-TIMER. I INTEND TO REPAY AN OLD FRIEND'S DEBT.
RECOIL YOUR DAMNED HANDS. I DO NOT FEAR THEM. I'M QUITE FAMILIAR WITH THEM.
YOU KNOW I REMAIN HERE. WHERE ON EARTH WOULD I GO? I'VE ALWAYS BEEN HERE.
WHAP
I KNOW MY PLACE.
THOUGH FOR FAR TOO LONG.

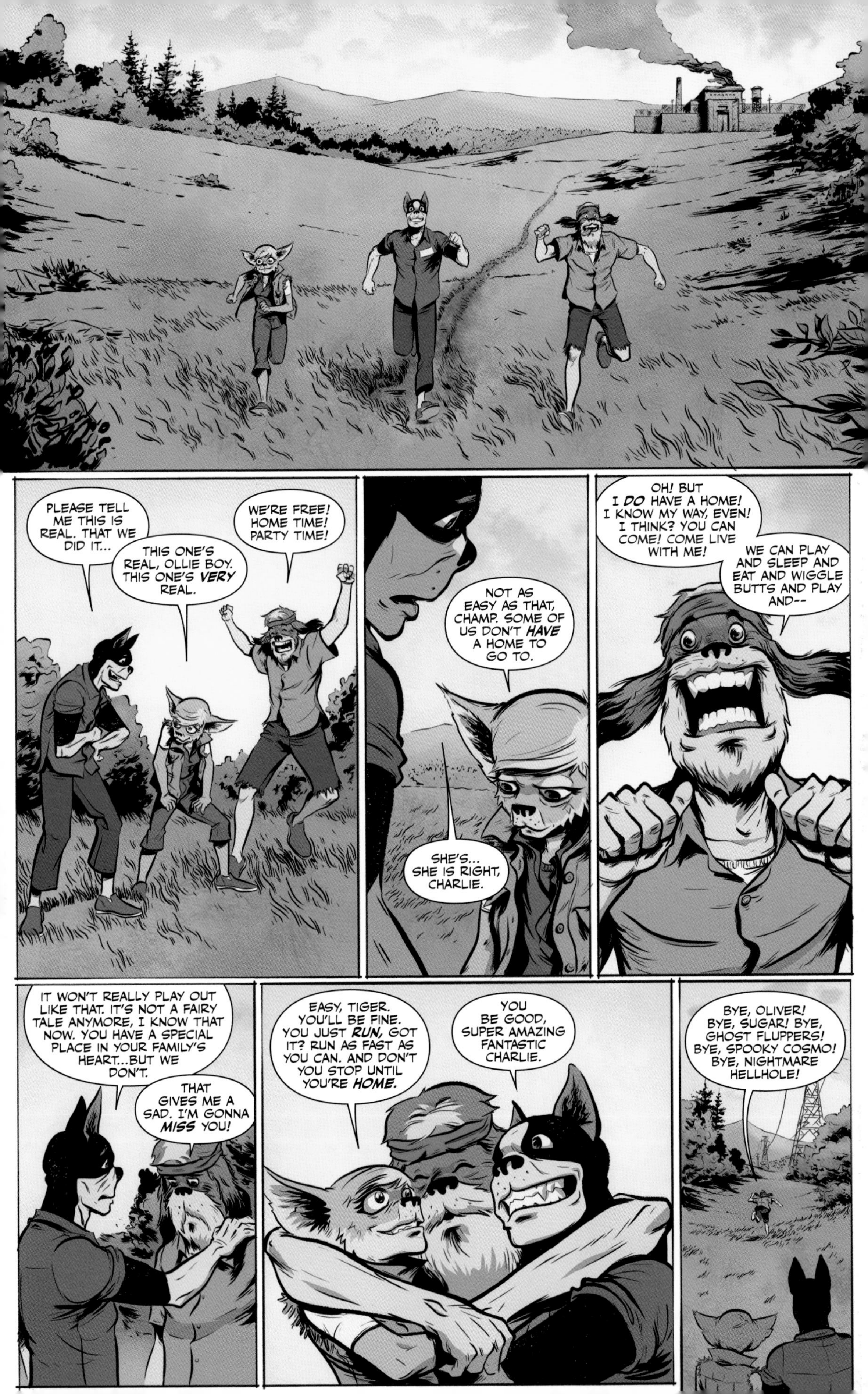
PLEASE TELL ME THIS IS REAL. THAT WE DID IT...
THIS ONE'S REAL, OLLIE BOY. THIS ONE'S VERY REAL.
WE'RE FREE! HOME TIME! PARTY TIME!
NOT AS EASY AS THAT, CHAMP. SOME OF US DON'T HAVE A HOME TO GO TO.
SHE'S... SHE IS RIGHT, CHARLIE.
OH! BUT I DO HAVE A HOME! I KNOW MY WAY, EVEN! I THINK? YOU CAN COME! COME LIVE WITH ME!
WE CAN PLAY AND SLEEP AND EAT AND WIGGLE BUTTS AND PLAY AND--
IT WON'T REALLY PLAY OUT LIKE THAT. IT'S NOT A FAIRY TALE ANYMORE, I KNOW THAT NOW. YOU HAVE A SPECIAL PLACE IN YOUR FAMILY'S HEART...BUT WE DON'T.
THAT GIVES ME A SAD. I'M GONNA MISS YOU!
EASY, TIGER. YOU'LL BE FINE. YOU JUST RUN, GOT IT? RUN AS FAST AS YOU CAN. AND DON'T YOU STOP UNTIL YOU'RE HOME.
YOU BE GOOD, SUPER AMAZING FANTASTIC CHARLIE.
BYE, OLIVER! BYE, SUGAR! BYE, GHOST FLUPPERS! BYE, SPOOKY COSMO! BYE, NIGHTMARE HELLHOLE!

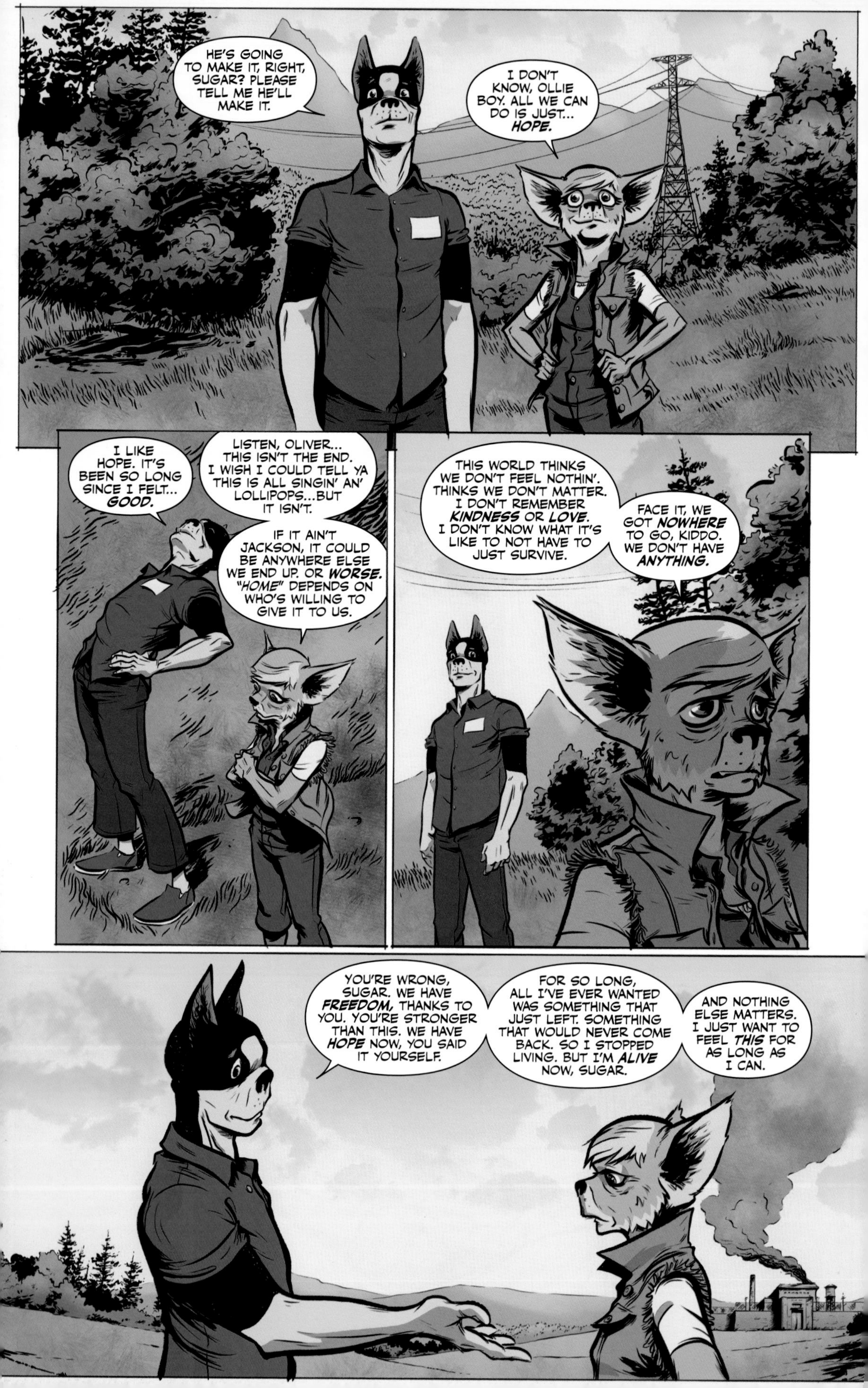
HE'S GOING TO MAKE IT, RIGHT, SUGAR? PLEASE TELL ME HE'LL MAKE IT.
I DON'T KNOW, OLLIE BOY. ALL WE CAN DO IS JUST... HOPE.
I LIKE HOPE. IT'S BEEN SO LONG SINCE I FELT... GOOD.
LISTEN, OLIVER... THIS ISN'T THE END. I WISH I COULD TELL YA THIS IS ALL SINGIN' AN' LOLLIPOPS...BUT IT ISN'T.
IF IT AIN'T JACKSON, IT COULD BE ANYWHERE ELSE WE END UP. OR WORSE. "HOME" DEPENDS ON WHO'S WILLING TO GIVE IT TO US.
THIS WORLD THINKS WE DON'T FEEL NOTHIN'. THINKS WE DON'T MATTER. I DON'T REMEMBER KINDNESS OR LOVE. I DON'T KNOW WHAT IT'S LIKE TO NOT HAVE TO JUST SURVIVE.
FACE IT, WE GOT NOWHERE TO GO, KIDDO. WE DON'T HAVE ANYTHING.
YOU'RE WRONG, SUGAR. WE HAVE FREEDOM, THANKS TO YOU. YOU'RE STRONGER THAN THIS. WE HAVE HOPE NOW, YOU SAID IT YOURSELF.
FOR SO LONG, ALL I'VE EVER WANTED WAS SOMETHING THAT JUST LEFT. SOMETHING THAT WOULD NEVER COME BACK. SO I STOPPED LIVING. BUT I'M ALIVE NOW, SUGAR.
AND NOTHING ELSE MATTERS. I JUST WANT TO FEEL THIS FOR AS LONG AS I CAN.

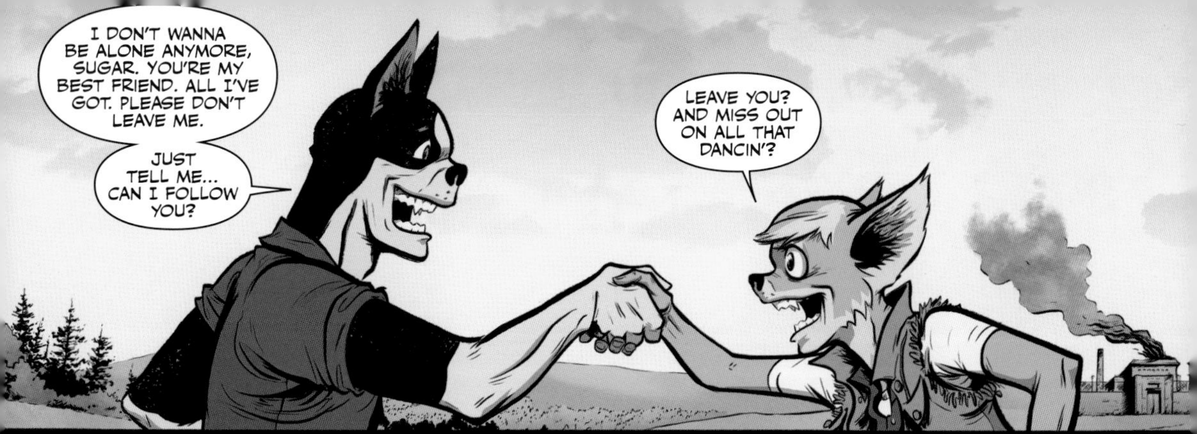
I DON'T WANNA BE ALONE ANYMORE, SUGAR. YOU'RE MY BEST FRIEND. ALL I'VE GOT. PLEASE DON'T LEAVE ME.
JUST TELL ME... CAN I FOLLOW YOU?
LEAVE YOU? AND MISS OUT ON ALL THAT DANCIN'?

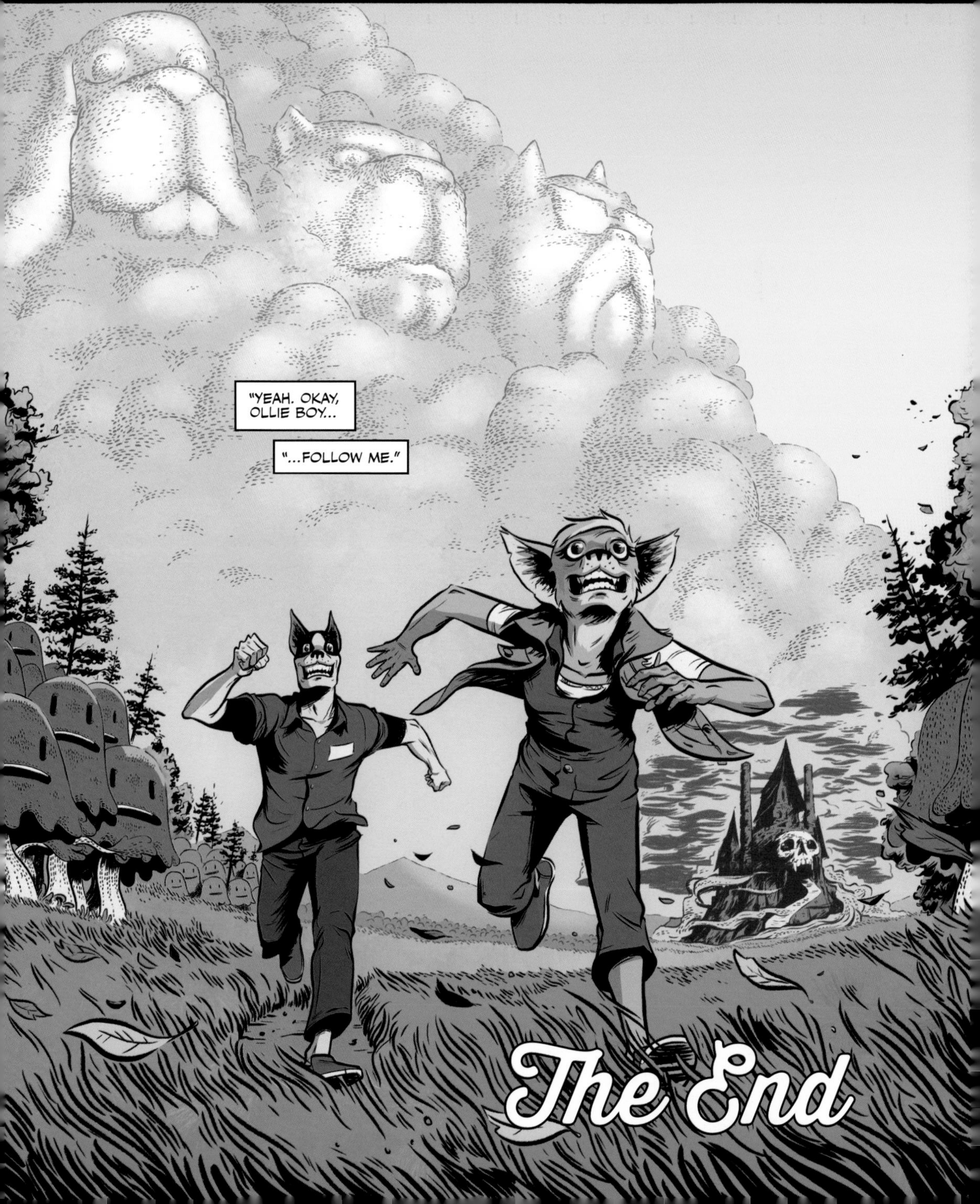
"YEAH. OKAY, OLLIE BOY...
"...FOLLOW ME."
The End

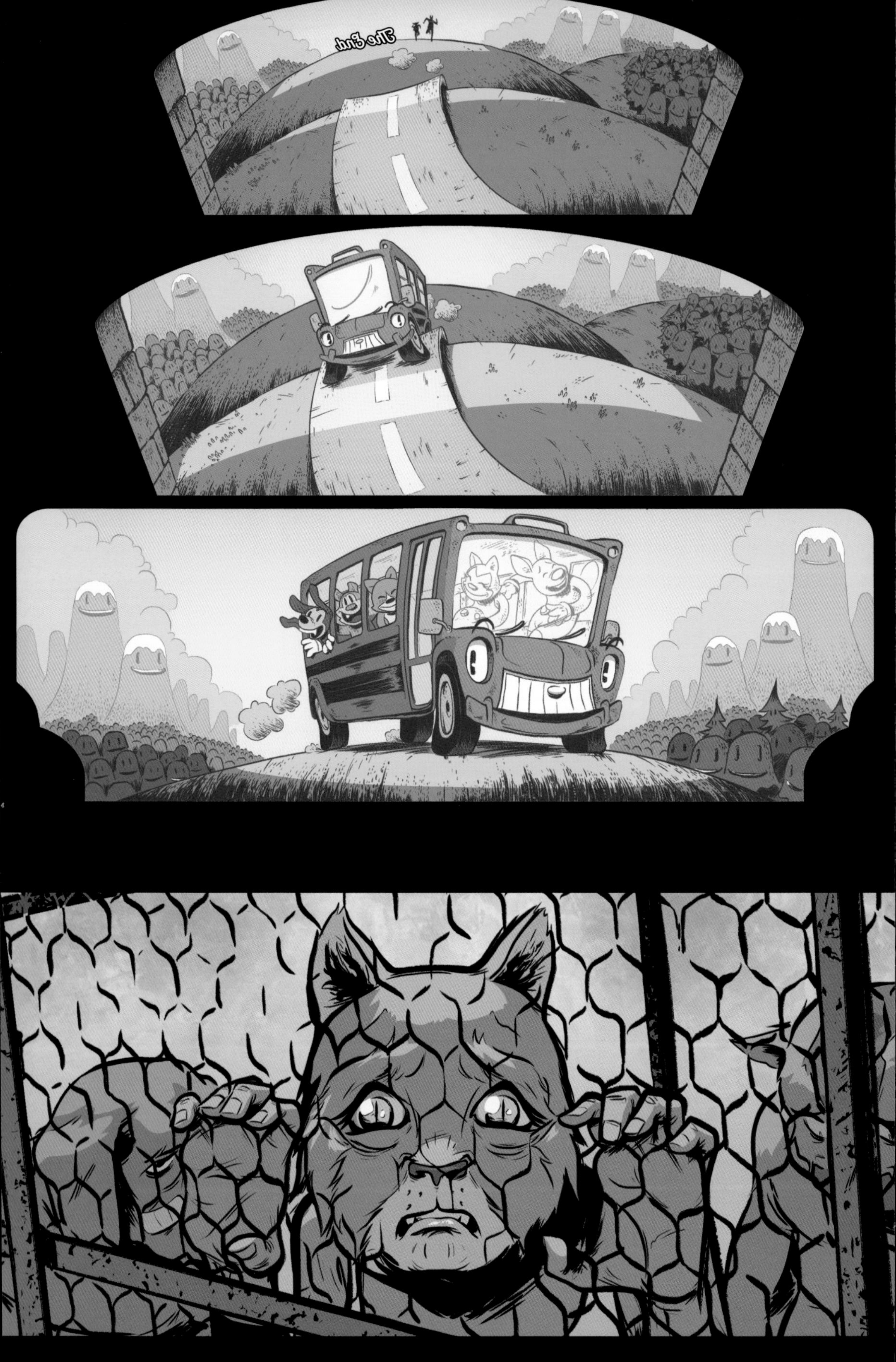
The End.

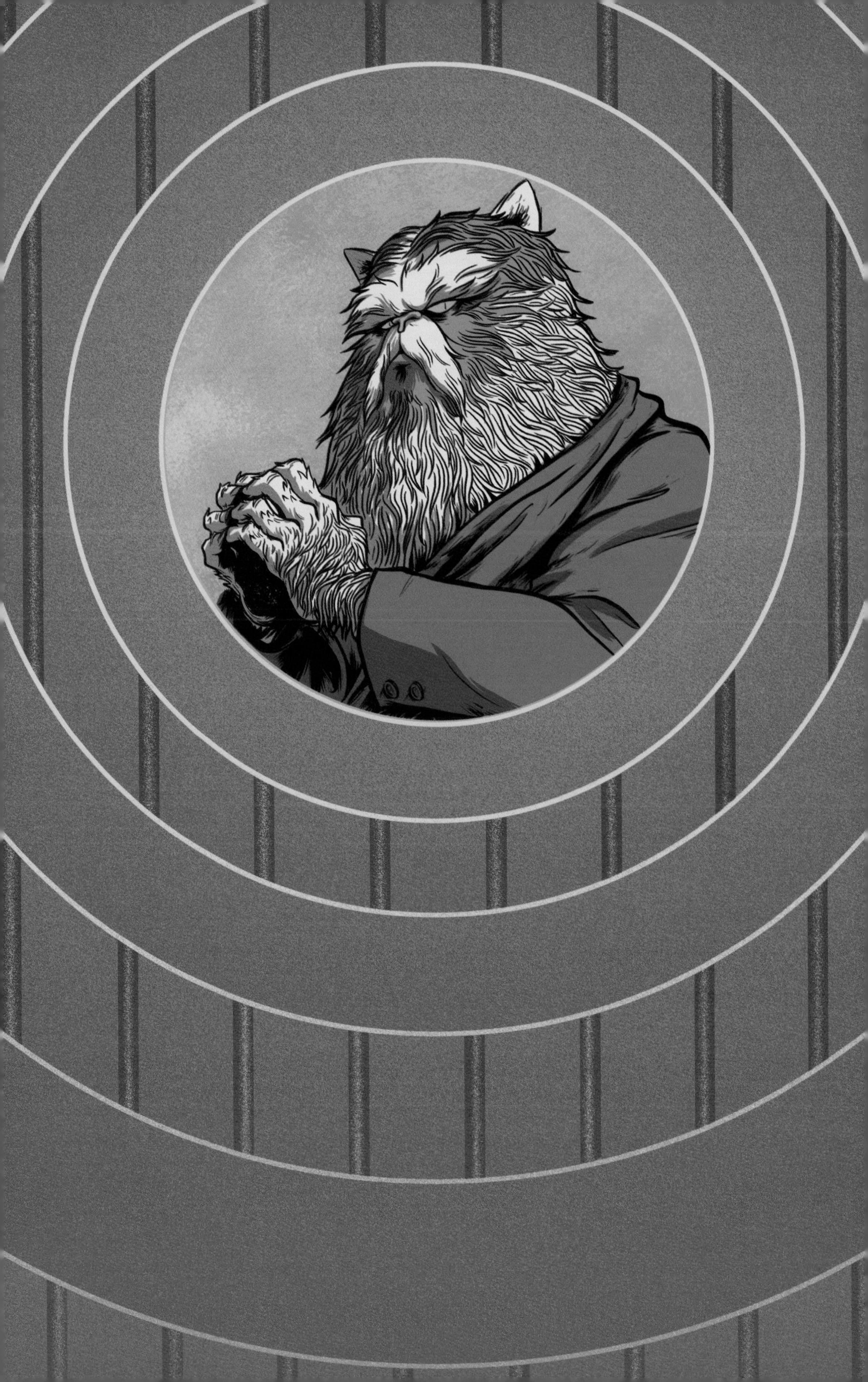

Cover Gallery

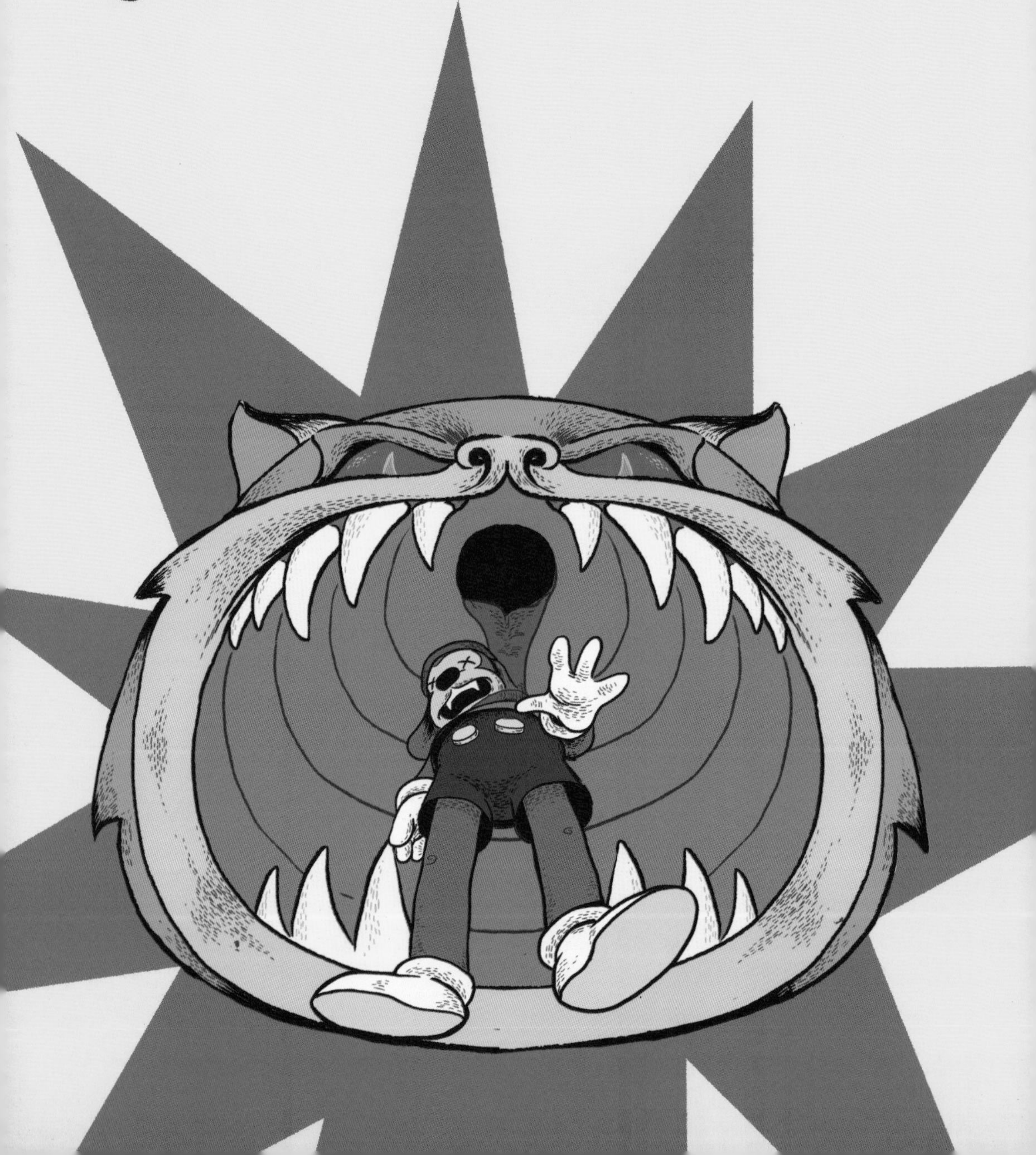

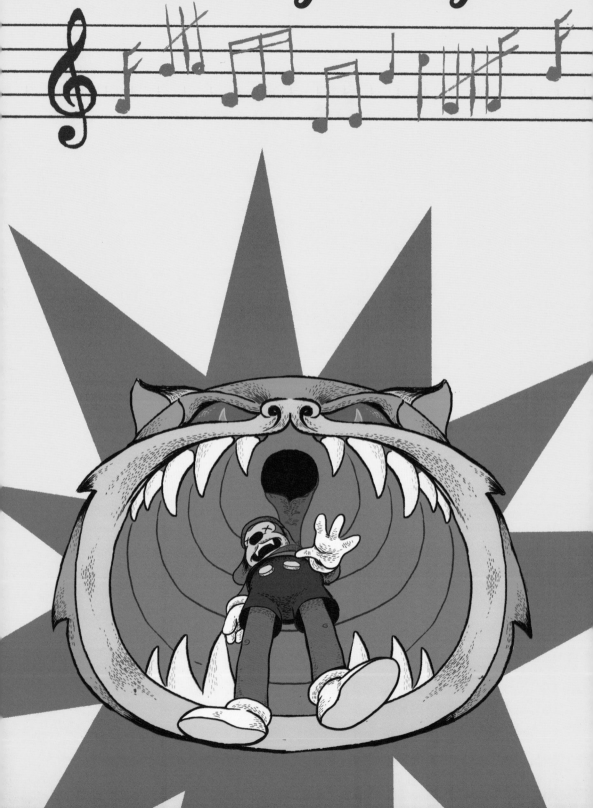

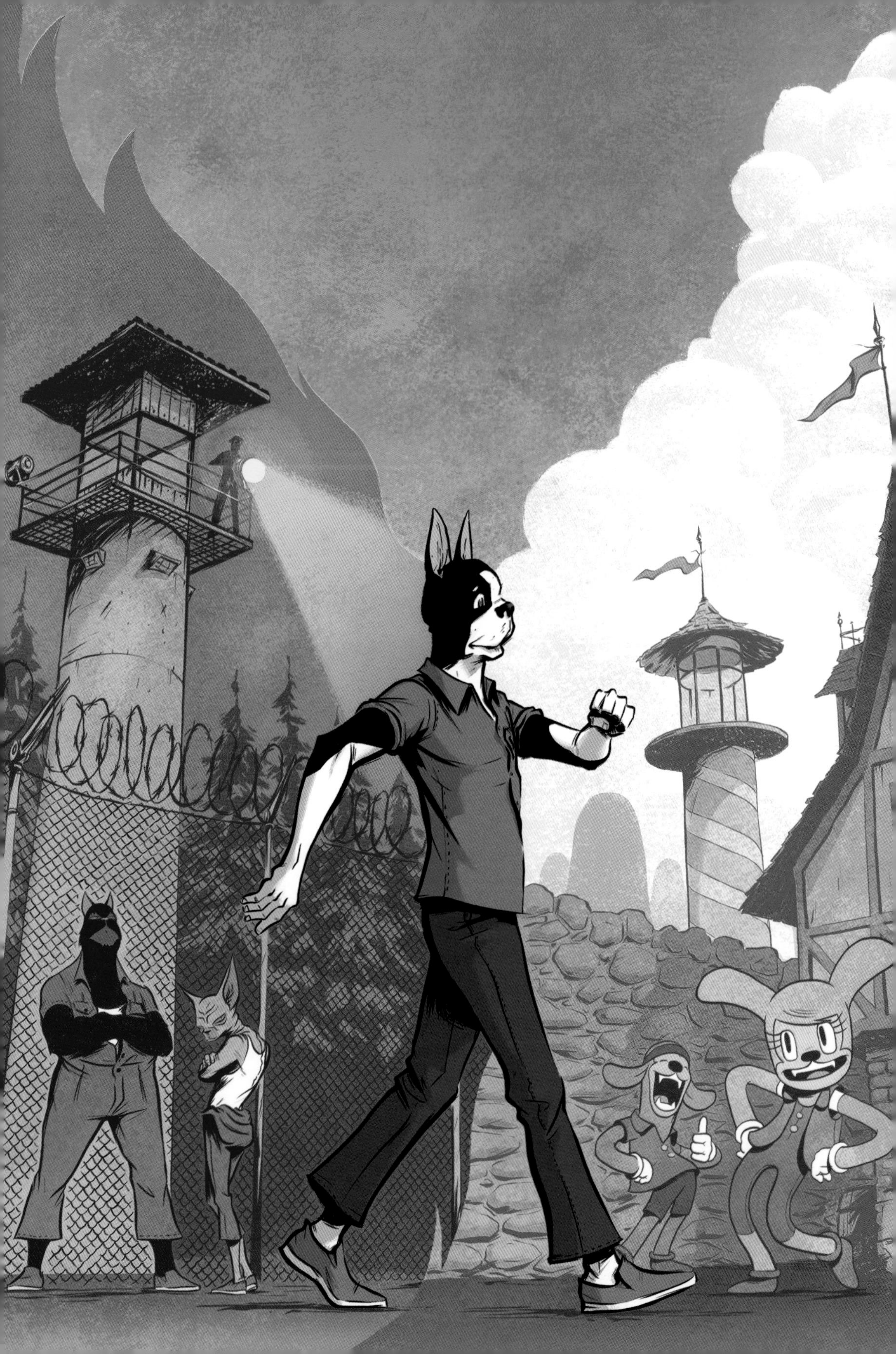

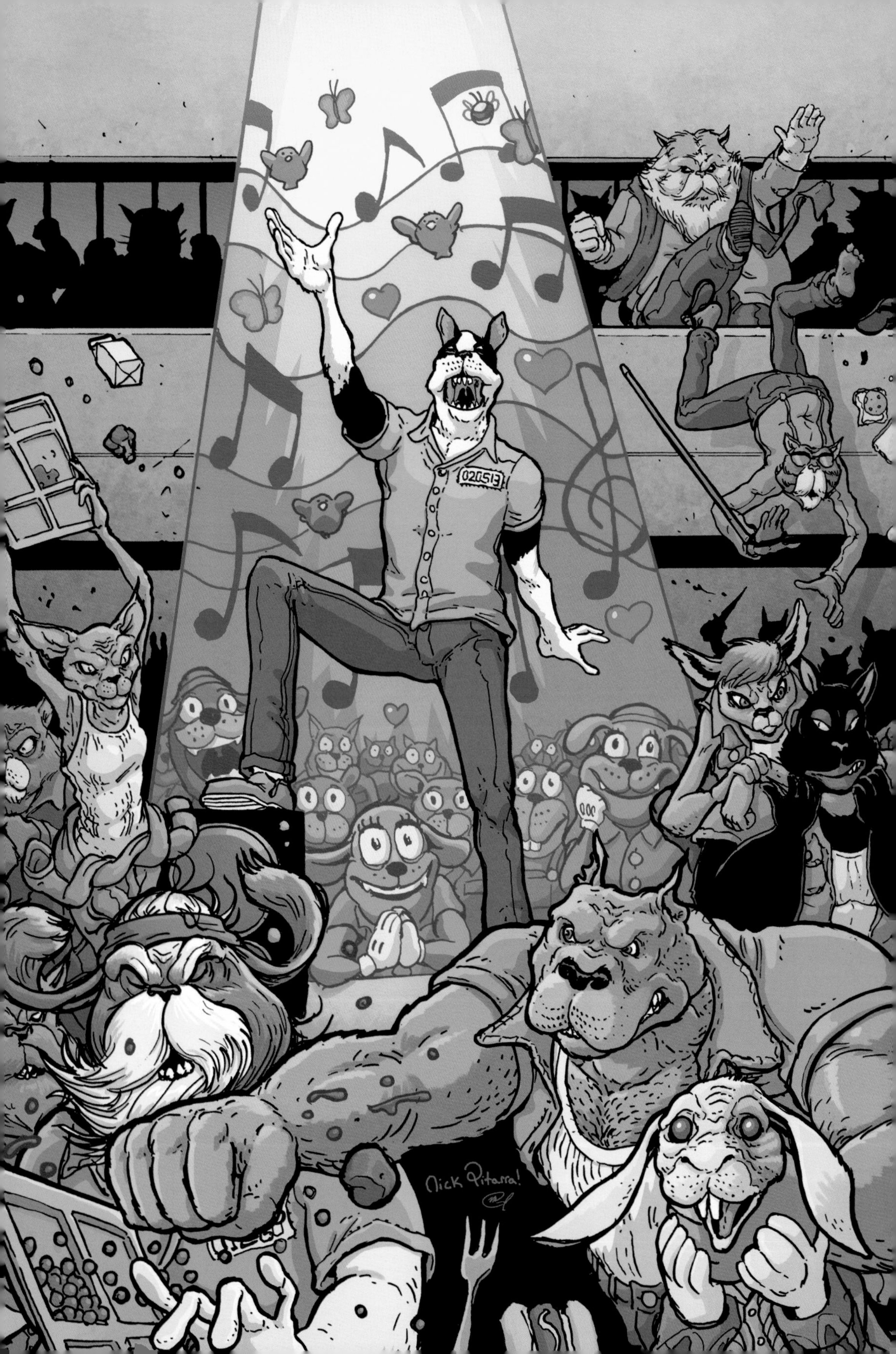
020513
Nick Pitarra!

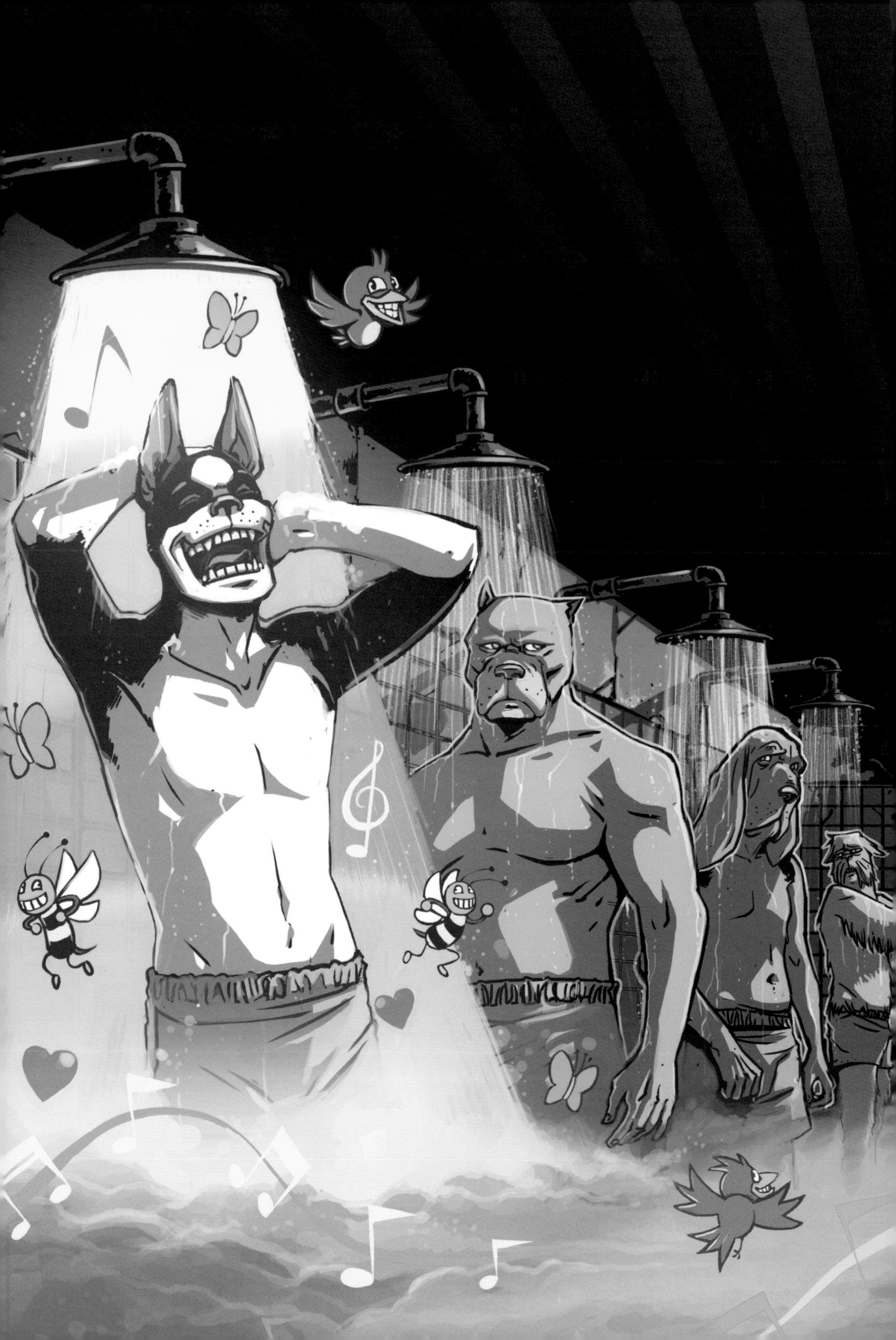

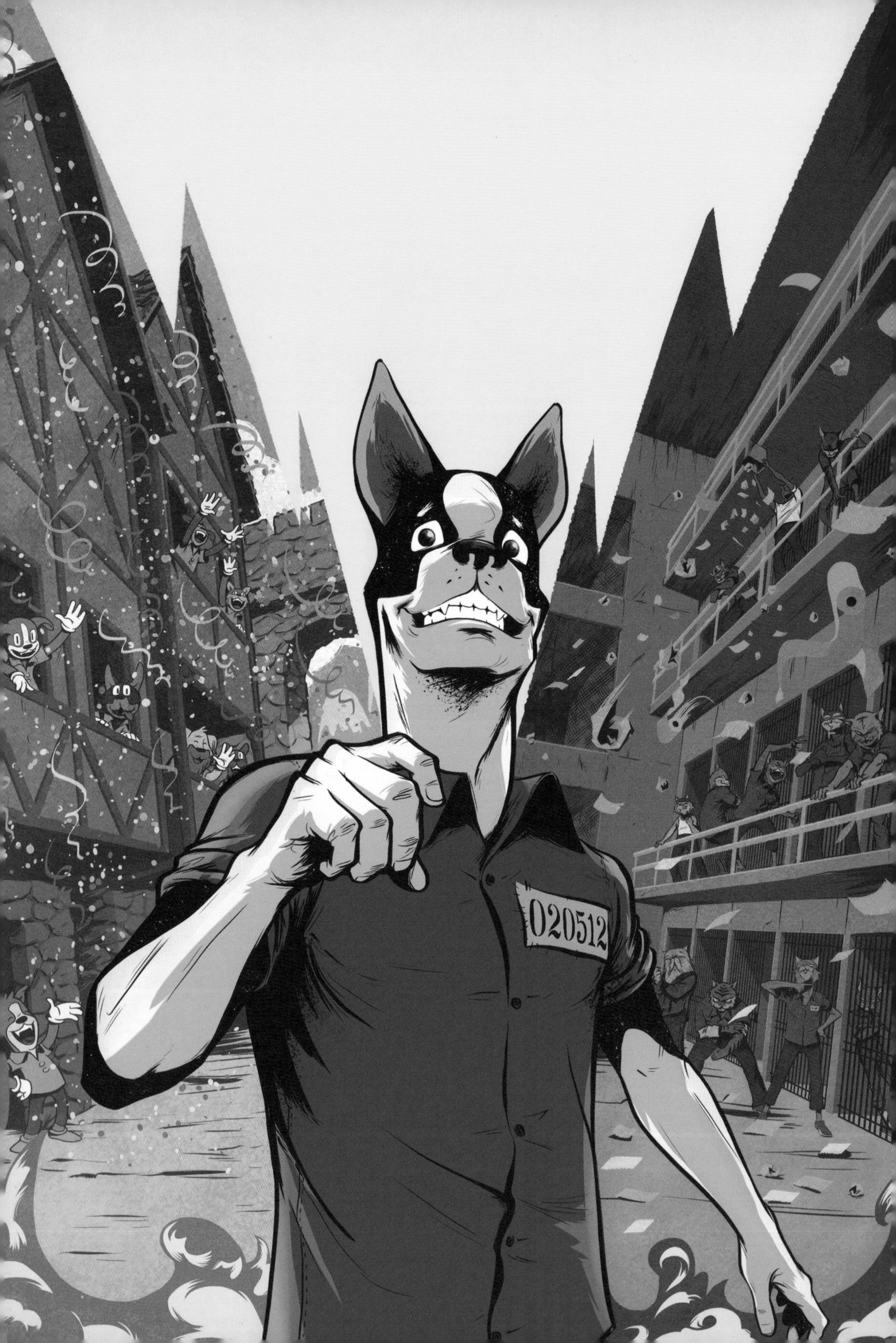
020512

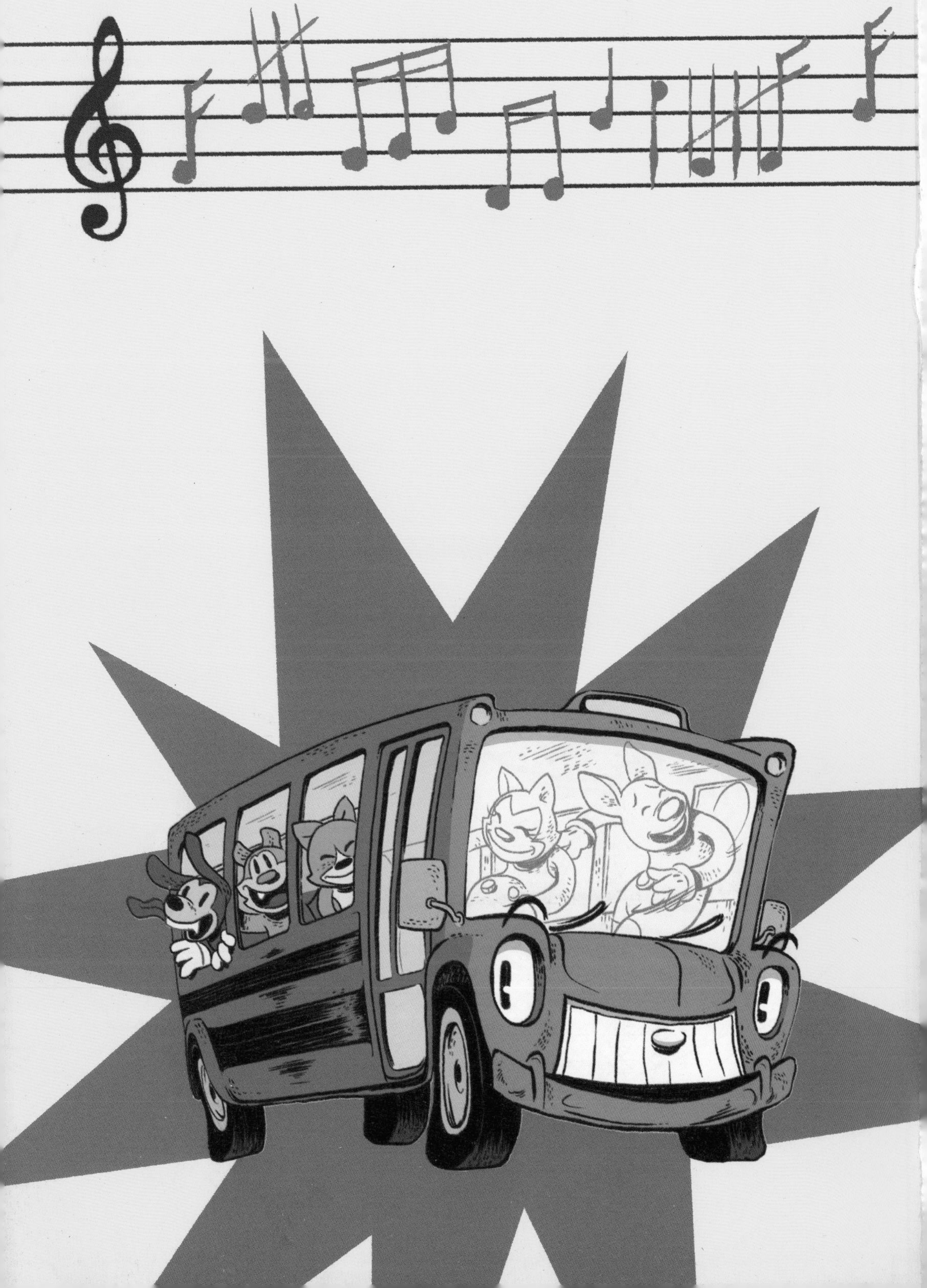

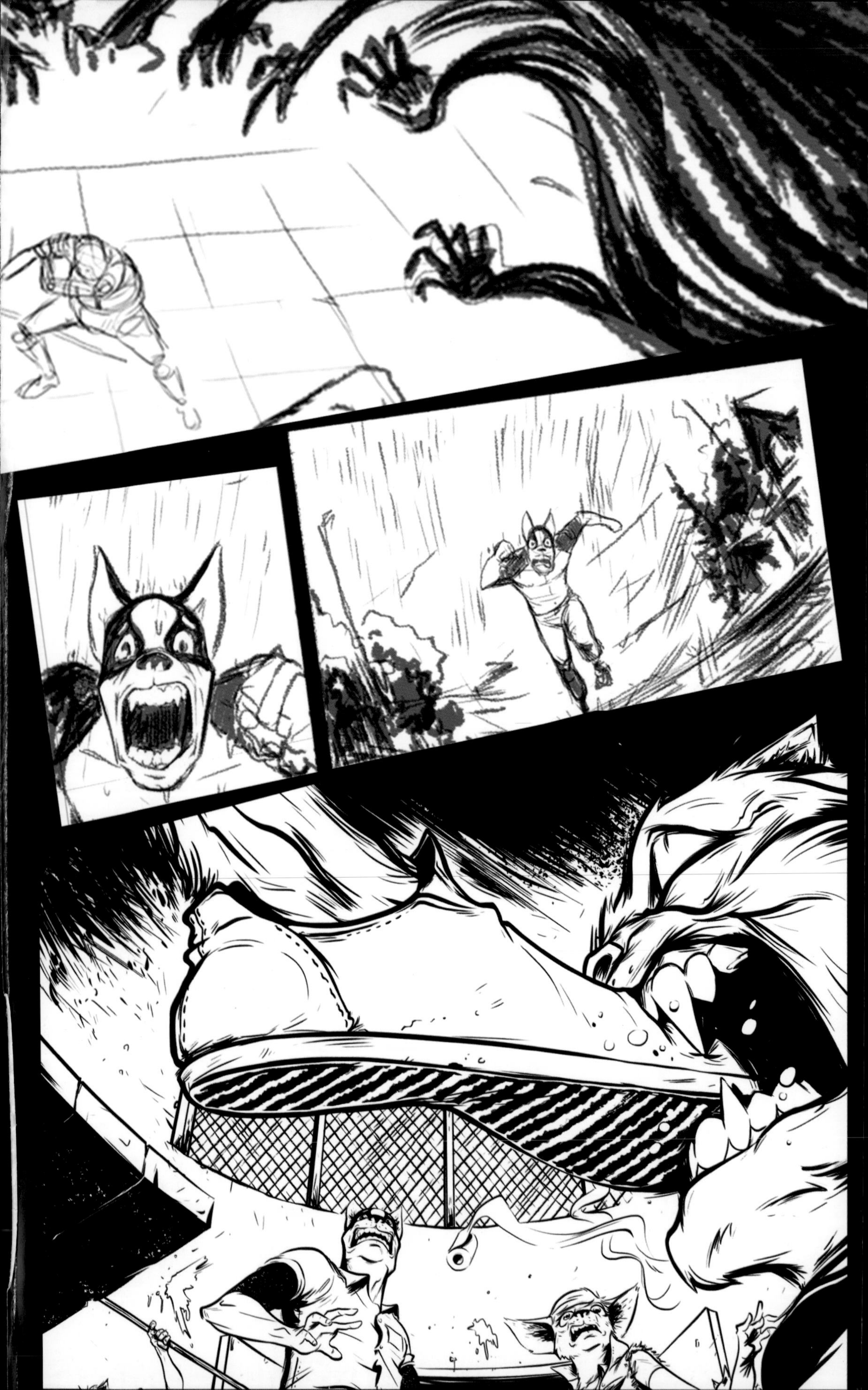

Daniel Bayliss

SKETCHBOOK

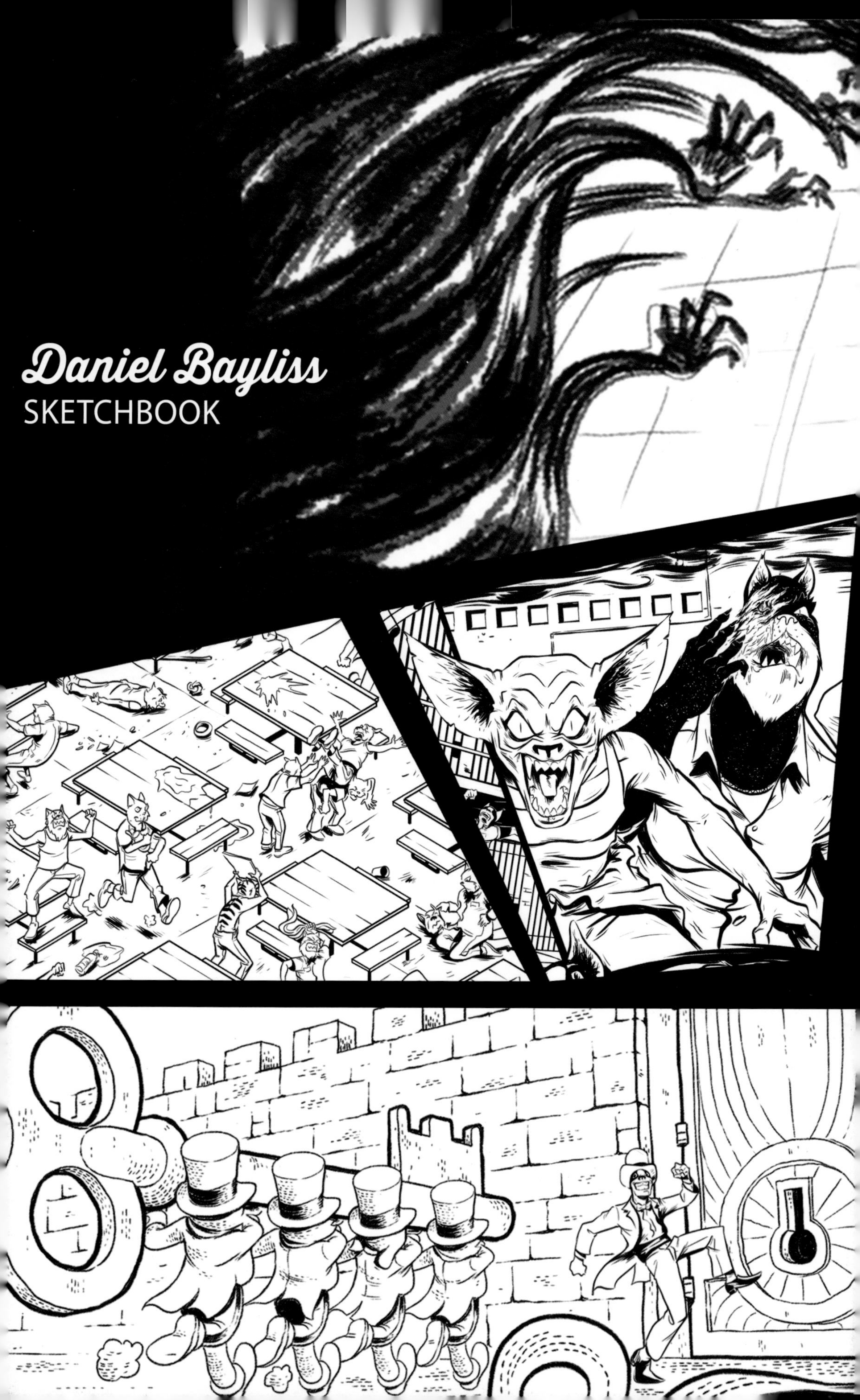

Issue #4 Cover by
Daniel Bayliss

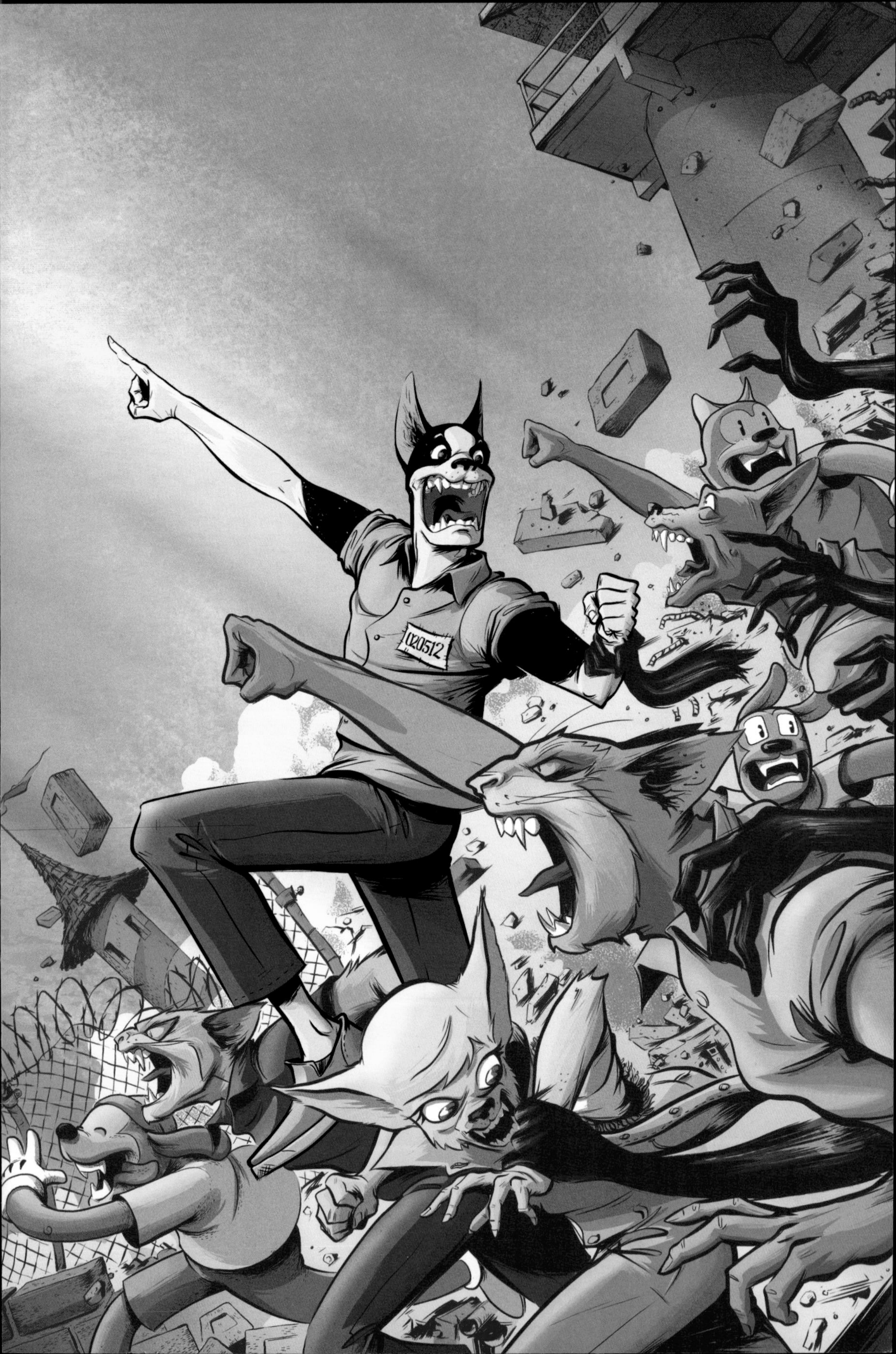
020512

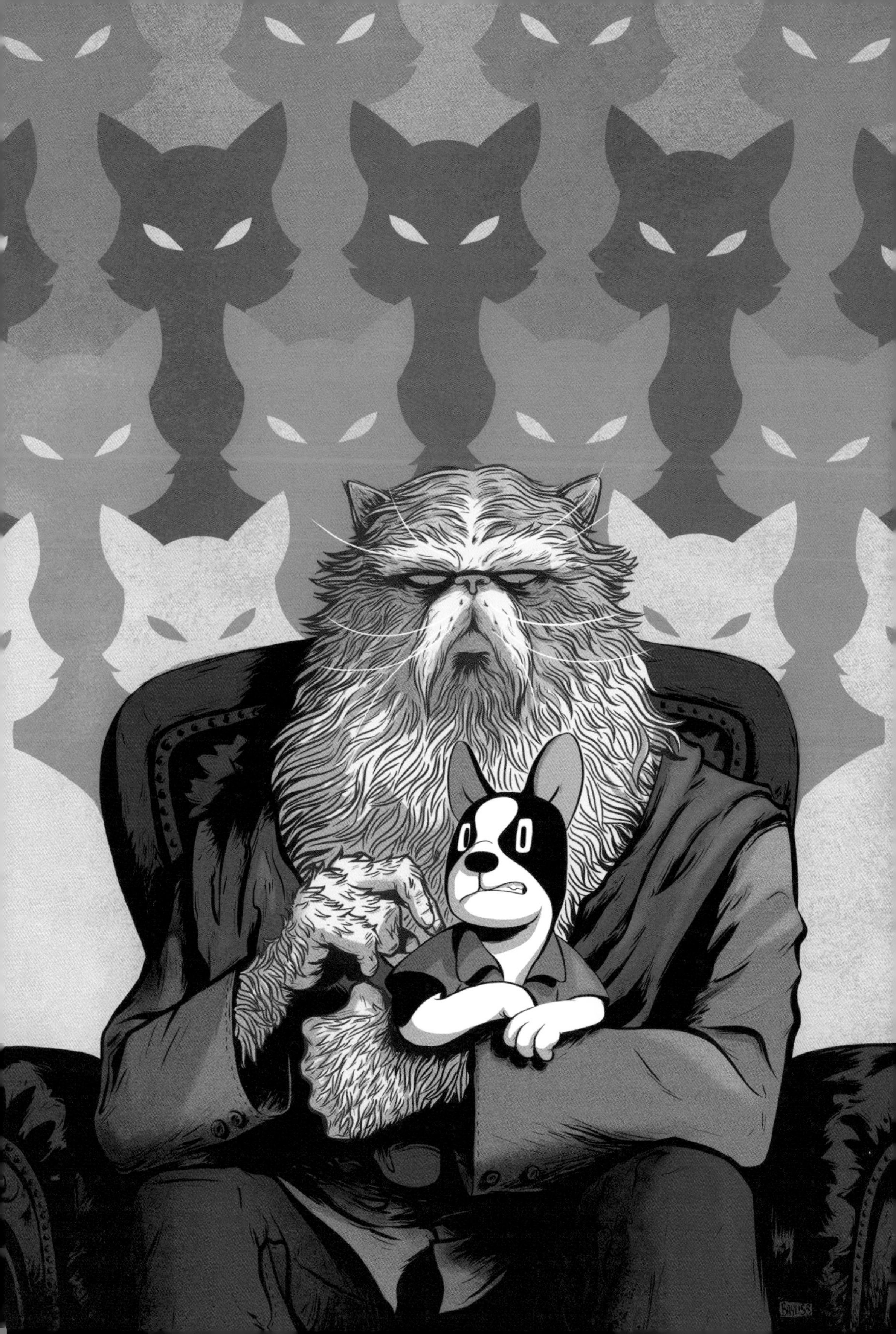

Issue #2 Cover by
Daniel Bayliss

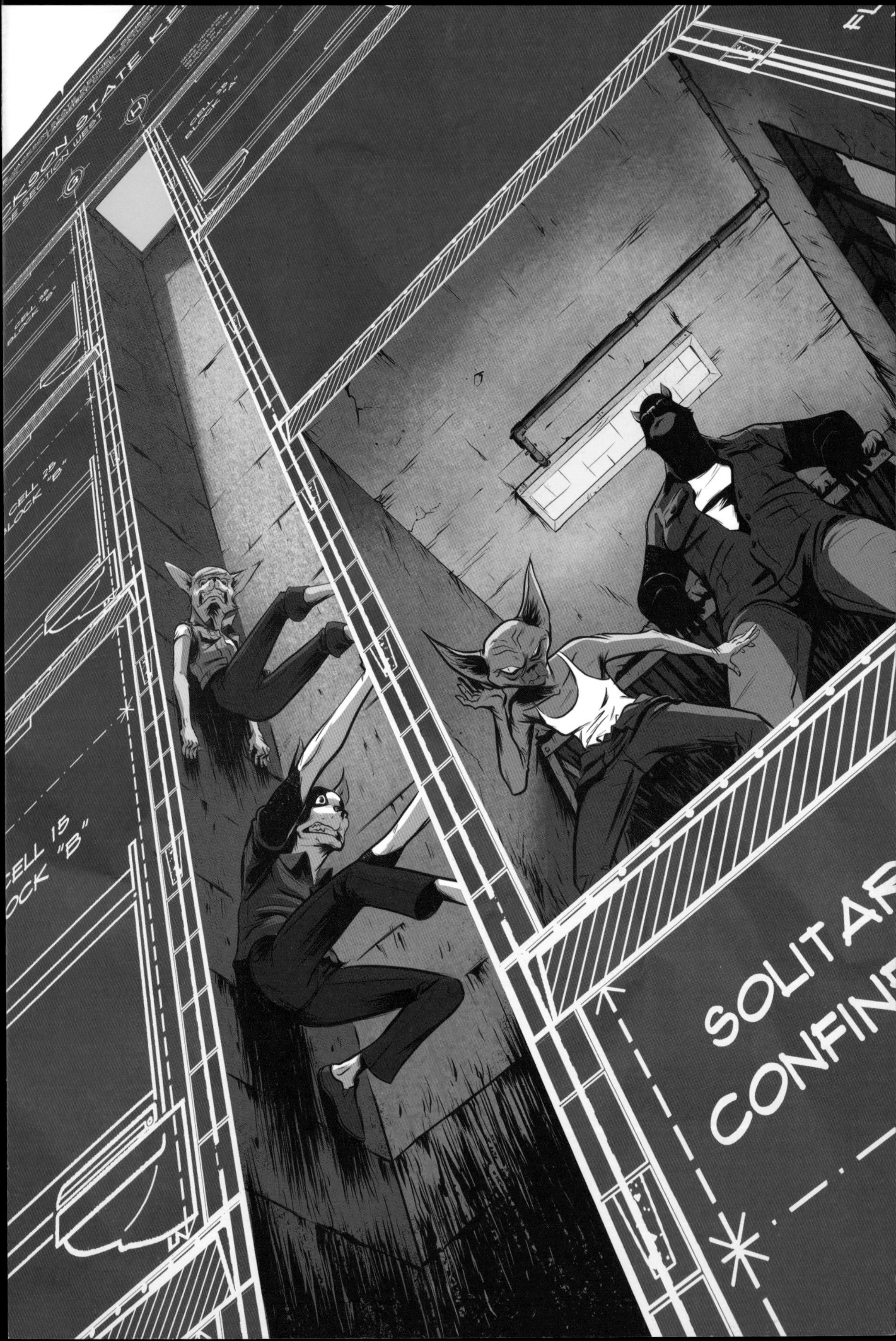
CELL 15
BLOCK "B"
SOLITAR
CONFINE